Visual QuickStart Guide

CORELDRAW 4

INCORPORATING

CorelTRACE

& CorelMOSAIC

Paul Webster

Webster & Associates

Peachpit Press

CorelDRAW 4 Visual Quickstart Guide
Webster & Associates

Peachpit Press, Inc.
2414 Sixth Street
Berkeley, CA 94710
(510) 548-4393 (phone)
(510) 548-5991 (fax)

Notice of Liability:

Trademarks:

First published 1993

ISBN: 1-56609-086-5

Printed and bound in the United States of America

 Printed on recycled paper

Why a Visual QuickStart Guide?

Virtually no one actually reads computer books; rather, people typically refer to them. This series of Visual QuickStart Guides has made that reference easier thanks to a new approach to learning computer applications.

While conventional computer books lean towards providing extensive textual explanations, a Visual QuickStart Guide takes a far more visual approach—pictures literally show you what to do, and the text is clear, concise commentary. Learning becomes easier, because a Visual QuickStart Guide familiarizes you with the look and feel of your software. Learning also becomes faster, since there are no long-winded passages.

It's a new approach to computer learning, but it's also solidly based on experience: Webster & Associates have logged thousands of hours of computer training, and have authored many books on computer applications.

Chapter 1 provides a general introduction to CorelDRAW.

Chapters 2 through 12 graphically overview the major CorelDRAW features. These chapters are easy to reference and, with the extensive use of screen shots, allow concepts to be quickly grasped.

Chapter 13 overviews the major CorelTRACE features.

Chapter 14 overviews the major CorelMOSAIC features.

Acknowledgments

The author wishes to acknowledge the assistance of the following people in the researching, writing, and editing of this book.

- Jenny Hamilton
- Sean Kelly
- Tony Webster

Contents

Chapter 5: The Edit Menu

Chapter 6: The Layout Menu

Chapter 7: The Effects Menu

Chapter 8: The Text Menu

Chapter 9: The Arrange Menu

Chapter 13: CorelTRACE

Chapter 14: CorelMOSAIC

INTRODUCING CORELDRAW 4

THE FIRST STEPS

The first step after buying CorelDRAW 4 is to install it on your machine. The first section of this chapter summarizes that very straightforward process. The rest of Chapter 1 looks at the components that make up the CorelDRAW 4 screen, explains what purposes they are used for, and describes the varied functions of a dialog box.

INSTALLATION GUIDE

You install CorelDRAW 4 from Windows. If CorelDRAW 4 is already installed on your machine, skip to the **Starting CorelDRAW 4** section in this chapter.

SUMMARY OF INSTALLATION

If you are installing CorelDRAW 4 from floppy disks, follow these steps. With Windows active, insert the CorelDRAW 4 disk number one into the appropriate drive.

Figure 1. Choose the *Run* command from the **File** menu in the Windows Program Manager.

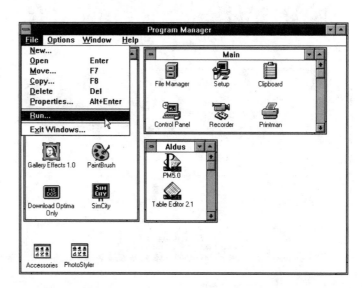

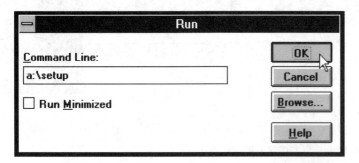

Figure 2. In the *Command Line* text box of the *Run* dialog box, type *a:* or *b: \setup*, and click on *OK.*

Figure 3. Once you've done this, it activates the CorelDRAW 4 Setup program. Click on the *Continue* button to move on.

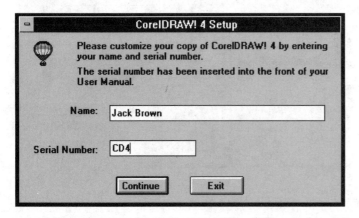

Figure 4. In the *CorelDRAW 4 Setup* dialog box you type your name and the serial number of the software. You can find this number on a piece of paper that is included in the diskette packet. Again, click on *Continue* once this is done.

Figure 5. The next dialog box is the *CorelDRAW Installation Options* dialog box. Here you are given two options for installing Corel-DRAW 4: *Full Install,* or *Custom Install.* Selecting the *Full Install* option installs all of CorelDRAW 4 and its associated programs onto your machine. If you do not want to install everything, choose the *Custom Install* option and you can choose what you want to install.

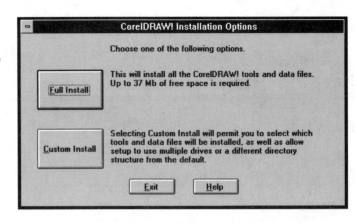

Figure 6. After clicking on the install option that you want, the installation process displays the *Destination Directory* dialog box. This shows where CorelDRAW 4 will go. Leave as is, or type in your own path to indicate where you want to install it.

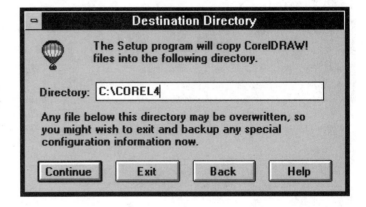

Figure 7. If you choose the *Custom Install* option, you can now specify which applications you want to install. You can see how much room is available and how much disk space the items you select will take up on your machine. Once you have selected the items you want installed, click on the *Continue* button.

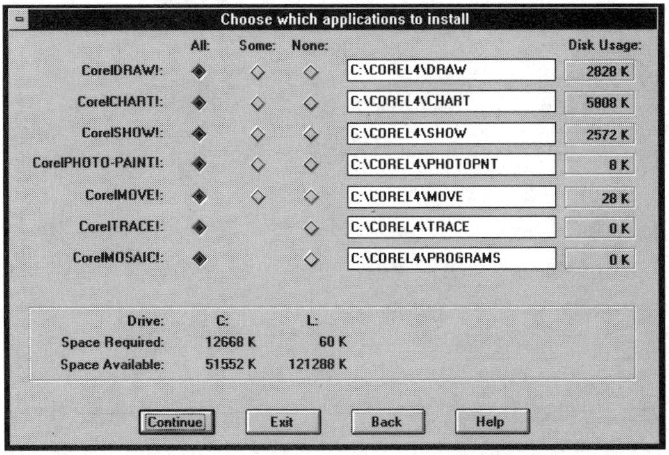

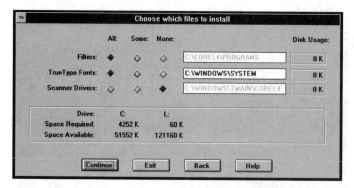

Figure 8. You then must decide which filters, fonts, and/or scanner drivers you want to install. Clicking on the *Some* option activates a further dialog box where you can make your choices for each option.

Otherwise, select the *All* or *None* options and click on *Continue*.

Figure 9. You are now ready to install CorelDRAW 4. Click on the *Install* button to move on. Just insert the remaining disks one by one when the program prompts you to.

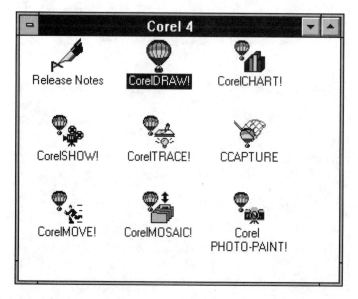

Figure 10. Once CorelDRAW 4 has completed the installation process, the Corel 4 group appears in the Windows Program Manager, displaying all the programs you included in the installation.

Figure 11. If you are installing the CD-ROM version of Corel-DRAW 4, you follow the same steps as previously described; put the CD in the CD player and type the directory letter of your CD player and *setup* in the *Run* dialog box. For example, if your CD player is the *e* drive, type *e:\setup*.

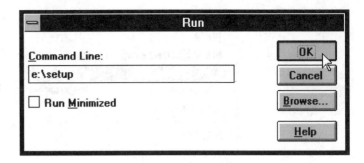

You also have the option of running CorelDRAW 4 directly from the CD without having to install it. In this case you would type *e:\setup2* in the *Run* dialog box. When you use CorelDRAW 4 this way, it installs certain files on your hard disk; they are copied into a Corel40 directory. These include TrueType fonts (you have the choice of which ones you want to install in your Windows *System* directory), scanner drivers, and various *ini* files, registration files, *dll* files among others.

STARTING
CORELDRAW 4

Figure 12. To start CorelDRAW 4, double-click on the CorelDRAW 4 icon in your Corel 4 Program Group (Figure 10).

After starting CorelDRAW 4, your screen looks like this. You are in a new, untitled CorelDRAW 4 file.

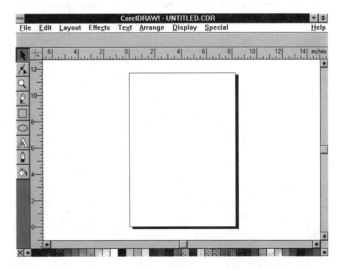

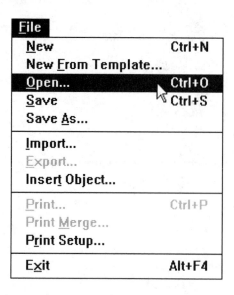

Figure 13. From the **File** menu, select the *Open* command to open an existing file. This activates the *Open Drawing* dialog box.

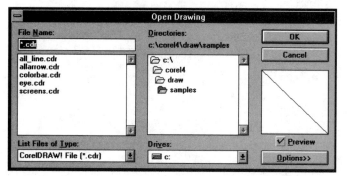

Figure 14. The *Open Drawing* dialog box gives you access to the computer's drives and directories. Find and select the desired file from the list of files in this dialog box, then click on the *OK* button. Alternatively, double-clicking on the filename opens the file.

For more information on the options available in this dialog box, see Chapter 4.

THE SCREEN

Figure 15. This figure shows the CorelDRAW 4 screen and its components.

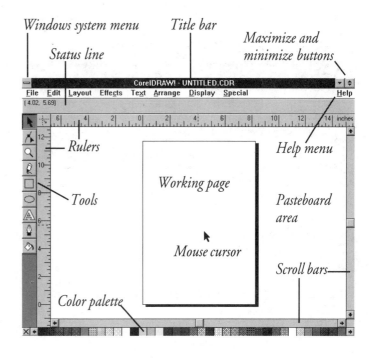

Windows system menu
Title bar
Maximize and minimize buttons
Status line
Rulers
Help menu
Working page
Tools
Pasteboard area
Mouse cursor
Scroll bars
Color palette

SCREEN COMPONENTS

MENU BAR

Figure 16. Clicking on a menu bar command with the mouse produces a menu of options. Each option performs a unique function. Menus are used for most Windows programs.

TITLE BAR

The title bar contains the name of the CorelDRAW 4 publication. If you have not yet given it a name, it reads *UNTITLED.CDR.*

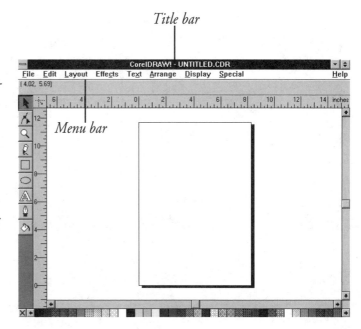

Title bar
Menu bar

Maximize and minimize buttons

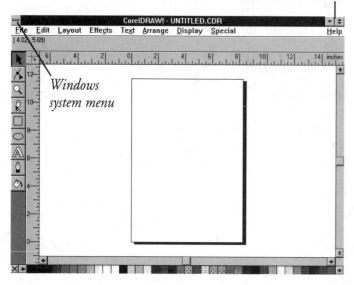

Windows
system menu

MAXIMIZE AND MINIMIZE BUTTONS, AND WINDOWS SYSTEM MENU

Figure 17. Using the single down-arrow minimizes the window to an icon in the bottom left of the screen. You can double-click on this icon to reactivate the window. Use the up- and down-arrow button to reduce the size of the window to the size you had it before.

The Windows **System** menu activates a menu of options that you will find in every Windows application. From this menu you can maximize, minimize, or close the current application.

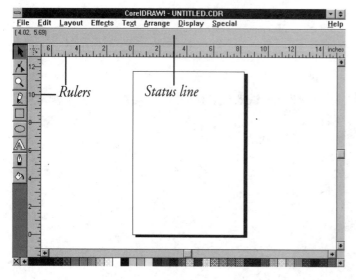

Rulers   Status line

STATUS LINE AND RULERS

Figure 18. The status line is a bar of information that indicates what object you have selected, as well as its dimensions; the font and point size of selected text; outline and color of a selected object; the angle of rotation; as well as other vital pieces of information. It tells the position of the mouse on the page in relation to the rulers. It also displays current information when you are moving and resizing objects.

You use the rulers to measure distance and placement of objects on the page. For more information on the rulers, see Chapter 10.

WORKING PAGE AND PASTEBOARD AREA

Figure 18. The working page represents the area of the page that prints.

This is like a desk on which you place your page. You can place objects on the pasteboard; they are saved with the file but will not print, unless you select the *Fit To Page* option in the *Print Options* dialog box.

See the *Print* command in **Chapter 4, The File Menu,** for more information.

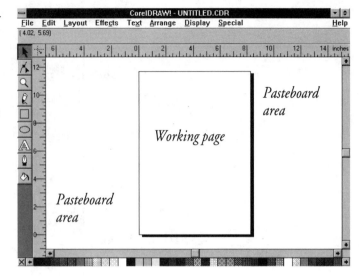

MOUSE CURSOR

Figure 20. The mouse cursor is the icon that moves around the screen, corresponding to where you move your mouse. The mouse cursor changes shape when you select a new tool from the Toolbox.

The icon in (a) indicates that you have selected the Pick Tool.

The icons in (b) and (c) show the Shape Tool and Zoom Tool, respectively.

(a)

(b)

(c)

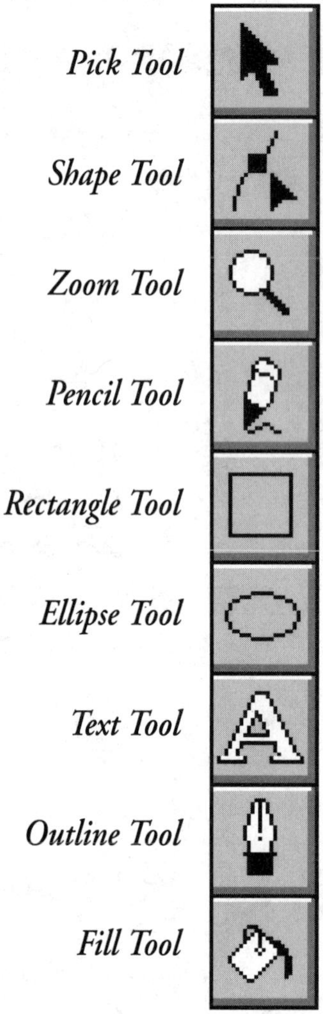

TOOLBOX

Figure 21. You can select the tool icons in the Toolbox with the mouse. These different tools have a wide range of functions and uses which we explain in detail in Chapters 2 and 3.

Pick Tool

Shape Tool

Zoom Tool

Pencil Tool

Rectangle Tool

Ellipse Tool

Text Tool

Outline Tool

Fill Tool

SCROLL BARS AND THE COLOR PALETTE

Figure 22. You use the scroll bars with the mouse to move different parts of the screen into view. Scroll bars are common to most Windows applications.

The Color Palette is a bar, running along the bottom of the screen, which lets you apply colors to selected objects quickly. For more information, see Chapter 10.

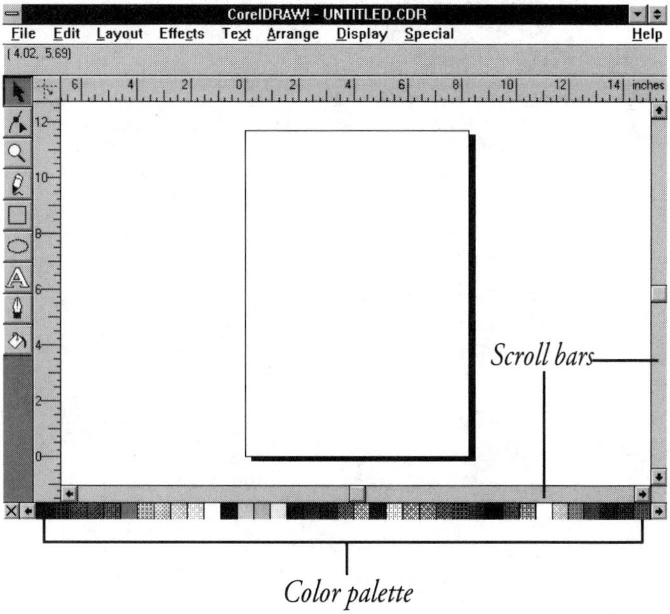

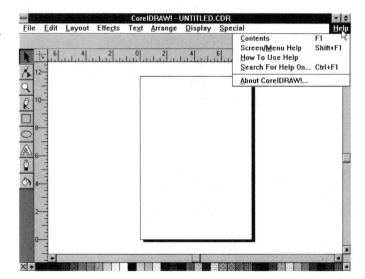

Scroll bars

Color palette

THE HELP MENU

Figure 23. The **Help** menu provides you with online help on how to use CorelDRAW 4.

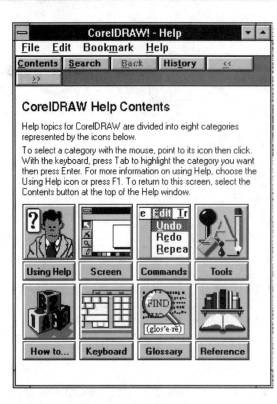

Figure 24. You can activate this *Help* screen through the *Contents* command from the **Help** menu; alternatively, you can use the F1 key. Follow the instructions in the *Help* window to find information on any topic related to Corel-DRAW 4.

Pressing the Shift+F1 keys, when there is no *Help* dialog box on screen, activates this icon: ♔?. Clicking with this cursor on any menu item or screen component gives you context-sensitive help for that menu item or screen component.

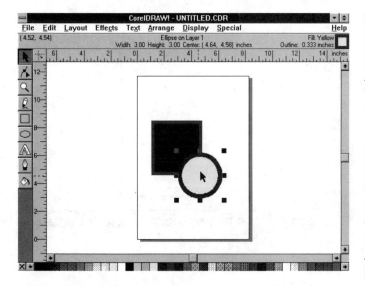

PREVIEW MODE

Figure 25. By default, Corel-DRAW 4 works in *full-color view* mode. This mode displays all objects in full color. To select a filled object in this mode, click inside the object (on the filled part).

The other option is *wireframe* mode. *Wireframe* mode is much faster, as it displays only the outlines of the various objects. To move between the two modes, select the *Edit Wireframe* command from the **Display** menu. Alternatively, press the Shift+F9 keys. For more information, see Chapter 10.

DIALOG BOXES

You can select and activate dialog box options in a number of different ways.

Figure 26. Clicking on the ◇ button next to the option you want to select activates radio buttons in dialog boxes. When you select a radio button, it assumes a recessed shaded appearance (◆).

Radio buttons are mutually exclusive—you can select only one option at a time from each section containing these buttons.

The *Page Setup* dialog box to the right shows examples of radio buttons. See the *Portrait* and *Landscape* options in the top right corner and the *Display* section in the bottom left.

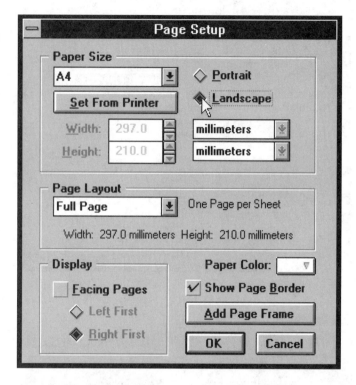

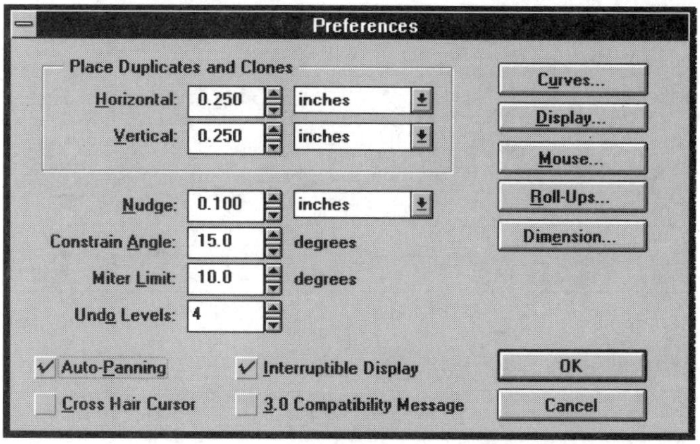

Figure 27. To mark and unmark check boxes, you click on them with the mouse. An active check box has a check mark in it (✔). You can select more than one check box in a section at one time.

In this example, we have selected the *Auto-Panning* and *Interruptible Display* check boxes at the bottom of the *Preferences* dialog box.

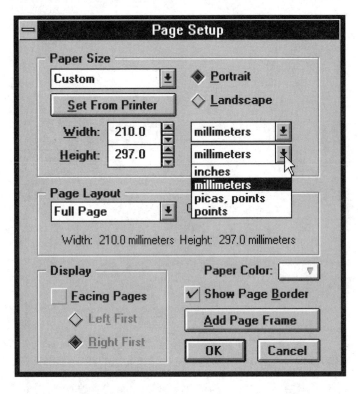

Figure 28. Clicking on a down-arrow (▣) in a dialog box activates a drop-down list. In this example, we have clicked on the unit of measurement option in the *Page Setup* dialog box to display the drop-down list of options from where you can select a new unit of measurement.

When you change the unit of measurement, the associated value in the text box changes accordingly.

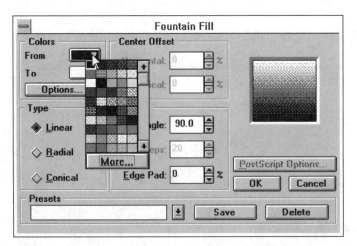

Figure 29. Some dialog boxes, such as the *Fountain Fill* dialog box, have buttons that open pop-up palettes or quick-pick palettes, from where you can select a color or an item.

Figure 30. Certain buttons in dialog boxes open a further dialog box. The ellipsis (three periods) after the button command name indicates these buttons.

The *OK* button confirms your dialog box selections and returns you to the editing screen. Click on the *Cancel* button if you want CorelDRAW 4 to ignore any changes you have made within a dialog box.

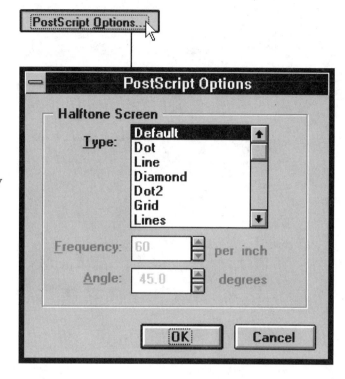

Figure 31. This dialog box shows two additional features—a text box and a list box. You enter or edit text within a text box, much like any text editing procedure. You can delete existing text with the Delete or Backspace keys. You can also highlight text by dragging across it with the cursor.

List boxes let you select an item from a group of items. Use the scroll bars if you need to view the item you want to select.

Text box

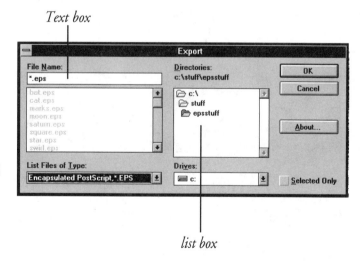

list box

(a)

| Width: | 210.0 | | millimeters | |
| Height: | 297.0 | | millimeters | |

Figure 32. You can change certain dialog box options by selecting the numeric value with the mouse (a) and typing a new value directly over the top (b).

(b)

| Width: | 250 | | millimeters | |
| Height: | 297.0 | | millimeters | |

(a)

| Width: | 255.0 | | millimeters | |
| Height: | 297.0 | | millimeters | |

Figure 33. You can also use the up or down arrows to the right of the frame to increase or decrease the value (a).

(b)   ── Put mouse here

| Width: | 260.0 | | millimeters | |
| Height: | 297.0 | | millimeters | |

Alternatively, hold the mouse down on the bar between the up and down arrows (b) and move the mouse up or down to change the value.

ROLL-UP WINDOWS

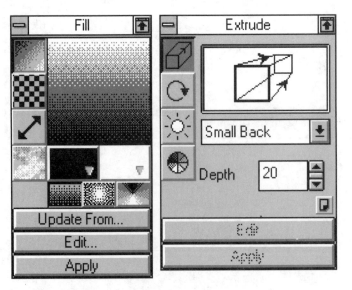

Figure 34. Roll-up windows can have all the features of a dialog box. They are constant dialog boxes that remain on screen until you remove them.

Many commands in Corel-DRAW 4 use roll-ups. For more information on each roll-up, see the specific command.

Figure 35. To reduce screen clutter, you can roll up or down the roll-up windows (hence their name) at any time. To do so, click on the arrow in the top right of the window.

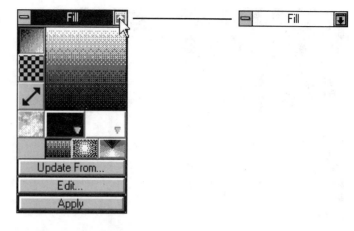

Figure 36. You can move a roll-up around the screen by holding the mouse down on the title bar of the roll-up and dragging it to a new position.

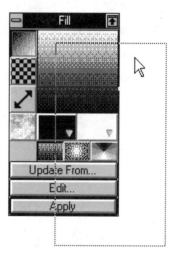

Figure 37. Clicking on the icon in the top left of a roll-up window displays this menu. Use the *Arrange* or *Arrange All* commands to arrange one or all of the roll-up windows currently on the screen.

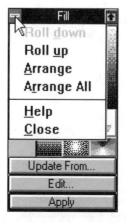

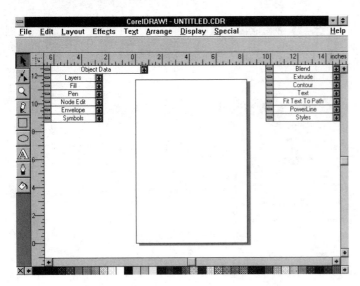

Figure 38. Selecting the *Arrange All* command from the menu of Figure 37 arranges all roll-up windows currently active.

In this example, all the available roll-ups in CorelDRAW 4 are open and arranged.

THE UTILITY, DRAWING, AND TEXT TOOLS

2

USING THE TOOLS

The CorelDRAW Toolbox contains all the tools you need to draw and manipulate objects. In this chapter you will learn the various functions of all tools except the Outline and Fill tools. You will also learn how to use the various tools in conjunction with each other, and with the menu commands.

Chapter 3 describes the Outline and Fill tools.

Figure 1. The Toolbox, at the left of the screen, contains all the CorelDRAW tools. Once you select it, a tool remains active until you select another from the Toolbox.

Pick Tool

Shape Tool

Zoom Tool

Pencil Tool

Rectangle Tool

Ellipse Tool

Text Tool

Outline Tool (see Chapter 3)

Fill Tool (see Chapter 3)

THE PICK TOOL

You can use the Pick Tool (▶) to select, resize, move, rotate, and skew objects. This is the tool that you use most of the time. If you are using a different tool from the Toolbox, press the Spacebar to select the Pick Tool.

SELECTING OBJECTS

(a)

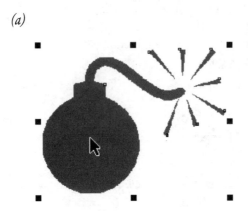

Figure 2. With the Pick Tool, click anywhere on a filled object to select that object (a). If the object has no fill, you click anywhere along the perimeter of the object to select it.

(b)

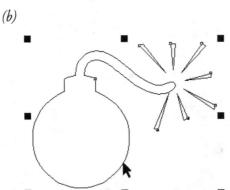

If you are in *wireframe* mode, you have to click on the edge of the object to select it (b).

Once selected, an object displays eight small handles around its edge. This is known as a highlight box. When you select an object, the status line indicates what sort of object it is, as well as its size, position, fill, and outline. To select more than one object, you can hold down the Shift key while clicking the Pick Tool on all the objects you want to select. Choose *Select All* from the **Edit** menu to select everything on the screen at once.

Use the Tab key to select the objects on the screen in turn automatically.

MARQUEE SELECTION

Figure 3. To select one or more objects, hold the mouse down and drag it over all the objects. This procedure selects all objects that fall entirely within the selection marquee (a).

(a)

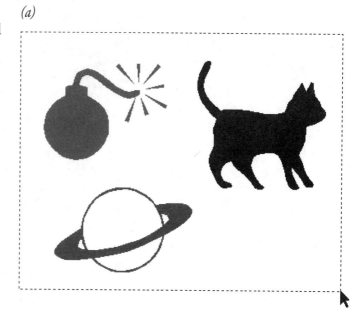

When you have selected multiple objects, all the objects are included in the one highlight box (b). You can now apply any option to these multiple objects that you could apply to a single selected object.

(b)

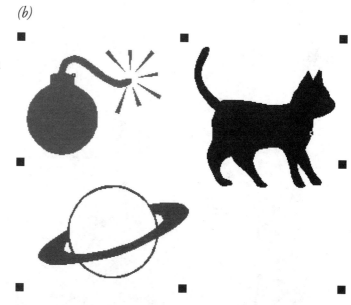

When you have more than one object selected, the status line indicates how many objects you have selected.

MOVING OBJECTS

Figure 4. In *full-color* mode, you can move a filled object with the Pick Tool if you hold the mouse button down when the cursor is anywhere on the object's interior, and drag the mouse. The object moves to where you release the mouse button.

If the object has no fill, or you are in *wireframe* mode, hold the mouse down on the border of the object, and then drag the mouse to the new position and release it. See also the *Nudge* command in Chapter 11, for another way of moving objects.

ROTATING AND SKEWING OBJECTS

Figure 5. Click twice on any objects (or once on any objects you've already selected) with the Pick Tool, to activate the *Rotate & Skew* handles (a).

To rotate an object, hold the mouse button down when the cursor is on any corner handle, and move the object in the direction you want it to rotate (b).

A crosshair appears when you put the cursor over a rotate handle

(a)   *(b)*

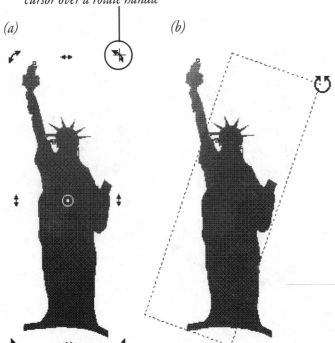

After releasing the mouse, you have rotated the object (c).

(c)

Figure 6. To skew an object, hold the mouse down on any middle handle and move it in the direction you wish to skew the object (a).

The result of skewing this graphic is shown in (b).

(a)

(b)

CENTER OF ROTATION

The (⊙) symbol that appears in the middle of an object when you activate the rotate and skew handles, shows the center of rotation. You can move this symbol if you drag it to a new position.

Moving this symbol changes the center of rotation of an object. The center of rotation symbol remains in the new position until you change it. See Chapter 7, on how to rotate and skew using the associated menu commands.

RESIZING OBJECTS

Figure 7. To resize an object, hold the mouse button down with the cursor on one of the eight selection handles and drag the mouse toward, or away from, the center of the object. The object then resizes accordingly.

Using one of the four corner handles to resize an object, as shown in this example, scales the graphic, keeping it in its true proportion.

(a)

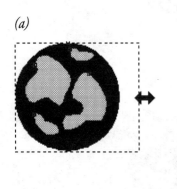

Figure 8. Using any of the four remaining handles (a) stretches or distorts the object, as in (b).

Clicking on the right mouse button after you have moved, rotated, skewed, mirrored, or resized objects leaves a copy of the original object behind.

(b)

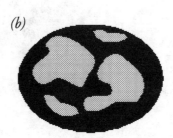

MIRRORING OBJECTS

Figure 9. To mirror an object horizontally, hold the mouse down on either side handle (a), press the Ctrl key, and drag the mouse across the object (b). Release the mouse before releasing the Ctrl key to mirror the object (c).

To mirror an object vertically, follow the same steps, but use either the top or bottom center handle.

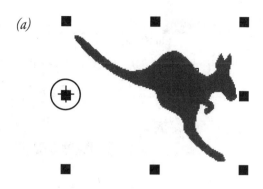

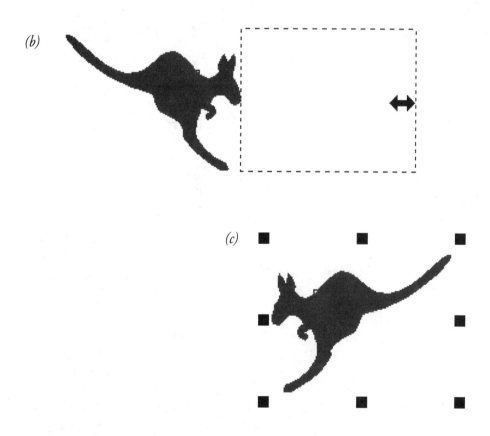

Edit	
Undo Stretch	Ctrl+Z
Redo	Alt+Ret
Repeat Stretch	Ctrl+R
Cut	Ctrl+X
Copy	Ctrl+C
Paste	Ctrl+V
Paste Special...	
Delete	**Del**
Duplicate	Ctrl+D
Clone	
Copy Attributes From...	
Select All	
Object	
Links...	

DELETING OBJECTS

Figure 10. To delete an object, first select it with the Pick Tool, then press the Delete key on the keyboard; alternatively, select *Delete* from the **Edit** menu.

THE SHAPE TOOL

Figure 11. The Shape Tool (✦) is directly below the Pick Tool in the Toolbox. Once this tool is selected, your mouse cursor looks like this. The F10 key also activates the Shape Tool.

Figure 12. Use the Shape Tool to manipulate objects you have placed or drawn on the page. Once you select an object with this tool, a series of nodes becomes apparent; you can move and manipulate these nodes and their properties.

You select objects with the Shape Tool the same way you select objects with the Pick Tool. In *wireframe* mode, and when the object has no fill in *full-color* mode, click on the perimeter of the object. If the object has a fill and you are working in *full-color* mode, click anywhere on the object.

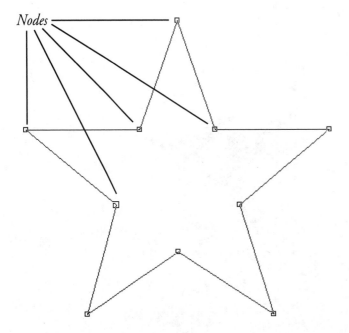

Nodes

To deselect an object selected with the Shape Tool, click on another object. Alternatively, you can select the Pick Tool and then click away from the object.

You can also use the Shape Tool to crop bitmaps, and modify rectangles, ellipses, and text.

MODIFYING RECTANGLES

Figure 13. To modify a rectangle with the Shape Tool, select one of its four corners (a) and move it towards the center to create the round-cornered rectangle shown in (b).

(a) 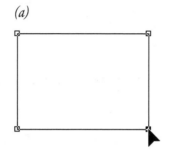 *(b)*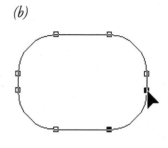

MODIFYING ELLIPSES

Figure 14. To modify an ellipse with the Shape Tool, move the node on the circumference of the ellipse to make an arc or a wedge (a).

If you drag the mouse inside the ellipse, you will create a wedge shape (b).

If you drag the mouse outside the ellipse, you will get an arc (c).

(a) 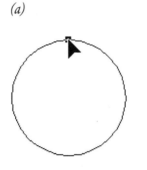 *(b)*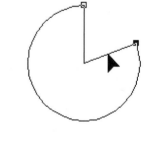

(c)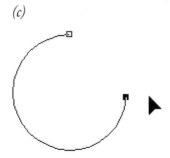

CONVERTING TO CURVES

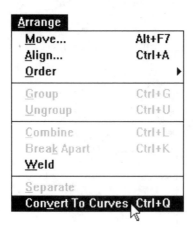

Figure 15. You can't change text, rectangles, and ellipses with the Shape Tool the same way as objects you have created with the Pencil Tool (see **The Shape Tool & Text** section later in this chapter). You must convert them to curves first. To do this, select the object with the Pick Tool and choose *Convert To Curves* from the **Arrange** menu.

You can covert Artistic Text to curves, but not Paragraph Text. Once you do this, a series of nodes appears along the object, which lets you change the shape of the object. Once you have converted an object to curves, you cannot change it back (unless you immediately choose *Undo* from the **Edit** menu). For more information, see the *Convert To Curves* command in Chapter 9.

SELECTING NODES

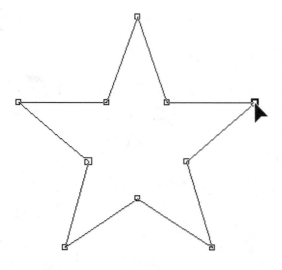

Figure 16. To select an individual node of an object selected with the Shape Tool, simply click on the node.

Figure 17. To select more than one node, hold down the Shift key and click on each node in turn (a).

(a)

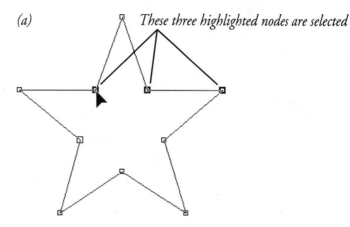

These three highlighted nodes are selected

Alternatively, use the Shape Tool to draw a selection rectangle around the nodes you wish to select. This procedure selects and highlights all nodes that fall inside this square.

(b)

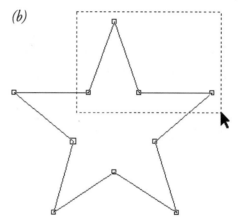

MOVING NODES

Figure 18. To move a node with the Shape Tool, hold the mouse down on a node and reposition it. Notice that some nodes, when selected, have control points attached to them, which you can also select and move when manipulating curves.

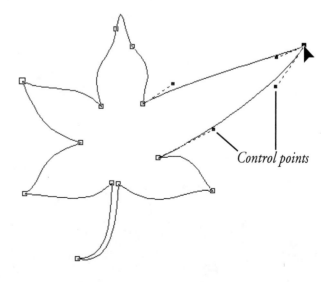

Control points

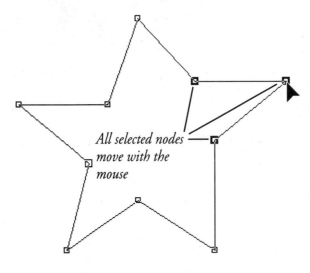

All selected nodes move with the mouse

Figure 19. You can move multiple nodes by selecting all the nodes you want to move and dragging a highlighted node to a new position. All the selected nodes move with the mouse.

You can also move nodes using the directional arrow keys on your keyboard. For more information on this procedure, see the *Nudge* option in the *Preferences* dialog box, from the **Special** menu.

MOVING CONTROL POINTS

Certain nodes have control points connected to them, which show when you select them (see Figure 18). Curved segment's nodes have control points, while straight (line) segments do not.

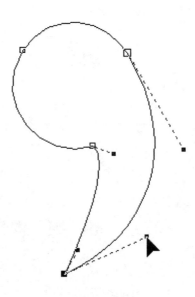

Figure 20. You can move a control point with the Shape Tool to change the shape of a curved segment. How this affects the shape of the object is determined by the type of node attached to the segment (see **Editing nodes** on the next page).

MOVING CURVED SEGMENTS

Figure 21. You can change the shape of the line by dragging the line segment with the mouse. The way the segment moves depends on what sort of curve it is.

For more information see the *Cusp*, *Smooth*, and *Symmet* options in the next section.

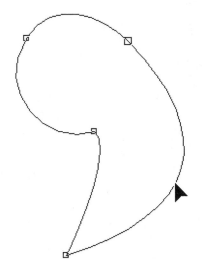

EDITING NODES

Figure 22. To change the properties of any nodes, double-click on an object, or one of its nodes, with the Shape Tool. This activates the *Node Edit* Roll-up window.

This option does not work with text, rectangles, or ellipses.

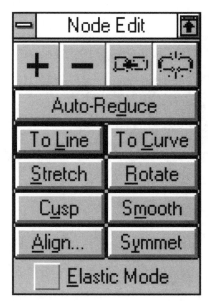

ADDING NODES

(a)

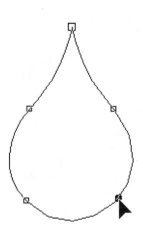

Figure 23. If the *Node Edit* Roll-up is not active, double-click on the segment where you want the node to appear. This places a black dot (•) on the line where you clicked the mouse and opens the *Node Edit* Roll-up (a).

If the *Node Edit* Roll-up is already open, click once on the line to add the black dot in the position you want to add the node.

(b)

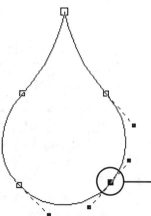

Click on the **+** button in the *Node Edit* Roll-up to add the node; this adds the node where the black dot is.

Alternatively, you can use the + key on the numeric keypad on your keyboard to add nodes where the black dot is.

You have now added a node to the object

If you click on the **+** in the *Node Edit* Roll-up when you have a node selected, this adds a node midway along the segment adjacent to the selected node.

You can add several nodes to an object at once by selecting the nodes next to the segments you want to add the nodes, then clicking on the **+** button in the *Node Edit* Roll-up.

DELETING NODES

Deleting nodes in an object is sometimes necessary to smooth out the object. The less nodes you use to create an object the better.

Figure 24. If the *Node Edit* Roll-up is not active, double-click on the node you want to delete, and then click on the — button when the *Node Edit* Roll-up appears.

If the *Node Edit* Roll-up is on, click on the node with the Shape Tool, and select the — button.

If you have multiple nodes selected, the — option in the *Node Edit* Roll-up or the Delete key on your keyboard removes all selected nodes.

JOINING NODES

You use the chain links icon ( ) in the *Node Edit* Roll-up option to join two nodes.

Figure 25. Select two nodes with the Shape Tool (they must be the last or first nodes of the same path), double-click on one of them to activate the *Node Edit* Roll-up, and then click on the chain links icon ( ) to join the nodes (a).

If the *Node Edit* Roll-up is already active, select the two nodes and choose this option.

(a)

Selected nodes

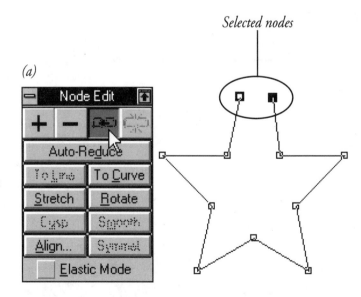

(b)

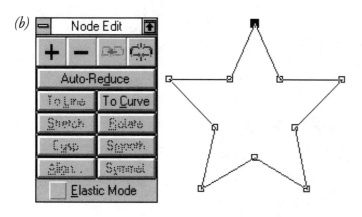

You have now joined the two nodes (b).

(a)

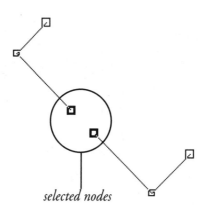

selected nodes

Figure 26. You can also join starting or ending nodes that belong to different subpaths of a path. All objects in CorelDRAW are known as paths. A path can contain several subpaths. When you select an object with the Shape Tool, the status line indicates how many subpaths (if any) are included in the one path.

The selected nodes in (a) belong to different subpaths of the same path. If you now clicked on the chain links icon ( ), the nodes will join and the two subpaths will become one path (b).

(b)

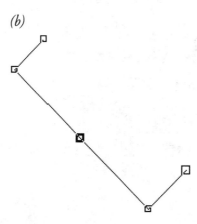

Figure 27. To join two separate paths (which differ from sub-paths), first select them both with the Pick Tool. Then, choose *Combine* from the **Arrange** menu (a).

(a)

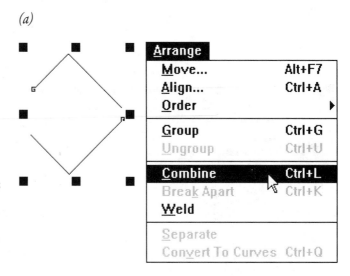

Now select the two nodes you wish to join with the Shape Tool and choose the chain links icon from the *Node Edit* Roll-up. If this Roll-up is not active, double-click on one of the selected nodes to activate the *Node Edit* Roll-up (b).

This procedure joins the selected nodes (c).

(b)

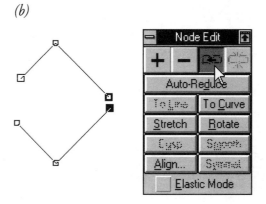

(c)

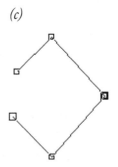

BREAKING NODES

Use the broken chain (⊂⊃) option in the *Node Edit* Roll-up to break a line or a closed object.

Figure 28. If the *Node Edit* Roll up is active, click once on the node or line segment where you want to break the object (a). If the Roll-up is not active, double-click on the node or line segment to activate it.

Click on the broken chain (break) icon from the *Node Edit* Roll-up window (b).

This breaks the section of the line where you clicked the mouse (c). You can then move these nodes separately with the Shape Tool.

(a)

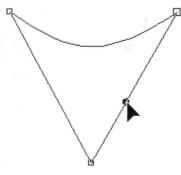

(b)

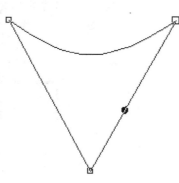

(c)

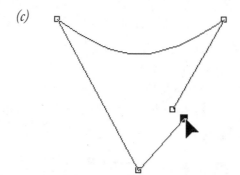

AUTO REDUCE

Figure 29. You can use the *Auto Reduce* option to let CorelDRAW remove any unnecessary nodes from an object that you think has too many nodes.

Marquee select the object with the Shape Tool to select all the nodes (a).

Click on the *Auto Reduce* option in the *Node Edit* Roll-up (b).

CorelDRAW removes all the nodes from the object that aren't necessary for its shape (c).

(a)

(b)

(c)

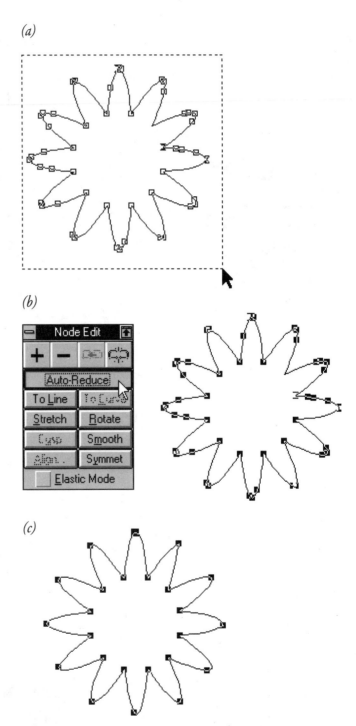

TO LINE

The *To Line* option converts the distance between two nodes from a curve to a straight line. You can access this option only if the selected segment is a curve.

(a)

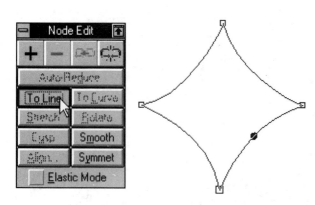

Figure 30. If the *Node Edit* Roll-up is not active, double-click on the segment that you want to convert to a straight line. This adds a black dot along the line and activates the *Node Edit* Roll-up. Now, click on the *To Line* option (a).

If the *Node Edit* Roll-up is active, click on the segment that you want to convert to a straight line, and then choose the *To Line* option.

(b)

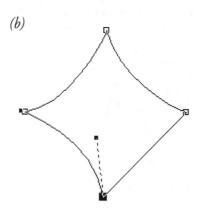

CorelDRAW converts the curved line to a straight line (b).

If the line is actually concave, as in this example, you will see the change in the line from curve to straight. If the line is a curve but is in a straight position, you will not necessarily notice any change in the line.

What will happen though, is the control points of the nodes connected to this line disappear. Straight lines do not have any control points attached to their nodes.

TO CURVE

The *To Curve* option changes the distance between two nodes from a straight line to a curve.

Figure 31. Double-click on the straight line to activate the *Node Edit* Roll-up and choose the *To Curve* option (a).

If the *Node Edit* Roll-up is already active, click once on the straight line you want to convert to a curved line, and then click on the *To Curve* option.

You can now manipulate the line as a curve. Notice the control points attached to the nodes on either side of the line (b).

(a)

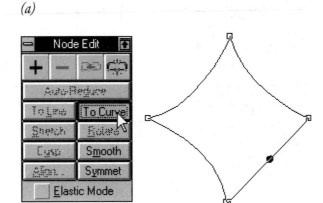

(b)

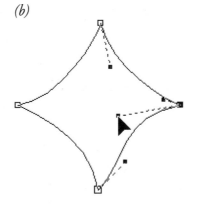

STRETCH

You can resize sections of a curved object using the *Stretch* option in the *Node Edit* Roll-up.

(a)

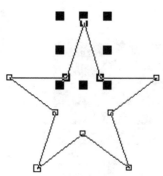

Figure 32. Select two or more nodes with the Shape Tool and click on the *Stretch* button. Eight selection handles appear around the selected nodes as though you had selected an object with the Pick Tool (a).

(If your *Node Edit* Roll-up is not active, double-click on one of the selected nodes to open it.)

Use the mouse to resize the section that has the selected nodes in it (b).

The segments with the selected nodes resize accordingly (c).

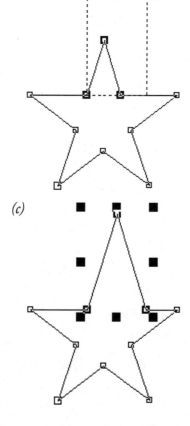

(b)

(c)

ROTATE

You can rotate and skew sections of a curved object using the *Rotate* option in the *Node Edit* Roll-up.

Figure 33. Select two or more nodes with the Shape Tool and click on the *Rotate* option in the *Node Edit* Roll-up. Rotate and skew handles appear around the selected nodes (a).

Use the mouse to rotate (b) or skew (c) the area containing the selected nodes.

(a)

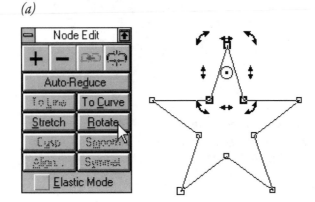

(b)   *(c)*

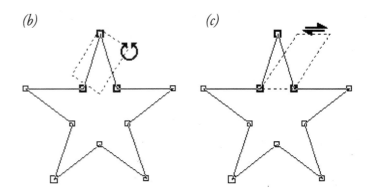

CUSP

Figure 34. You can use the *Cusp* option in the *Node Edit* Roll-up to change a selected node's attributes. This allows you to move the control points on either side of the node independently without affecting another part of the line. A cusp node lets you make a sharp change in direction in a line.

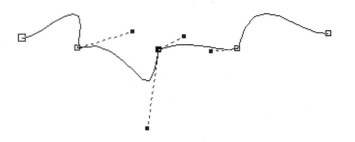

SMOOTH

Figure 35. The *Smooth* option converts a sharp point to a smooth point. Unlike the *Cusp* option, the control points of a *Smooth* node, when you move them, affect the lines on both sides of the node. This allows the control points to run along a straight line on either side of the node.

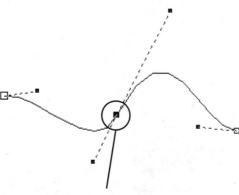

We applied the Smooth option to this middle node, causing the control points on either side of the node to run in a straight line. Moving one of the control points therefore affects the other control point.

SYMMET

Figure 36. The *Symmet* option is similar to the *Smooth* option, but the control points move the line in opposite directions of equal distance.

The control points of a node which you have given the *Symmet* option to (in this case the middle node), move in the opposite direction but at an equal distance. This option also moves the line on either side of the node the same way.

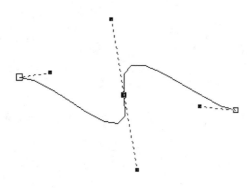

ALIGN

Figure 37. To use the *Align* command in the *Node Edit* Roll-Up, you must first have two nodes selected with the Shape Tool. After double-clicking on one of the selected nodes, you then click on the *Align* option.

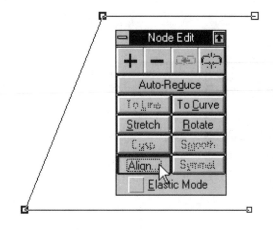

In this example, we selected the top and bottom nodes on the left-hand side of the object. We then double-clicked on one of the nodes to open the *Node Edit* Roll-Up, and then on the *Align* option to activate the *Node Align* dialog box of Figure 38.

Figure 38. In the *Node Align* dialog box, you can align nodes horizontally, vertically, or by their control points. This is useful for technical drawings where you need a high degree of accuracy. For this example, we selected the *Align Vertical* option for the two selected nodes in Figure 37.

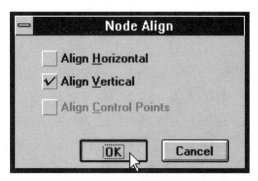

Figure 39. The above method has now vertically aligned the two nodes.

You can also use the *Align* option to line up the edges of objects. You can align objects from different paths if they are first combined through the **Arrange** menu.

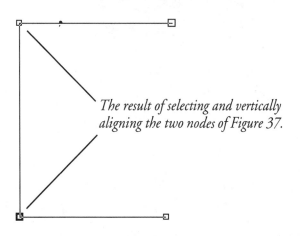

The result of selecting and vertically aligning the two nodes of Figure 37.

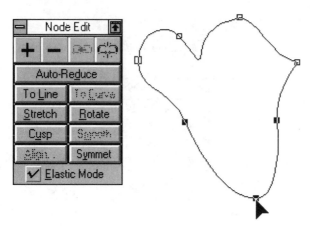

ELASTIC MODE

Figure 40. Choosing the *Elastic Mode* option when you have two or more nodes selected affects the way you can move the selected nodes. As you move any one of the selected nodes, the other selected nodes move in different amounts.

CROPPING BITMAPS

Figure 41. To crop a bitmap, select it with the Shape Tool; selection handles appear around its edge (a).

(a)

Hold the mouse down on any handle and drag it towards the center of the bitmap. You may reverse this procedure to reveal any part which you have covered (b).

In this example we are cropping the bitmap from the bottom middle handle.

(b)

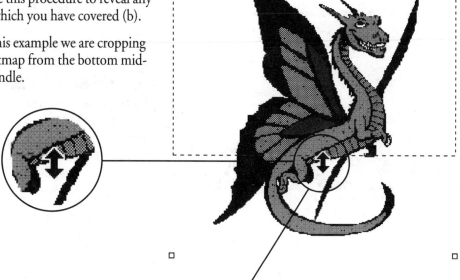

Drag a selection handle toward the center of the bitmap to crop it.

The result of cropping the bitmap from the bottom (c).

For information on manipulating text with the Shape Tool, see **The Shape Tool and Text** section later in this chapter.

(c)

THE SHAPE TOOL AND TEXT

You can use the Shape Tool with text in various ways.

MOVING INDIVIDUAL LETTERS

(a)

(b)

Figure 42. If you select text with the Shape Tool, each letter displays a node to the bottom left (a).

You can move each letter independently if you select a node and reposition the letter (b). You can move more than one letter at a time if you hold down the Shift key to select multiple nodes.

Alternatively, select multiple nodes using marquee selection.

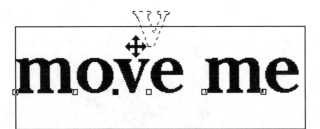

Figure 43. You can move individual letters with both Artistic and Paragraph Text.

MODIFYING KERNING AND LEADING

Figure 44. To modify the kerning or inter-letter spacing of a text string, first position the Shape Tool over the right arrow marker (a).

(a)

Then, drag the marker to the right to increase the spacing, or to the left to decrease the spacing. We are dragging the marker to the right (b).

(b)

You increase the spacing between the letters when dragging to the right (c).

(c)

If you hold down the Ctrl key as you drag the right arrow marker, you increase or decrease the inter-word spacing only.

You can move the arrow marker at the left of the selected text block up or down (d). This modifies the leading (line spacing) of the text. This works only if there is more than one line of text.

(d)

Modifying kerning and leading works with both Artistic and Paragraph Text.

CHANGING SINGLE CHARACTER ATTRIBUTES

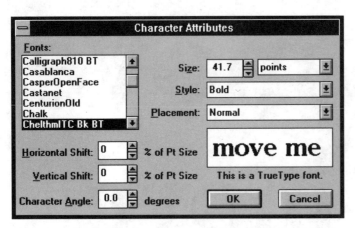

Figure 45. If you double-click on any node to the left of a letter with the Shape Tool, you activate the *Character Attributes* dialog box. Here you can change font, point size, position, and angle of any letter or letters. For more information, see Chapter 8.

Figure 46. In this example, we changed the font, point size, and character angle of the letter "o."

Figure 47. In this diagram, we have arbitrarily changed all characters of this text string.

Figure 48. Changing single character attributes also works with Paragraph Text.

Figure 49. You can also change the outline and fill of individual letters. By selecting a single letter with the Shape Tool, as previously described, you can then change the fill and outline of this letter without affecting the rest of the text.

For more information on outline and fill options, see Chapter 3.

THE ZOOM TOOL

Figure 50. Use the Zoom Tool (🔍) to change the viewing size and position of the screen. Selecting the Zoom Tool activates the Zoom Tool fly-out.

Included in the Zoom Tool are five different options as displayed here.

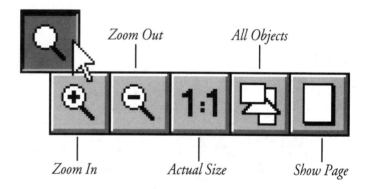

Zoom Out   *All Objects*

Zoom In   *Actual Size*   *Show Page*

Figure 51. The *Zoom In* tool enlarges the section that falls within the area you selected by dragging the mouse. You can also press the F2 key to activate the *Zoom In* tool.

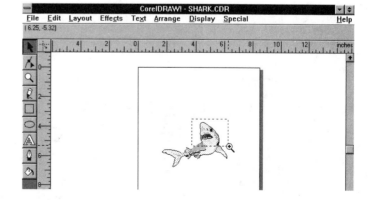

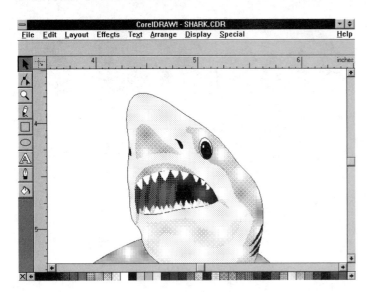

Figure 52. The section defined in Figure 51 now fills the entire working screen. You may use this tool continuously in order to enlarge an area you wish to view more closely.

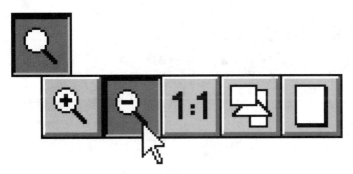

Figure 53. Selecting the *Zoom Out* option in the Zoom Tool fly-out takes the page view back to the size it was before you magnified it or, by a factor of two each time you press the mouse, if there was no previous zoom in. You can also activate the *Zoom Out* tool by pressing the F3 key.

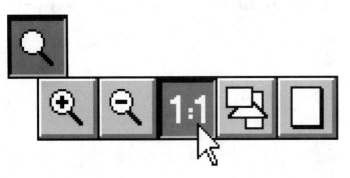

Figure 54. When you select the *Actual Size* option, the screen displays the drawing at the size it prints.

Figure 55. Selecting the *All Objects* option displays all objects in the current file, even if they are outside the working page. You can also use the F4 key for this.

Figure 56. Selecting the *Show Page* option displays the whole working page, taking you back to the view of Figure 51. Alternatively, you can use the Shift and F4 keys.

THE PENCIL TOOL

Figure 57. The Pencil Tool (ℓ) is the drawing tool; you operate it in either *Freehand* or *Bezier* mode. By default, *Freehand* mode is active when you first select the Pencil Tool.

Alternatively, you can use the F5 key to activate the Pencil Tool.

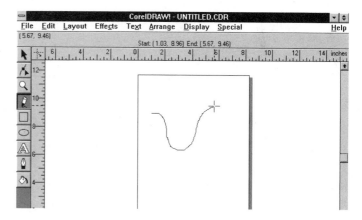

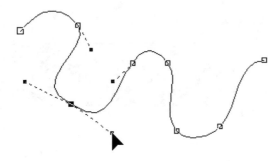

FREEHAND MODE ✎

Figure 58. To draw curved lines in this mode, hold the mouse down and drag it on the page the same way you would with a pencil. After you release the mouse, the line will display a series of nodes; you can then manipulate these nodes with the Shape Tool.

(a)

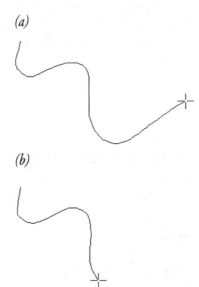

(b)

Figure 59. When you are drawing lines with the Pencil Tool in *Freehand* mode, you can erase what you have drawn before you release the mouse. If you are not happy with the curves you are drawing (a), hold down the Shift key and drag the mouse back over the line you have just drawn.

The line disappears as you drag the mouse back over it (b). Stop dragging the mouse when you have erased the part of the line you don't want.

STRAIGHT LINES

Figure 60. To draw a straight line in *Freehand* mode, click the mouse once on the page, move it to the end point of the line, and click the mouse once more to end the line.

You can continue drawing from this line by connecting a new line to it. To do this, click the mouse (with the Pencil Tool still active) directly over the last node of the line. Corel-DRAW assumes you want to connect the lines and joins them up for you. The *AutoJoin* option in the *Preferences - Curves* dialog box lets you adjust the distance from the node that CorelDRAW uses to assume you want to connect new lines with existing lines.

Figure 61. To change the direction of straight lines, double-click the mouse at the point you want to change direction. This adds a node in the spot you double-clicked while still allowing you to continue drawing straight lines with the Pencil Tool.

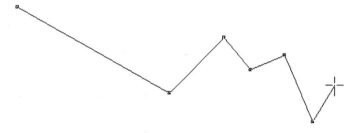

CLOSED OBJECTS

Figure 62. To create a closed object in *Freehand* mode, begin drawing as if you were creating a straight line, but double-click in the second position, so you can continue the line in a different direction. Repeat this procedure to create as many nodes as you need for the shape of the object.

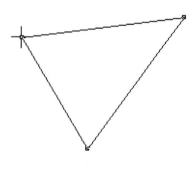

To close the object, click the mouse once on top of the starting point. If you didn't close the object, the right side of the status line reads *Open Path* if you select the object with the Pick Tool. If this is the case, you can join the start and end nodes using the *Join* command from the *Node Edit* Roll-up.

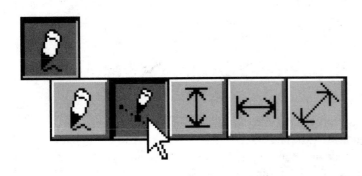

BEZIER MODE

Figure 63. To activate *Bezier* mode, hold the mouse down on the Pencil Tool in the Toolbox until the fly-out menu appears. Select the *Bezier* option as shown. This remains active until you change it back to *Freehand* mode. Drawing in *Bezier* mode gives the nodes slightly different qualities, making it easy to draw curves.

Note: You may find it easier to draw an object using straight lines as previously described. You can add the curved sections later using the Shape Tool and the options in the Node Edit Roll-up.

DRAWING CURVES

Figure 64. Hold the mouse down and begin to draw. Notice that you can manipulate built-in control points in order to define the direction and angle of the curve (a).

Click once somewhere else to continue this curve. Repeat this to draw any shape you like (b).

To draw a straight line in *Bezier* mode, click the mouse button at the starting point, move it elsewhere on the page, and click the mouse button again.

(a)

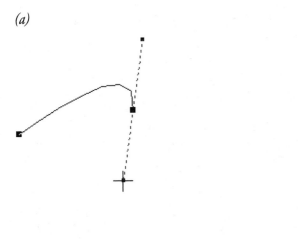

(b)

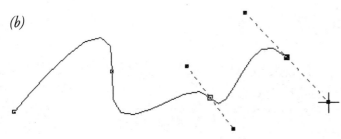

When drawing a closed object in *Bezier* mode, you click the mouse once only at each change of direction. To close an object, click on the beginning node, as in *Freehand* mode. To stop drawing an object that is not a closed object, click once again on the Pencil Tool in the Toolbox.

AUTOTRACE

With the Pencil Tool, you can trace TIF, PCX, GIF, and BMP images imported into CorelDRAW. Do not confuse this feature with CorelTRACE, which is a separate tracing utility that comes with CorelDRAW.

You can trace bitmaps in *full-color* or *wireframe* mode, with either *Freehand* or *Bezier* mode active.

Figure 65. In this figure, we are looking at a bitmap file in *wireframe* mode. You may find it easier to trace the bitmap in this mode, because if it has a black outline or fill (*full-color* mode), it would be hard to see where you were tracing.

Figure 66. Select the bitmap with the Pick Tool, and then choose the Pencil Tool. Note the new shape of the mouse pointer (+–). This indicates you can now use the Pencil Tool for tracing.

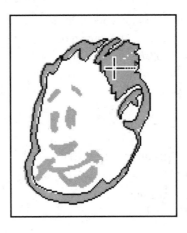

Figure 67. Click the mouse on the section of the graphic that you want to trace. After a few seconds, this procedure displays an outline around the selected area.

Repeat this process until you are satisfied with the results. Once you have finished, you can move or delete the underlying bitmap, and also edit and color the traced image like any other drawing in CorelDRAW.

DIMENSION LINES

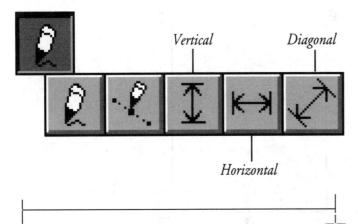

Vertical   *Diagonal*

Horizontal

Figure 68. The three remaining options on the Pencil Tool fly-out are for drawing dimension lines. You can use these tools to draw lines for technical drawings to measure and label vertical (☐), horizontal (⟵⟶), and diagonal (⤢) distances.

Figure 69. To draw a line with any of the dimensional line drawing tools, first select the tool from the Pencil Tool fly-out. Then, click the mouse where you want to start drawing the line and move the mouse either horizontally, vertically, or diagonally (depending on the tool you have selected).

A line from where you first clicked the mouse follows the mouse as you drag it. In this example we used the horizontal tool.

Figure 70. Click the mouse once again in the position that you want to end the dimension line. You can then drag the mouse to establish the extension line height.

The extension lines appear at opposing ends of the dimension line. Then, click the mouse once more to finish the line. The dimension text appears along the line where you clicked the mouse.

You can also select and edit this text independently of the dimension line through the commands in the **Text** menu. For more information on formatting this text, see Chapter 11.

THE RECTANGLE TOOL

Figure 71. Use the Rectangle Tool (▤) to create rectangles and squares. To draw a rectangle with this tool, drag the mouse diagonally in any direction. Release the mouse button to stop drawing the rectangle.

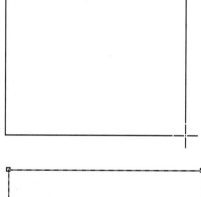

Figure 72. You can resize and move a rectangle with the Pick Tool. Note that the status line always reflects the width and height of a selected rectangle.

DRAWING SQUARES

To draw a square, hold down the Ctrl key while drawing with the Rectangle Tool, and do not release it until you release the mouse button.

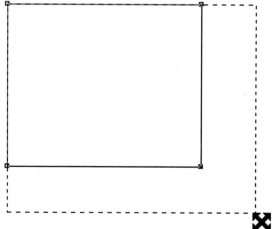

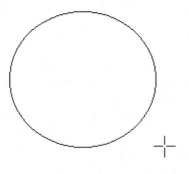

THE ELLIPSE TOOL

Figure 73. Use the Ellipse Tool (◯) to create circles and ellipses. To draw an ellipse, select the tool, drag the mouse diagonally to a new position, and release the button.

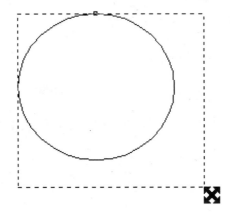

Figure 74. You can resize and move an ellipse with the Pick Tool. The status line always reflects the width and height of a selected ellipse.

DRAWING CIRCLES

To draw a perfect circle, hold down the Ctrl key while drawing the circle, and do not release it until you release the mouse button.

THE TEXT TOOL

You use the Text Tool in CorelDRAW (𝔸) to add text to the page. You can then go on to edit, manipulate, and format this text using the Pick Tool, the Shape Tool, and the options in the **Text** menu (see Chapter 8). You can also use the Text Tool to place Symbols on the page.

You can add text to the page in two different ways: Artistic Text and Paragraph Text. In this section we discuss the differences between Artistic Text and Paragraph Text and how you apply them to your documents.

ARTISTIC TEXT

We will look at Artistic Text first. You use Artistic Text when you want to create a special effect with your text.

Figure 75. After you have selected the Text Tool, click anywhere on the page. The text entry cursor appears on the screen where you clicked with the mouse. You can now type and edit text directly on the screen.

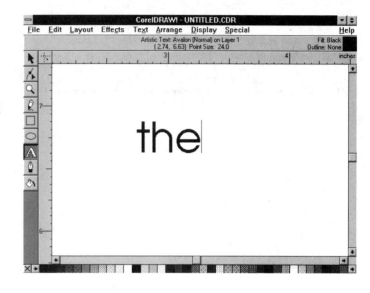

Figure 76. To edit the text attributes, make sure the insertion point is still in the text string you want to edit. Select *Edit Text* from the **Text** menu to open the *Artistic Text* dialog box.

    You can also select text with the Pick Tool when choosing this command. When working with Artistic Text, you have a limit of 250 characters in each text block.

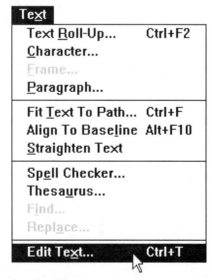

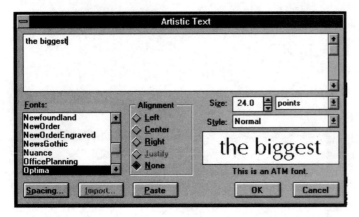

Figure 77. You can edit the text in the text entry window at the top of the *Artistic Text* dialog box and change the typeface by selecting a different option from the *Fonts* list. Changing the *Justification* options affects the alignment of text in relation to where on the page you clicked the Text Tool.

You can also alter the size and style of the text through this dialog box, among other things. For more information on the options available in this dialog box, see Chapter 8.

EDITING ARTISTIC TEXT

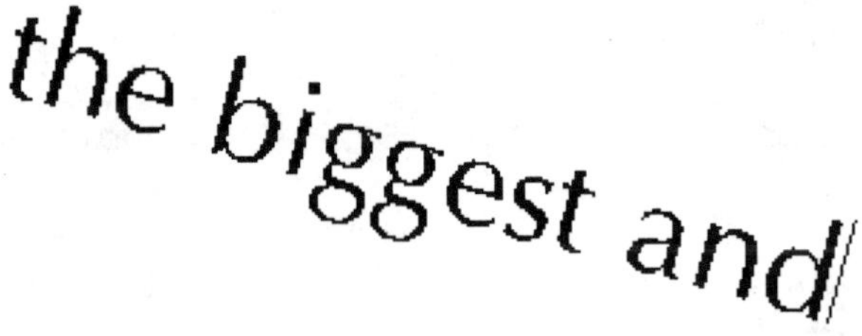

Figure 78. You can directly edit Artistic Text that you have manipulated. Note the insertion point at the end of this rotated text block.

the biggest and

To put the insertion point back into a text block after working with another object, click anywhere on the text block with the Text Tool. You can also select the text with the Pick Tool, then choose the Text Tool from the Toolbox. Doing either automatically inserts the text cursor at the end of the text block.

If you have applied an envelope, extrusion, or perspective to your Artistic Test, you can edit it through the *Artistic Text* dialog box. When you click the Text Tool on text that you have applied any of these effects to, it automatically activates the *Artistic Text* dialog box.

Figure 79. You can also highlight text with the Text Tool (in the same way you would in a word processing program). You do this by holding the mouse down (with the Text Tool selected) and dragging across the text. You can then directly edit the text.

the biggest and

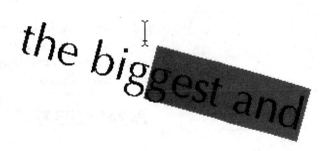

Figure 80. You can (a) move, (b) rotate, (c) skew, and (d) resize Artistic Text with the Pick Tool in the same way as you can other objects in CorelDRAW.

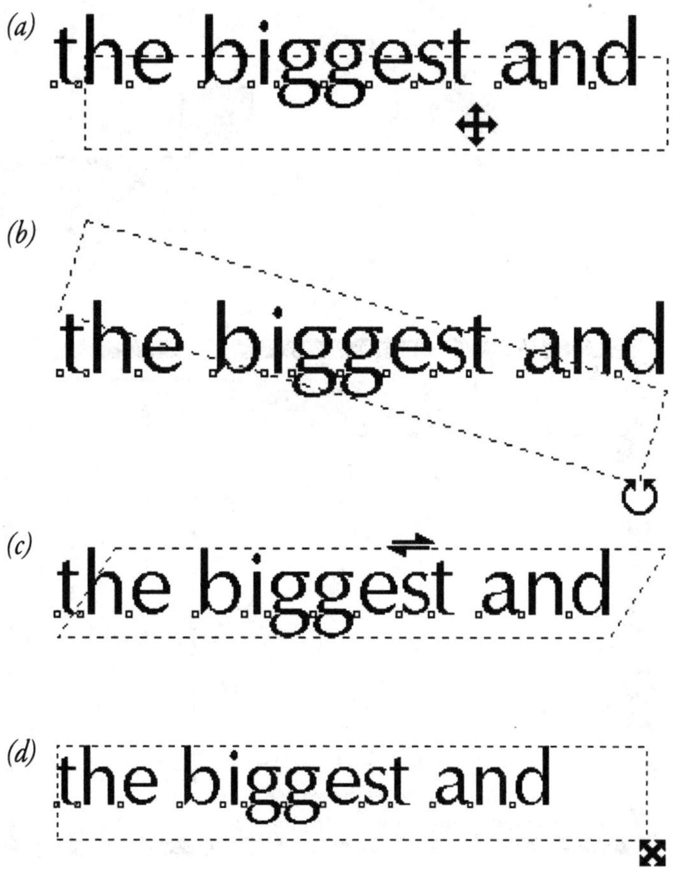

(a)
the biggest and
(b)
the biggest and
(c)
the biggest and
(d)
the biggest and

To change the shape of text with the Shape Tool, the same way you can for other curved objects, you must convert the text to curves. For more information see the *Convert To Curves* command in Chapter 9.

PARAGRAPH TEXT

Use Paragraph Text to add lengthy blocks of text to a Corel-DRAW file. Paragraph Text has an advantage over Artistic Text, in that you have more formatting options available.

Figure 81. To place Paragraph Text on the page, hold down the mouse on the Text Tool in the Toolbox and select the Paragraph Text option (▤).

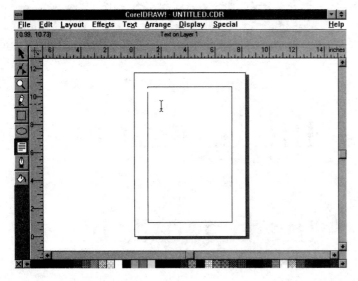

Figure 82. Once you have selected the Paragraph Text Tool, you can click the tool once on the page to add a paragraph text frame.

Figure 83. Alternatively, to create a Paragraph Text frame, drag the mouse down and to the right, releasing the button to display the text frame. This frame is the same size as the area covered with the mouse.

Figure 84. Both the Paragraph Text frames created in the previous two figures are the same except for the size. You can now type the text directly into the Paragraph Text frame, no matter how you created it.

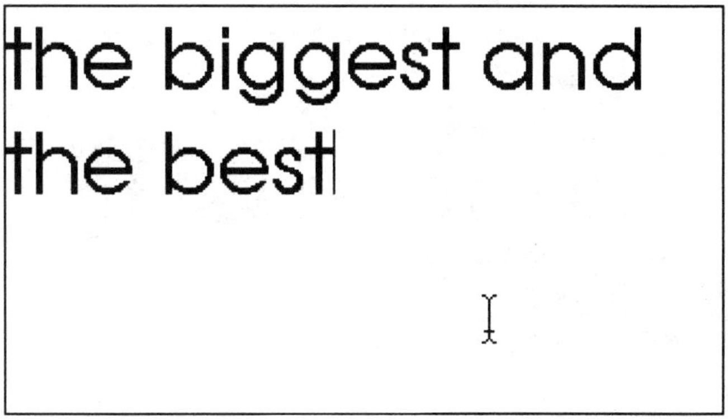

the biggest and the best

You can edit the text directly on the screen, as with Artistic Text, or through the *Paragraph Text* dialog box. To activate the *Paragraph Text* dialog box, make sure the insertion point is still in the text, or that you have selected it with the Pick Tool. Then, choose *Edit Text* from the **Text** menu.

Figure 85. The *Paragraph Text* dialog box functions the same way as the *Artistic Text* dialog box, but with a number of exceptions. In the *Paragraph Text* dialog box, you can choose the *Justify* and *Import* options. For more information on the *Paragraph Text* dialog box, see the *Edit Text* command in Chapter 8.

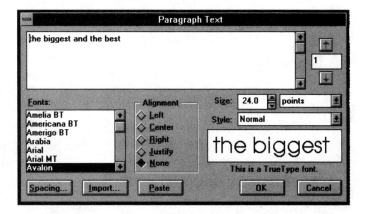

(a)

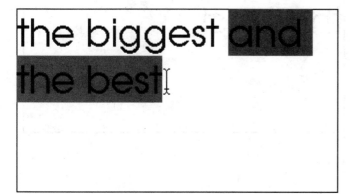

EDITING PARAGRAPH TEXT

Figure 86. To edit Paragraph Text on screen, insert the text cursor back into the text block and edit it directly (a).

You can also drag across Paragraph Text with the Text Tool before you start editing (b).

(b)

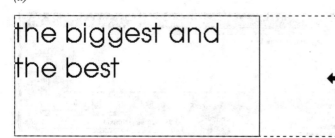

(a)

Figure 87. You cannot resize Paragraph Text by resizing the Paragraph Text frame (a).

Resizing the Paragraph Text frame with the Pick Tool resizes the text frame only, and can change the layout of the text (b). You must resize the text through the *Size* option in the *Paragraph Text* dialog box.

(b)

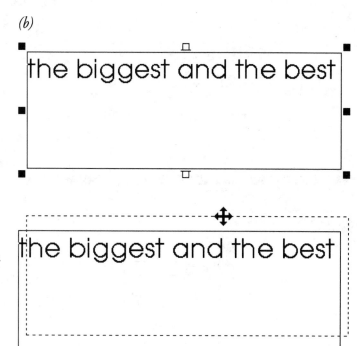

Figure 88. You can move a Paragraph Text frame with the Pick Tool by holding the mouse button down when the cursor is on the border of the frame, or on the actual text, and dragging it to a new position.

If you press the right mouse button or the + key on the numeric keypad on your keyboard while you are moving Paragraph Text, the original text block remains behind and you make a copy of it.

Figure 89. You can also rotate Paragraph Text in the same way you rotate all other objects in Corel-DRAW. Once you have rotated Paragraph Text, you can still edit it on screen.

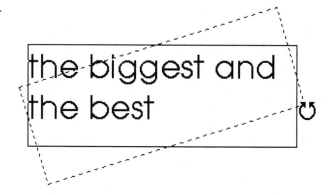

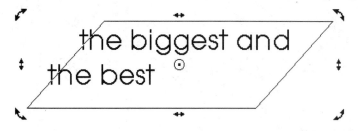

Figure 90. You can also skew Paragraph Text. When you skew Paragraph Text, however, the actual text frame skews but the text itself does not. It only reformats to adjust to the new shape of the text frame.

FLOWING PARAGRAPH TEXT

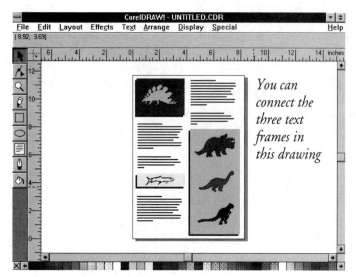

You can connect the three text frames in this drawing

Figure 91. You can flow Paragraph Text into separate text frames. These text frames can be on the same page or on different pages. This lets you resize frames without losing text, because if you shrink a text frame, the text then flows into the next connected frame.

Flowing Paragraph Text
Figure 91. You can flow Paragraph Text into separate text frames. These text frames can be on the same page or on different pages. This lets you resize frames without losing text, because if you shrink a text frame the text then flows into the next connected frame.

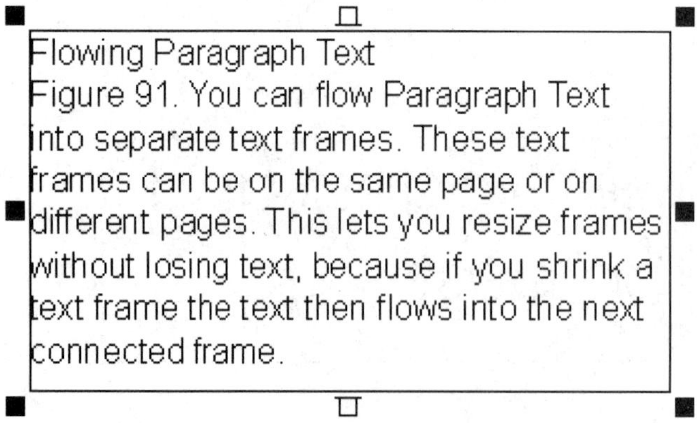

Figure 92. When you select a Paragraph Text frame that has not flowed into another frame, you will see a hollow box at the top (□) and bottom (□) of the text frame.

Figure 93. If you want to flow the text from the bottom of the frame, click on the bottom box (□). This changes the cursor to the icon indicated in this figure.

You would use this option, for example, if there wasn't enough room in the column or page to fit the whole text frame. You could reflow the remaining text in a frame in the next column or the next page.

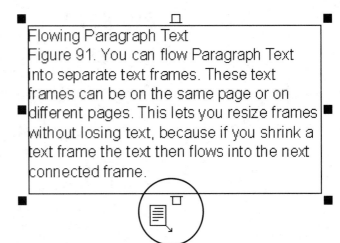

Flowing Paragraph Text
Figure 91. You can flow Paragraph Text into separate text frames. These text frames can be on the same page or on different pages. This lets you resize frames without losing text, because if you shrink a text frame the text then flows into the next connected frame.

Figure 94. Immediately after clicking on the hollow box, draw a frame with the mouse the size you want the new text frame (a).

When you release the mouse, the text flows into this frame (b). When you select the frame with the Pick Tool, the hollow box at the top of the frame has a plus symbol in it (⊞). This shows that the text block is connected to the bottom of another text frame.

If you want to flow the text from the top of the frame, follow the steps just described, but click on the hollow box (□) at the top of the text frame.

(a)

(b)

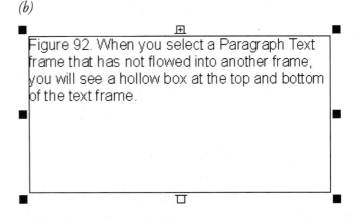

Figure 92. When you select a Paragraph Text frame that has not flowed into another frame, you will see a hollow box at the top and bottom of the text frame.

PASTING TEXT

You can paste text directly onto the page from the Windows Clipboard; this text may have come from another Windows application. You can place this as either Artistic Text or Paragraph Text.

Before pasting text, make sure you have copied some text from a Windows application other than CorelDRAW. If you plan to place the text as Artistic Text, do not copy more than 250 characters. When you paste text into CorelDRAW, you should probably place it as Paragraph Text, because Artistic Text is not as manageable.

(a)

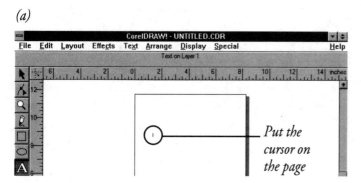

Figure 95. To paste the text as Artistic Text, select the A Text Tool and click on the page where you want the text to appear (a).

(b)

Now, choose *Paste* from the **Edit** menu (b).

Edit	
Undo Current Text Editing	Ctrl+Z
Redo	Alt+Ret
Repeat	Ctrl+R
Cut	Ctrl+X
Copy	Ctrl+C
Paste	Ctrl+V
Paste **Special**...	
De**lete**	Del
Duplicate	Ctrl+D
Clone	
Copy Attributes From...	
Select **All**	
Object	
Links...	

The text you copied now appears on the page as Artistic Text, on one line (c).

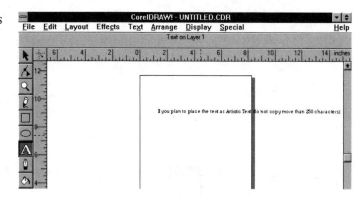

Figure 96. To paste the text as Paragraph Text, select the ▤ Text Tool and draw a frame on the page where you want the text (a).

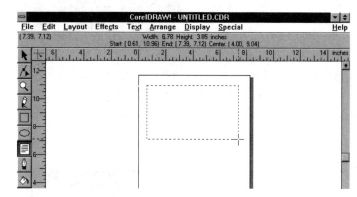

After you choose *Paste* from the **Edit** menu, the text you copied now appears in the frame (b).

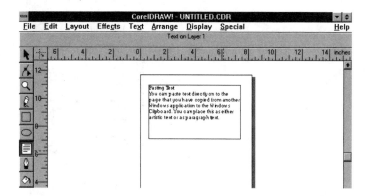

Symbols

CorelDRAW comes with over 5,000 thematic symbols covering a wide range of subjects. If you have installed the symbols, you can access them very easily, and at any stage.

Figure 97. Use the Text Tool to place symbols on the page. To activate the *Symbols* Roll-up, hold the mouse down on the Text Tool and select the ☆ icon from the fly-out that appears.

The *Symbols* icon is active in the Toolbox until you change it.

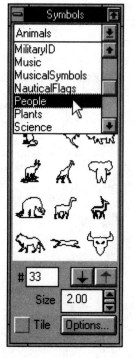

Figure 98. At the top of the *Symbols* Roll-up is a drop-down list that contains all the available symbol categories. Select the category you want to view.

Use the scroll bar and arrows to see all available categories.

Figure 99. To place a symbol on the page, first hold the mouse down on the symbol to display a box around it.

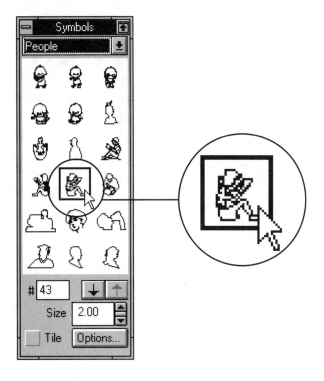

Figure 100. Then, drag the mouse out onto the page and a copy of the symbol moves with the mouse.

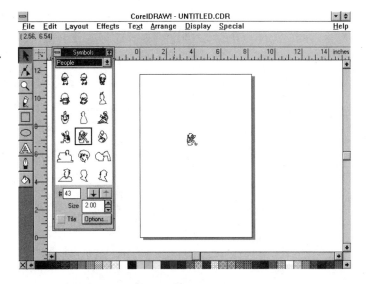

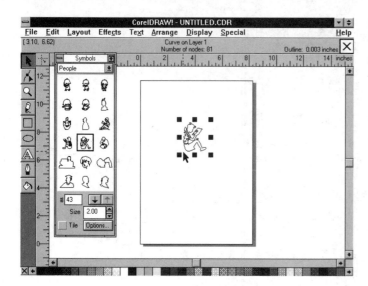

Figure 101. Release the mouse where you want the symbol to appear.

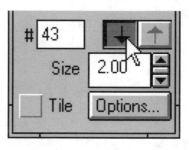

Figure 102. Click the arrows (↓ ↑) below the frame of symbols to access all symbols available in each category.

If you know the number of the symbol, you can type the number into the # frame, and a box automatically appears around the corresponding symbol. You can then drag this symbol onto the page.

The *Size* option lets you set the size of the symbol on the page. The default size for a symbol is 2 inches.

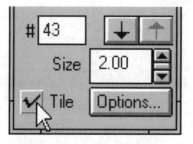

Figure 103. Check the *Tile* option in the *Symbols* Roll-up if you want to create a continuous tile pattern from a single symbol.

Figure 104. Click on the *Options* button at the bottom of the *Symbols* Roll-up to open the *Tile* dialog box. The *Horizontal* and *Vertical* options let you size each tile.

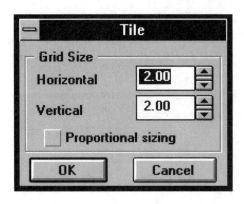

If you check the *Proportional sizing* option, you need change only one value and CorelDRAW changes the other value to match.

To ensure that the symbol tiles do not overlap, make sure the *Horizontal* and *Vertical* values in the *Tile* dialog box are the same as or smaller than the actual tile size.

Figure 105. When you drag a symbol on to the page with the *Tile* option checked, a continuous tile pattern of the symbol appears.

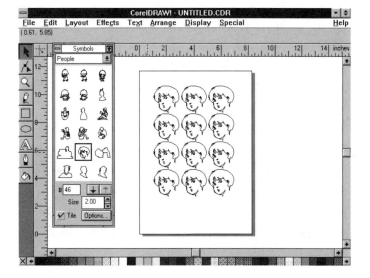

OUTLINE AND FILL TOOLS 3

THE OUTLINE AND FILL TOOLS

When you have drawn an object or placed some text on the page, and want to color it, you use the Outline and Fill tools. You also use the Outline Tool to change the thickness of an object's outline.

THE OUTLINE TOOL

Figure 1. Clicking on the Outline Tool (✒) in the Toolbox opens the Outline Tool fly-out menu. The options in this fly-out menu determine the outline color and thickness of an object.

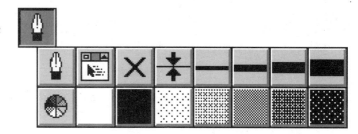

THE OUTLINE PEN

Figure 2. To open the *Outline Pen* dialog box, select the first option in the top row of the Outline Tool fly-out menu (✒). After you have made any changes in this dialog box, click on the *OK* button to apply these changes to the selected line or object.

Before opening this dialog box, make sure you have the required object selected with the Pick Tool.

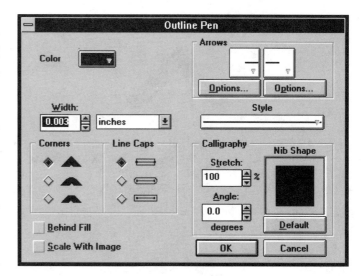

75

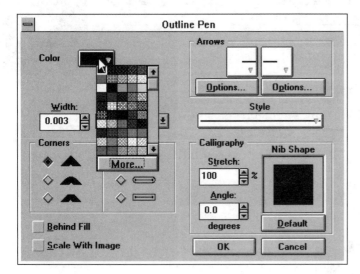

COLOR

Figure 3. The first option in the *Outline Pen* dialog box is the *Color* option. Clicking the mouse on the color swatch shows a quick-pick palette that you can select a different color from. This swatch always displays the current outline color of the selected object.

Selecting the *More* button at the bottom of the quick-pick palette activates the *Outline Color* dialog box. For more information on this dialog box, see **Outline Color** later in this chapter.

WIDTH

The *Width* option in the *Outline Pen* dialog box tells you the outline thickness of the currently selected object. Change this figure to alter the outline width.

CORNERS

Figure 4. You use the *Corners* options to modify the corners of the outline of an object, and you can also use them at the intersection of two lines.

LINE CAPS

The three *Line Caps* options affect the end of a line. When you select the top option, the outline, no matter how thick, will not extend past the end of the line. Selecting the second option rounds off the end of a line; the third option extends the end of a line for a distance equal to half the line thickness.

BEHIND FILL

Figure 5. The *Behind Fill* option lets you send the outline of a selected object behind the fill of the object. You will find this option useful when working with very thick outlines.

In this example, the two text characters have the same outline, yet the outline of the text character on the left is behind the fill.

SCALE WITH IMAGE

The *Scale With Image* option lets you scale the thickness of the outline when you resize an object. In other words, you thicken the outline when you enlarge the object, and you thin it when you reduce the object.

ARROWS

Figure 6. The *Arrows* section of the *Outline Pen* dialog box lets you apply an arrowhead to either or both ends of a line. The left-hand arrow icon represents the start of a line, and the right-hand arrow icon represents the end of a line.

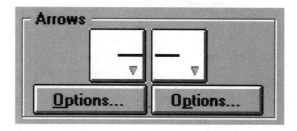

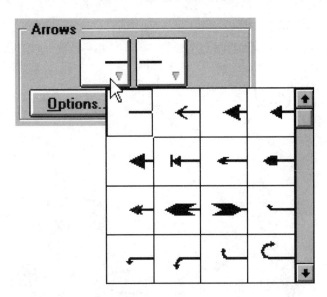

Figure 7. When you click the mouse on either arrow icon, you activate a pop-up palette containing different arrowheads.

You can use the scroll bar to the right of this pop-up palette to choose the arrowheads you can't see. Click on the arrowhead you want on the line.

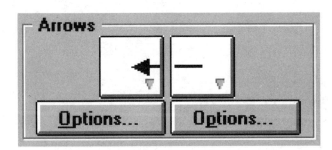

Figure 8. The arrowhead you select from the pop-up palette appears in the corresponding arrow icon.

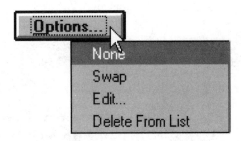

Figure 9. Selecting the *Options* button underneath each arrowhead icon displays a pop-up list. The *None* command lets you remove an arrowhead from the above icon. Use the *Swap* command to swap the current left and right arrowheads.

Figure 10. To activate the *Arrowhead Editor* dialog box, click on the *Edit* command from the *Options* pop-up list (Figure 9). Here you can resize, move, and change the direction of an arrowhead.

The *Delete From List* command in the *Options* pop-up list removes the last arrowhead selected. You would use this command if you have created your own arrowhead, but later wanted to delete it.

For more information on creating arrowheads, see Chapter 11.

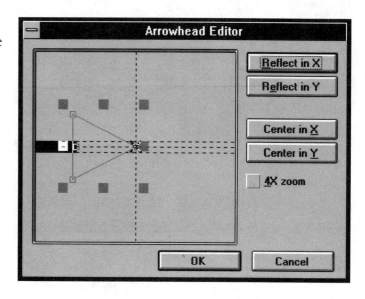

Figure 11. The thickness of a line determines the size of an arrowhead. You can view arrowheads in *full-color* mode only, not *wireframe* mode.

You cannot copy or cut arrowheads to the Windows Clipboard.

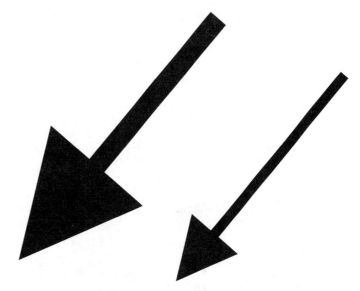

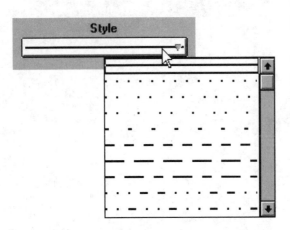

STYLE

Figure 12. The *Style* option in the *Outline Pen* dialog box lets you apply different dashed and dotted patterns to a selected outline. Click on the *Style* display field to open the associated pop-up menu.

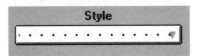

Figure 13. Select the dashed or dotted pattern you want. Clicking on *OK* in the *Outline Pen* dialog box applies the current *Style* to the outline of the selected object.

CALLIGRAPHY

The options in this section of the *Outline Pen* dialog box let you apply a calligraphic outline to an object.

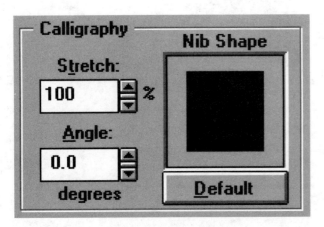

Figure 14. You can adjust the *Stretch* and *Angle* settings to create the calligraphic outline. As you alter these settings, the *Nib Shape* square changes to reflect this.

Figure 15. You can hold the mouse button down with the cursor on the *Nib Shape* square and move it around until you get the right angle and stretch. The *Stretch* and *Angle* settings change accordingly when you alter the *Nib Shape* square.

Clicking on the *Default* button returns the *Nib Shape* square back to the normal settings of 100% *Stretch* and 0.0 *Angle*.

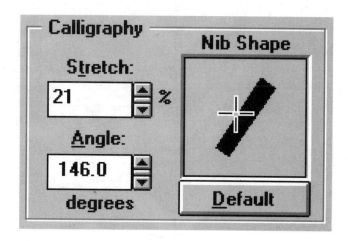

Figure 16. You can vary the *Width*, *Angle*, and *Stretch* options in the *Outline Pen* dialog box to create examples similar to this.

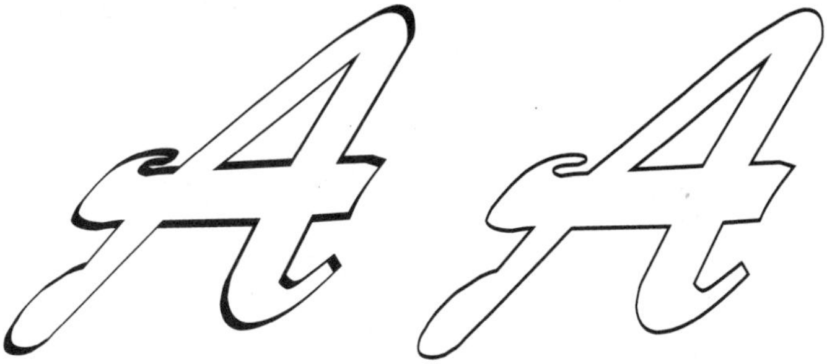

PEN ROLL-UP

Figure 17. To display the *Pen* Roll-up, select the second option (▤) in the top row of the *Outline Tool* fly-out menu of Figure 1.

This window gives you a chance to change some of the pen options without having to open the *Outline Pen* dialog box discussed above.

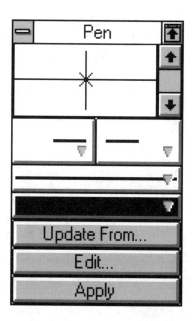

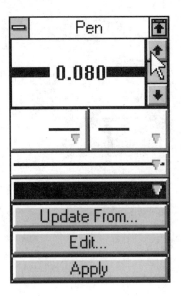

Figure 18. The first option in the *Pen* Roll-up is a means of adjusting the thickness of a line or an object outline.

As you click on the up or down scroll arrow to alter the thickness, the new thickness of the line appears. Each click on the arrow changes the amount by 0.01 of an inch.

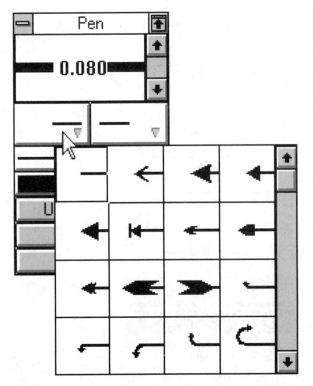

Figure 19. Below the thickness field is the arrowhead option. As with the arrowhead options in the *Outline Pen* dialog box, the left arrowhead icon represents the start of a line and the right is the end.

Clicking on either icon displays the arrowhead pop-up menu as shown. Choose the arrowhead design you want from this menu.

Figure 20. The next option is the *Style* list. Click on the display field to view the options available for dashed or dotted lines.

This option is the same one discussed in Figures 12 and 13.

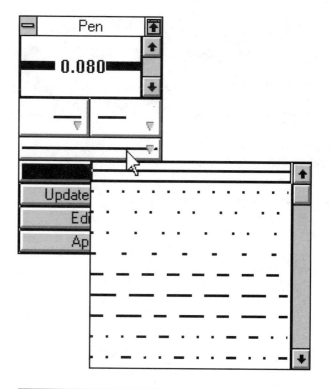

Figure 21. The next field is the outline color field. Click on the color bar to get a quick-pick color palette, where you can choose a different outline color.

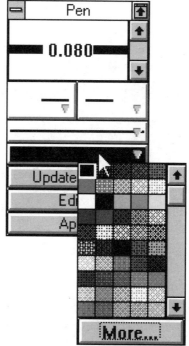

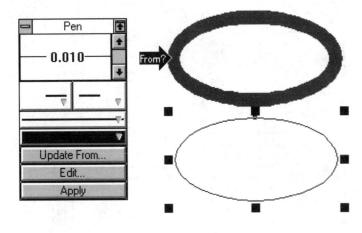

Figure 22. Clicking on the *Update From* button lets you copy an outline from one object to another.

First, select the object you want to copy the outline to (the bottom ellipse). Click on the *Update From* button and, using the *From?* arrow (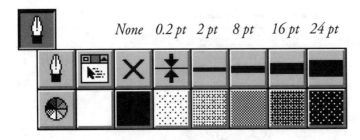), click on the object you want to copy the outline from (the top ellipse). You then must click on the *Apply* button to complete the process.

In this example, you are copying the thick outline of the top ellipse to the one below it.

You can re-apply the same outline to other objects by selecting them first and clicking on the *Apply* button.

Clicking on the *Edit* button in the *Pen* Roll-up opens the *Outline Pen* dialog box for more editing.

You must use the *Apply* button to apply any changes you make in the *Pen* Roll-up window to the selected object.

Figure 23. The remaining options in the top row of the Outline Tool fly-out menu determine the thickness of an outline. This figure shows the different thicknesses available.

OUTLINE COLOR

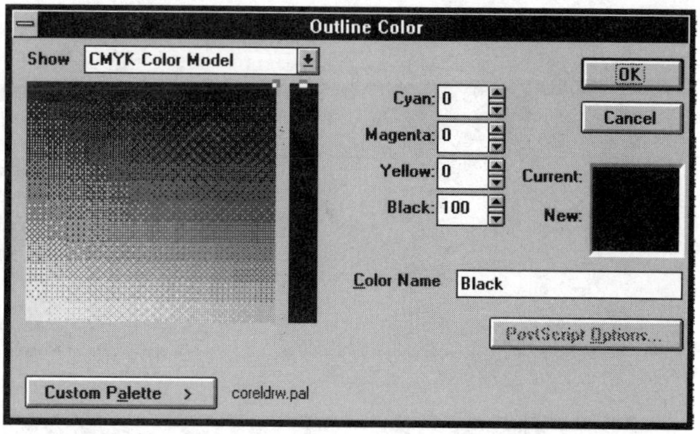

Figure 24. Choosing the first option (●) in the bottom row of the Outline Tool fly-out opens the *Outline Color* dialog box. Pressing Shift+F12 also opens this dialog box.

Make sure you have selected the object you want to change before choosing this option.

SHOW

Figure 25. Your first choice in the *Outline Color* dialog box is the method of coloring. Click on the *Show* drop-down list to view the color methods available.

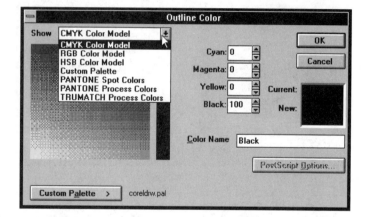

CMYK COLOR MODEL

The *CMYK Color Model* option (seen in the previous two figures) lets you create a color using a mixture of cyan, magenta, yellow, and black—which are known as process colors.

Process colors use percentages of cyan, magenta, yellow, and black to make up a single color. If you are adding many colors to your drawing and are planning on printing it commercially, it is best to use process colors.

To create a color using the *CMYK Color Model*, change the values in the edit frames, to the right of the dialog box, for each of the four colors available.

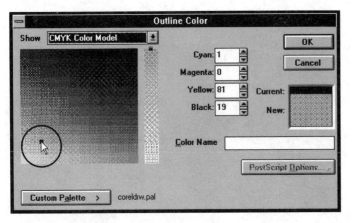

Figure 26. Alternatively, hold the mouse button down with the cursor on one of the two colored boxes at the left of the dialog box. The large box adjusts the settings for cyan and magenta, while the long thin bar adjusts the yellow setting.

RGB COLOR MODEL

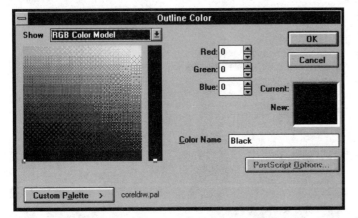

Figure 27. The *RGB Color Model* option uses percentages of red, green, and blue. Mixing or selecting colors is done the same way as for the CMYK color model.

The large visual selector box, in the case of the RGB color model, adjusts red and green, and the long thin box adjusts the blue component.

HSB COLOR MODEL

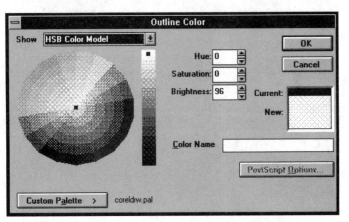

Figure 28. You manipulate the *HSB Color Model* options through the variation of hue, saturation, and brightness.

You can use the percentage boxes to create a color, or the color wheel to determine the hue and saturation. The long thin bar determines the brightness.

CUSTOM PALETTE

Figure 29. The *Custom Palette* option in the *Show* drop-down list lets you select one of the custom palettes that come with Corel-DRAW, or one you may have created and saved yourself.

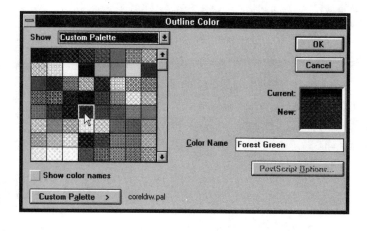

To select a color from the palette, click on the required color. The name of the color appears in the *Color Name* edit box. Use the scroll bar to the right of the palette to choose colors that aren't showing.

The default palette in Corel-DRAW is the *coreldrw.pal* palette. For more information on opening and saving palettes, see the **Custom Palette Menu** section later in this chapter.

Figure 30. Click on the *Show color names* option to view the *Custom Palette* colors by name. The *Search String* edit box lets you type in the name of the color (if you know it) to automatically select it.

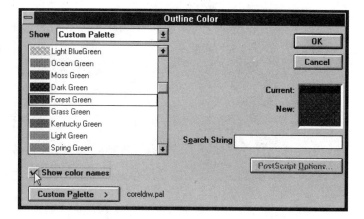

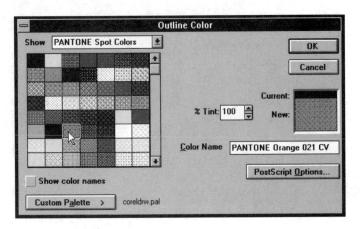

PANTONE SPOT COLORS

Figure 31. The *PANTONE Spot Colors* option lets you select a Pantone color. The Pantone library of colors is recognized by printers world wide.

You can use Pantone colors if you are using no more than four colors in your drawing. Click on the color you want from the palette. Use the scroll bar to see palette colors not showing.

As with the *Custom Palette*, you can click on the *Show color names* option if you want to see the names of the *PANTONE Spot Colors*. The *Search String* edit box lets you type in the number of the color (if you know it) to select it automatically.

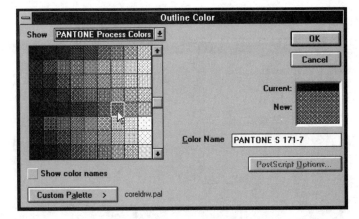

PANTONE PROCESS COLORS

Figure 32. The *PANTONE Process Colors* option provides a library of Pantone colors that are made up of four colors: cyan, magenta, yellow, and black. Click on the color you want from the palette. Use the scroll bar to see colors that aren't showing.

You can click on the *Show color names* option to view the *PANTONE Process Colors* by name. Type the number of the color (if you know it) into the *Search String* edit box to select it automatically.

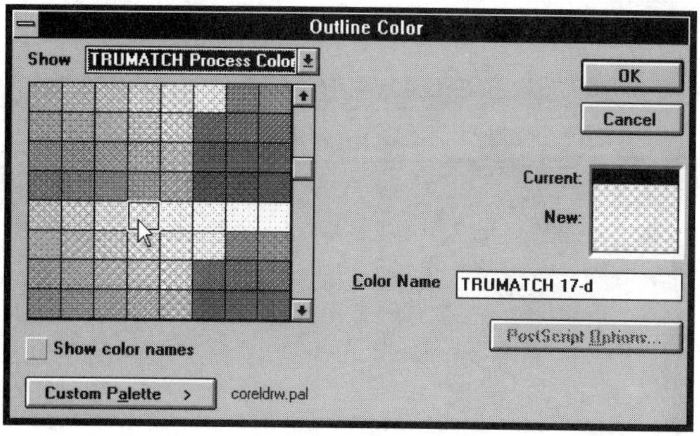

Figure 33. The *TRUMATCH Process Colors* option provides another library of process colors that are made up of four colors: cyan, magenta, yellow, and black. Click on the color you want from the palette. Use the scroll bar to see colors not currently displayed.

If you click on the *Show color names* option you'll see the *TRUMATCH Process Colors* by name. The *Search String* edit box lets you type in the number of the color (if you know it) to select it automatically.

CUSTOM PALETTE MENU

Figure 34. Clicking on the *Custom Palette* button pops-up a menu.

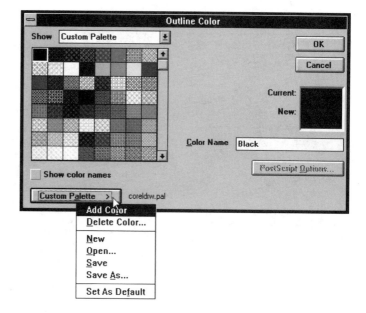

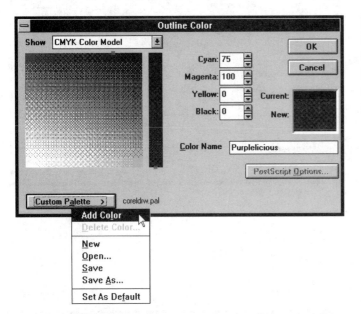

ADD COLOR

Figure 35. After creating a color from one of the three process color models (*CMYK, RGB,* or *HSB*), insert a name for the color in the *Color Name* edit box, and choose the *Add Color* command.

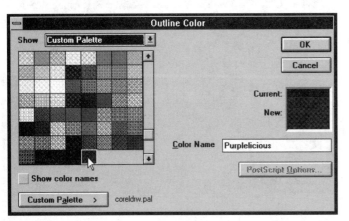

Figure 36. This command then adds the color to the end of the colors in the currently loaded custom palette.

DELETE COLOR

Figure 37. To remove a color from the currently loaded palette, select the color by clicking on it and choose *Delete Color* (a).

(a)

You are then asked to confirm your decision to delete the selected color (b). Click on *Yes* to delete the color, or *No* to cancel the procedure.

(b)

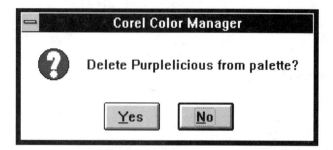

NEW

Figure 38. Selecting *New* from the *Custom Palette* menu opens an empty palette. The palette is automatically called *untitled.pal*.

You can then add colors you have created and named from the three process color model options (*CMYK, RGB, HSB*).

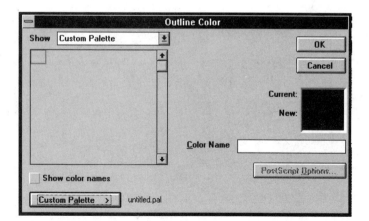

You can drag a color square to another position on the palette and release the mouse button

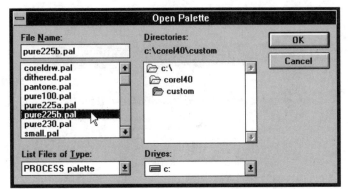

Figure 39. In any custom palettes you have open or create, you can change the order the colors appear in the palette by holding the mouse down on a color square and dragging it to a new position on the palette.

OPEN

Figure 40. The *Open* command from the **Custom palette** menu of Figure 34 lets you open a different custom palette (a). This can be one of the palettes that comes with CorelDRAW or a palette you have created yourself.

Double-click on the palette name from the list of files in the *Open Palette* dialog box. The palette you chose is now displayed in the *Outline Color* dialog box (b).

(a)

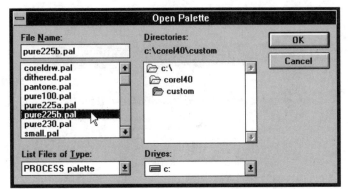

(b)

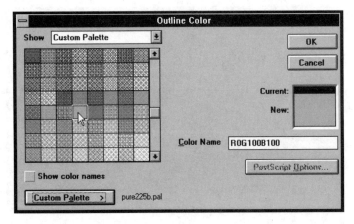

SAVE/SAVE AS

The *Save* command from the *Custom Palette* pop-up menu lets you save any changes you made to the currently loaded custom palette; e.g. adding or deleting colors. As well as naming and saving a new palette, you can use the *Save As* command to save a palette under a different name, allowing you to make changes to this palette without affecting the original.

Figure 41. The *Save As* command from the *Custom Palette* menu opens the *Save Palette As* dialog box, where you can name the new palette. You might like to save it in the same directory as the custom palettes that come with Corel-DRAW. CorelDRAW automatically places a *pal* extension on the name you type into the *File Name* text box.

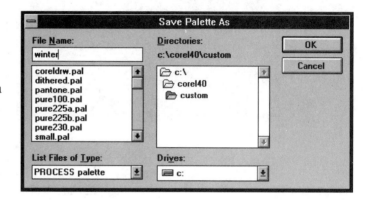

SET AS DEFAULT

Use the *Set As Default* command in the *Custom Palette* pop-up menu to save the current palette as the default palette. This palette will then display each time you open CorelDRAW.

CURRENT/NEW SWATCH

Figure 42. The outline color of your selected object displays in the *Current* swatch. When you select a new color from any of the methods in the *Outline Color* dialog box, this color appears in the *New* swatch. This lets you compare the current color with any new color you create or select.

POSTSCRIPT OPTIONS

Figure 43. Click on the *PostScript Options* button in the *Outline Color* dialog box to activate the *PostScript Options* dialog box. You can access the *Halftone Screen* options in this dialog box only if you are using the *PANTONE Spot Colors* method.

The options available in the *Type* list provide you with a range of various shapes of halftone dots, lines, and ellipses. You cannot display them on screen, but they will print.

The *Frequency* option determines the number of times it displays the screen pattern per inch. The *Angle* option determines the angle at which it places the pattern. You must click on any option other than *Default* from the *Type* list to access the *Frequency* and *Angle* options.

Click on *OK* in the *PostScript Options* dialog box and the *Outline Color* dialog box to return to the drawing with the new color applied to the outline of the selected object(s).

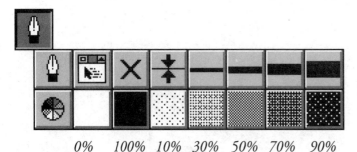

0%   100%   10%   30%   50%   70%   90%

Figure 44. The remaining options in the bottom row of the Outline Tool fly-out let you apply a color quickly to an outline, from white (no color) to full color (in percentages).

CONVERTING SPOT TO PROCESS

Figure 45. If you have a specific color you want to convert from *Spot* color to *Process*, follow these steps. First, select the Pantone spot color you want to change from the *PANTONE Spot Colors* palette.

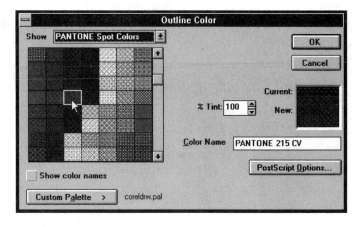

Figure 46. Next, choose the *CMYK Color Model* from the *Show* drop-down list (a), and you will see that CorelDRAW has converted the Pantone color to the closest possible mix of process colors (b).

(a)

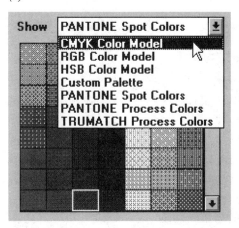

(b)

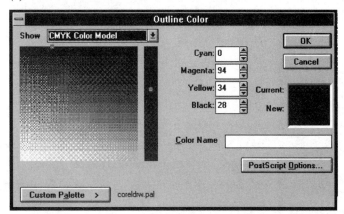

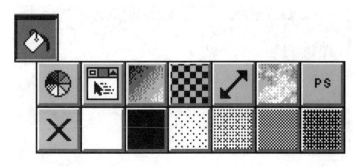

THE FILL TOOL

Figure 47. You use the Fill Tool to determine the fill of an object. Click on the Fill Tool (✍) in the Toolbox to open the Fill Tool fly-out menu. You can apply a fill to any closed object.

Make sure you have selected the object you want changed before selecting options in the Fill Tool fly-out.

UNIFORM FILL

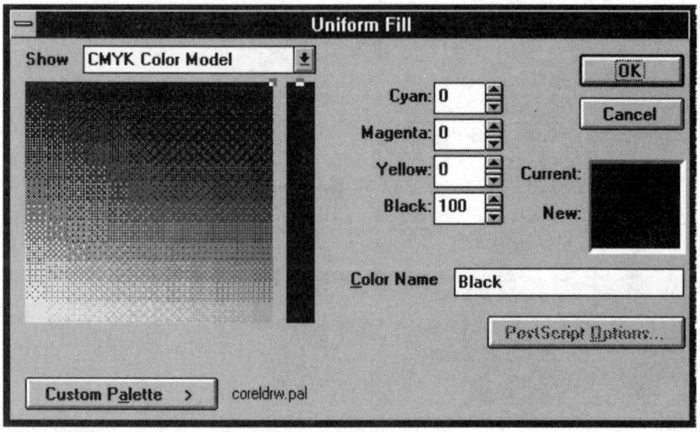

Figure 48. Selecting the first option from the top row of the Fill Tool fly-out (●) activates the *Uniform Fill* dialog box. You can also press Shift+F11 to activate this dialog box. The options in this dialog box function the same way as the *Outline Color* dialog box options, described previously.

The second option in the Fill Tool fly-out (▦) gives you the *Fill* Roll-up window. For more information on the options in this Roll-up, see the **Fill Roll-up** section later in this chapter.

FOUNTAIN FILLS

Figure 49. Clicking on the *Fountain Fill* icon (■) from the Fill Tool fly-out opens the *Fountain Fill* dialog box. Fountain fills range from one color to another.

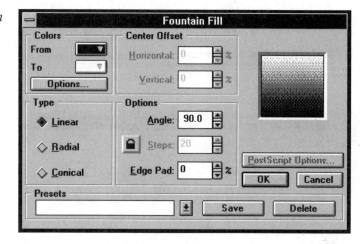

Figure 50. You select the two colors you are going to use in the fountain fill in the *Colors* section of the dialog box. When you click on the *From* color swatch, a quick-pick color palette appears.

The colors that appear in this palette are the colors that are in the currently loaded custom palette. Click on the color you want as the starting color for the *From* color in the fill. If you want to select a different color, or create your own, click on the *More* button at the bottom of the quick-pick palette.

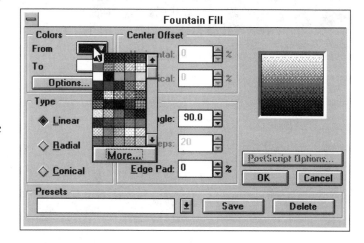

This opens another dialog box that is identical to the *Uniform Fill* dialog box and the *Outline Color* dialog box (explained earlier in this chapter).

Click on the *To* color swatch to select the color you want to bland to in the fountain fill. The *To* color quick-pick palette works the same way as the *From* quick-pick palette.

If you plan to color-separate a CorelDRAW file, you can use only spot (Pantone) colors in fountain fills when the two colors in the one fill are a tint of the same color. If they aren't tints of one color, they are converted to the closest equivalent process colors when separated.

FOUNTAIN FILL COLOR OPTIONS

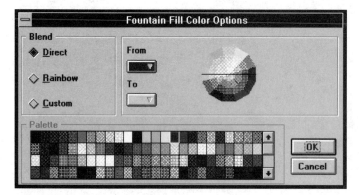

Figure 51. The *Options* button in the *Colors* section of the *Fountain Fill* dialog box activates the *Fountain Fill Color Options* dialog box.

The *Blend* options determine how the two colors in the fountain fill blend together. The *Direct* option blends the two colors in the fountain fill in a straight line.

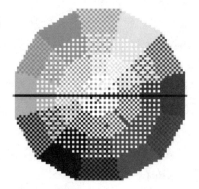

Figure 52. A line appears in the color wheel indicating the two colors you have selected in the fill.

In this example, the two colors in the fill are red and cyan, indicated by the line in the color wheel that stretches from red to cyan.

Figure 53. The *Rainbow* option allows you to blend two colors through a spectrum of colors. You also have the choice with a rainbow fountain fill whether the color spectrum is clockwise (↻) or anti-clockwise (↺). When you choose either direction, the line on the actual rainbow symbol changes to indicate the direction of colors.

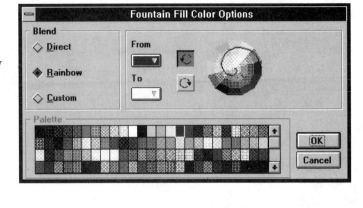

You can select the two colors for the Rainbow fill using the *From* and *To* quick-pick palettes in this dialog box. In this example the colors are blending from red to white.

Figure 54. You can add colors to the fountain fill with the *Custom* option. You can add up to 99 colors to a fountain fill from the palette at the bottom of the dialog box.

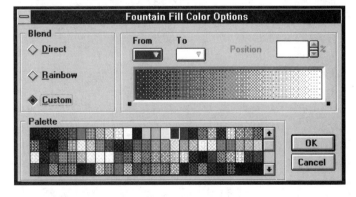

Figure 55. To add colors to the preview strip above the palette, click on one of the small black squares at both ends of the preview strip. Clicking on either square adds a color location marker (▲) to the preview strip. This color location marker remains selected until you add or select another one. A selected location marker is black, or white when it's not selected.

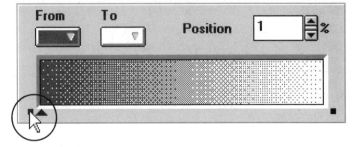

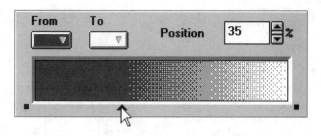

Figure 56. You can drag a color location marker along the preview strip. This changes the *Position* value and you will also notice a change in the preview strip.

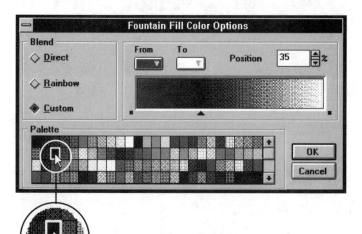

Figure 57. If you then click on a color from the color palette below, this adds the new color to the blend. This color will blend all the two colors on either side of it—in this case the start and end colors.

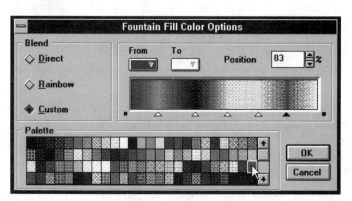

Figure 58. You can keep adding more and more location markers and colors to the preview strip until you are happy with the fill.

You can also change the start and end colors of the fill by selecting different colors from the *From* and *To* quick-pick palettes.

Figure 59. You can quickly and easily add a color location marker along the preview strip by double-clicking in the required position.

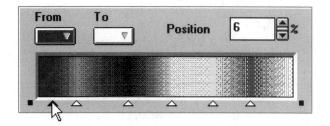

You can delete a color location marker by double-clicking on it.

Click on *OK* in the *Fountain Fill Color Options* dialog box to return to the *Fountain Fill* dialog box.

Figure 60. You have three choices in the *Type* section of the *Fountain Fill* dialog box of Figure 48.

The *Linear* option is the default setting for blending the two colors in the fountain fill in a straight direction (a).

The *Radial* option blends two colors along the radius of a circle (b), and the *Conical* option blends the colors in a cone fashion (c).

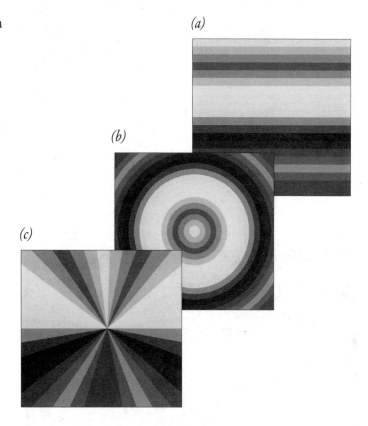

(a)

(b)

(c)

(a)

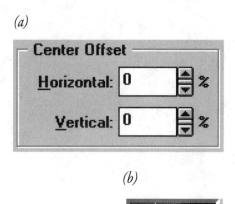

(b)

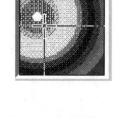

Figure 61. The *Center Offset* options within the *Fountain Fill* dialog box let you change the center of a fountain fill when you are using the *Radial* or *Conical Type* options.

You can alter the *Center Offset* values in the *Horizontal* and *Vertical* text boxes (a), or directly through the color display by holding down and dragging the mouse to reposition the center offset (b).

Figure 62. The *Options* features of the *Fountain Fill* dialog box do not work for all types of fountain fills.

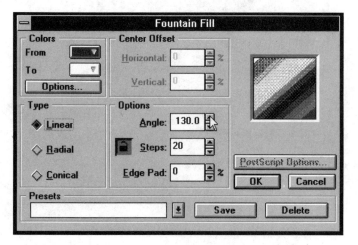

Figure 63. The *Angle* option applies only to *Linear* and *Conical* fountain fills. Here you can change the angle of the fountain fill.

When you change the *Angle* value it is reflected in the preview square.

Figure 64. With *Linear* fills you can change the angle of the fill directly in the preview square with the mouse.

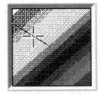

Figure 65. Click on the 🔒 icon to access the *Steps* option. Changing this value determines the amount of fountain fill steps that appear on screen and when you print the file. The *Steps* option in this dialog box overrides the fountain fill steps options in the *Preferences Display* and the *Print Options* dialog boxes.

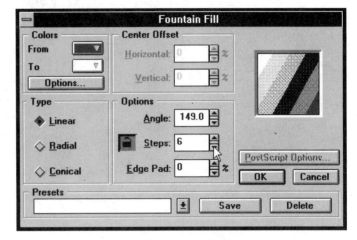

Figure 66. The *Edge Pad* option is available only for *Linear* and *Radial* fills. Choose this option to increase the amount of color at the start and end of the fill. A filled object acts as a window for the fountain fill, therefore the *Edge Pad* option is useful for asymmetrical options where part of the fill falls outside the object.

You cannot use a percentage higher than 45% in the *Edge Pad* option, and you can view your changes in the color display square. Compare the display square in this figure to the one above.

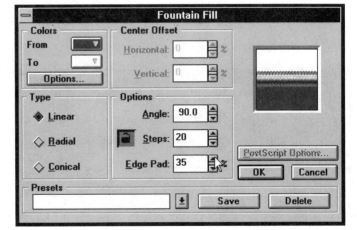

You can access the *PostScript Options* button in the *Fountain Fill* dialog box only if you are using Pantone spot colors. The options in this dialog box are discussed in the **Outline Color** section earlier in this chapter.

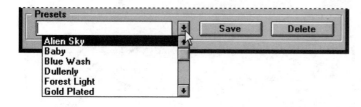

Figure 67. The *Presets* drop-down list contains some fountain fills that come with CorelDRAW. You can also save fountain fills that you have created yourself.

After creating the fill, type a name into the *Presets* text box and click on *Save*; this then adds the fill to the *Presets* list. If there are any fills in the *Presets* list that you do not want, select them and click on the *Delete* button.

Click on the *OK* button in the *Fountain Fill* dialog box to apply the fill to the selected object.

TWO-COLOR PATTERNS

Figure 68. You use the *Two-Color Pattern* icon (▦) in the Fill Tool fly-out menu to activate the *Two-Color Pattern* dialog box.

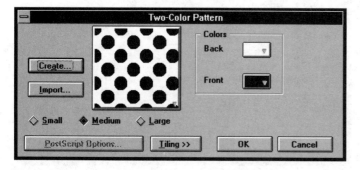

Figure 69. You can choose patterns directly by clicking on the large display grid, which pops up a palette. Choose the pattern you want from the palette that appears, and click on *OK* in the menu bar of the palette of patterns. The *Cancel* option removes the palette.

Delete item in this palette's **File** menu removes a pattern from the palette, and *Import pattern* lets you import a file into the *Two-Color Pattern* dialog box.

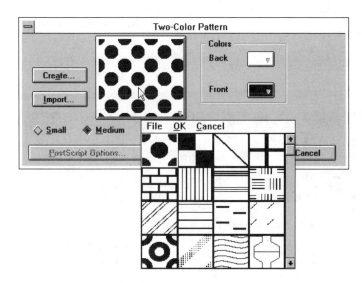

Figure 70. Clicking on the *Back* and *Front* color swatches lets you apply a foreground and background color to the pattern.

Clicking on the *More* button at the bottom of the quick-pick palettes opens a dialog box that works in the same way as the *Uniform Fill* dialog box.

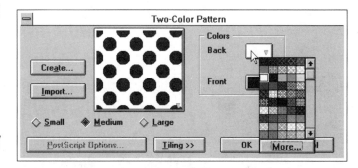

Figure 71. Clicking on the *Create* button in the *Two-Color Pattern* dialog box opens the *Two-Color Pattern Editor* dialog box. Here you create your own patterns which you can then add to the bottom of the pop-up palette.

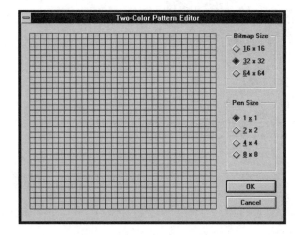

Clicking on the *Import* button, below the *Create* button in the *Two-Color Pattern* dialog box, gives you access to the *Import* dialog box. From here you can import a file to become a two-color pattern.

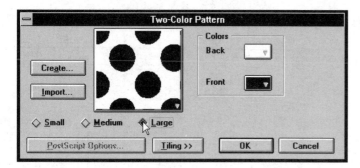

Figure 72. The *Small, Medium,* and *Large* options in the *Two-Color Pattern* dialog box let you change the tiling size to one of three preset figures.

Clicking on the *PostScript Options* button opens the *PostScript Options* dialog box. The options available here were described in the **Outline Color** section. You can access the PostScript options only if you are working with Pantone spot colors.

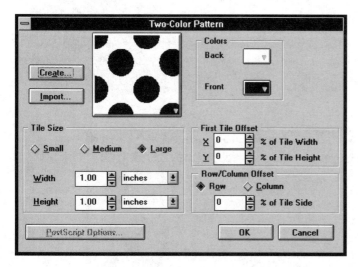

Figure 73. Selecting the *Tiling* button expands the *Two-Color Pattern* dialog box to include *Tile Size* and *Offset* options. You can insert your own size for each tile for *Width* and *Height.* The tiles in the display square change size according to the changes you make in the *Tile Size* section.

By altering the *X* and *Y* options in the *First Tile Offset* section, you can alter the position of the first tile of a pattern. The first tile of a pattern is in the top left corner.

The *Row/Column Offset* options let you offset the orientation of the row or column.

FULL-COLOR PATTERNS

Figure 74. The *Full-Color Pattern* icon (■) in the Fill Tool fly-out opens the *Full-Color Pattern* dialog box.

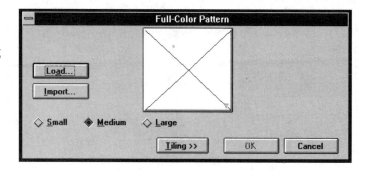

Figure 75. Click on the display square to bring up the pop-up palette of patterns, from where you can select your own fill pattern.

This works in the same way as selecting a two-color pattern, although the **File** menu in the palette of patterns has one further option available: the *Save Current Fill* command. When you import a file into the *Full-Color Pattern* dialog box, you can save the fill so it appears in the full-color palette of patterns.

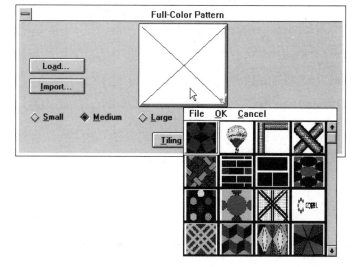

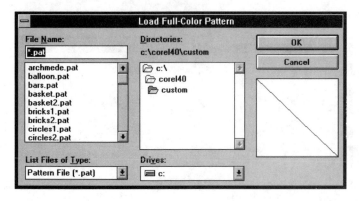

Figure 76. Clicking on the *Load* button in the *Full-Color Pattern* dialog box opens the *Load Full-Color Pattern* dialog box; from this box you can load a pattern file from anywhere on your machine. Full-color patterns have an extension of *pat*.

For more information about creating your own full-color patterns, see the *Create Pattern* command in Chapter 11.

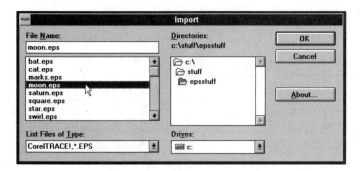

Figure 77. Selecting the *Import* button from the *Full-color Pattern* dialog box opens the *Import* dialog box. You can import a file to become a full-color pattern here.

The *List Files of Type* drop-down list at the bottom of the dialog box contains a list of file formats that you can import files from.

For more information on importing, see Chapter 4.

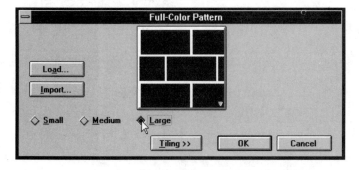

Figure 78. The *Small, Medium,* and *Large* options are three preset tile sizes. You can select any one of these for your full-color pattern.

Figure 79. As with the *Two-Color Pattern* dialog box, clicking on the *Tiling* button expands the *Full-Color Pattern* dialog box. The *Tile Size* options in the newly expanded dialog box give you control over the tile size, as discussed in the *Two-Color Pattern* dialog box section (Figure 72).

By altering the *X* and *Y* options in the *First Tile Offset* section, you can alter the position of the first tile of a pattern. The first tile of a pattern is in the top left corner.

The *Row/Column Offset* options allow you to offset the alignment of the row or column.

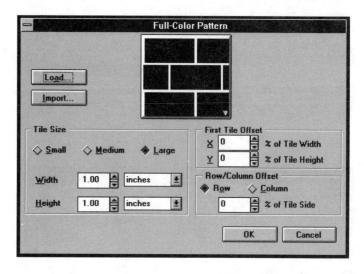

BITMAP TEXTURE FILLS

Figure 80. The *Bitmap texture* icon (▣) in the Fill Tool fly-out opens the *Texture Fill* dialog box. Bitmap texture fills look textured and you can change each fill to create literally millions of variations. They display on screen and can be printed on any laser printer.

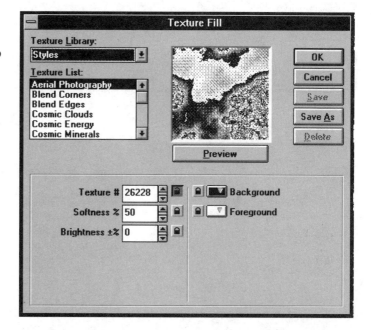

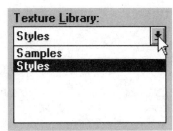

Figure 81. After opening the *Texture Fill* dialog box, choose a library from the *Texture Library* drop-down list.

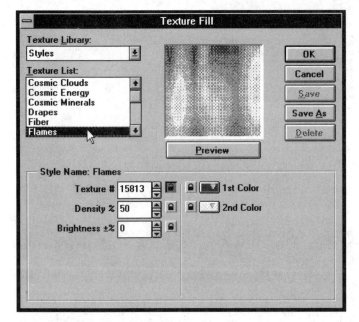

Figure 82. Then, from the *Texture List*, choose the texture name you want and the texture appears in the *Preview* window.

You can modify texture styles yourself with the parameters at the bottom of the dialog box. You can have CorelDRAW randomly modify texture styles by unlocking any or all of the parameters at the bottom of the dialog box.

You unlock options by clicking on the 🔒 icon so it looks like this (🔓). Click on the *Preview* button to let CorelDRAW randomly alter the texture using the unlocked parameters.

Each texture fill has 32,768 variations. You can also change the *Texture #* from 0 to 32,767 to alter the texture.

Figure 83. Each texture style has a specific range of parameters that you can use to change the texture; change these parameters yourself to create different variations of a style. In this example we changed the *Texture #*, *Density*, and *Brightness*, and clicked on the *Preview* button. Compare this to Figure 81.

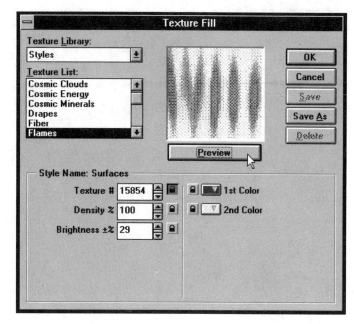

It is possible to save changes you have made to texture fills. There are two types of texture fills—style textures and user textures. Saving a *style* texture is different from saving a *user* texture.

You store style textures in the *Styles* library. You can make changes to any of the style textures, and these changes are assigned to the selected object, but you cannot save the new texture. Notice that when you have a texture selected from the *Styles* library, the *Save* button in the *Texture Fill* dialog box is dimmed.

Figure 84. You can however, use the *Save As* option to save a style texture under a different name. After changing the style texture, click on the *Save As* button. This opens the *Save Texture as* dialog box. Type the new name of the texture in the *Texture Name* edit box. In the *Library Name* list, select any library name other than *Styles*, because texture fills you create (user textures) can't be saved in the *Styles* library.

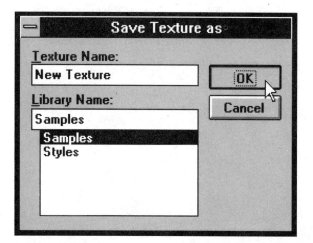

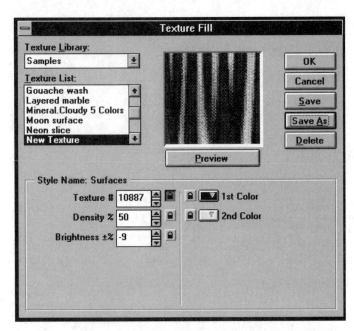

Figure 85. After clicking on *OK* in the *Save Texture as* dialog box, CorelDRAW adds the new texture to the style library that you have selected.

You can also create a new texture library by typing a new name in the *Library Name* text box in the *Save Texture as* dialog box.

User textures are derived from style textures. You can save changes to user textures, or you can use the *Save As* option with user textures so the original user texture remains unaffected.

Figure 86. Use the *Delete* option to delete user textures. After clicking on this button, confirm that you want to delete the texture fill.

POSTSCRIPT FILLS

Figure 87. Clicking on the *PS* option (▥) in the Fill Tool fly-out opens the *PostScript Texture* dialog box. You can fill the selected object with a variety of patterns from the list; however, you can see them only when you print to a Post-Script printer.

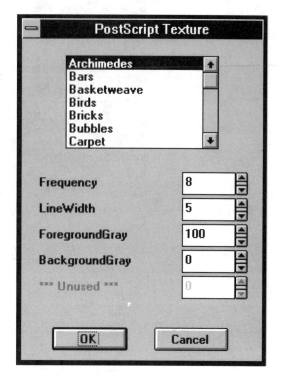

Use the options below the list of available fills to modify the size and shades of the fills. Appendix A of the CorelDRAW manual provides a comprehensive listing of available PostScript fills.

FILL ROLL-UP

Figure 88. Selecting the second option in the top row of the Fill Tool fly-out (▨) activates the *Fill Roll-up*. All the fill options available in this Roll-up are available in dialog boxes directly from the Fill Tool fly-out.

As with all Roll-ups, you must click on the *Apply* button at the bottom of the Roll-up to apply any changes to selected objects.

Fountain Fill —————

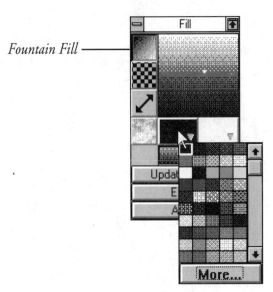

Figure 89. The first option in the *Fill* Roll-up (■) is *Fountain Fill.* This lets you apply a fill ranging from one color to another. Clicking on either of the two color buttons below the fountain fill display opens a color palette from where you can select a color.

The left palette button is the start color and the right palette button is the end color. Click on the *More* button at the bottom of the quick-pick palette to choose from all colors.

Figure 90. The options below the two color buttons let you choose a *Linear, Radial,* or a *Conical* fountain fill. In this example we have chosen the *Conical* option.

Figure 91. You can use the display square to change the fill angle or center offset of the fountain fill, as you can with the display square in the *Fountain Fill* dialog box described earlier (see Figures 60 and 64).

After clicking on the *Fountain Fill* button, click on the *Edit* button in the *Fill* Roll-up to access the *Fountain Fill* dialog box. This is this same dialog box that you open in the Fill Tool fly-out menu.

Figure 92. The next icon down in the *Fill* Roll-up window is the *Two-Color Pattern* fill button (▓). Clicking on this display square pops-up a palette where you can select a pattern to fill an object with. Use the scroll bar to see more patterns.

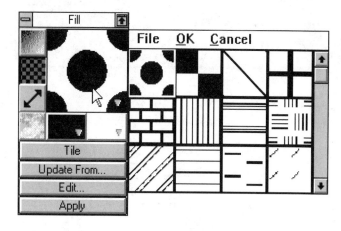

Figure 93. The pop-up palette for the two-color patterns has its own menu bar. Clicking on the **Cancel** option removes the pop-up palette without changing the pattern. You use the **OK** option to put the selected fill into the display square in the *Fill* Roll-up window.

The options available in the **File** menu let you remove the currently selected pattern from the pop-up palette and import a new pattern into the pop-up palette.

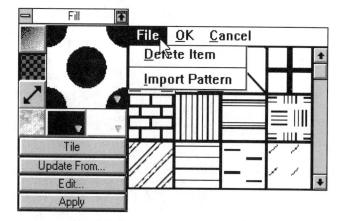

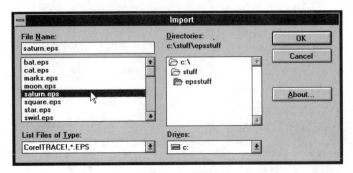

Figure 94. *Import Pattern* from the File menu in the pop-up palette opens the *Import* dialog box, where you can import a file to become a two-color pattern. Select a file format from the *List Files of Type* drop-down list.

For more information on importing see Chapter 4.

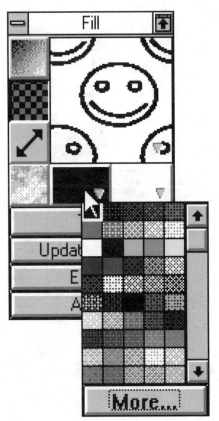

Figure 95. Once you have selected your two-color pattern and it is in the display square, you can use the two color buttons below to choose a foreground (left button) and a background (right button) color.

Click on the *More* button at the bottom of the quick-pick palette to see all the color models and options.

Figure 96. Use the *Tile* button below the color buttons in the *Fill* Roll-up to adjust tile size and orientation. Clicking on this button displays two squares over the top of your pattern, representing two adjacent tiles.

Before clicking on the *Tile* button, make sure you have selected the filled object with the Pick Tool.

Figure 97. Holding the mouse button down with the cursor on the left square and moving the mouse around adjusts the position of the tiles. Both squares move together.

Click on the *Apply* button to change the tile.

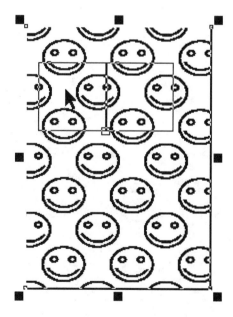

(a)

Figure 98. If you drag the node that's between the tiles (a), you change their size. After clicking on the *Apply* button, the size of the tiles changes, as in (b).

(b)

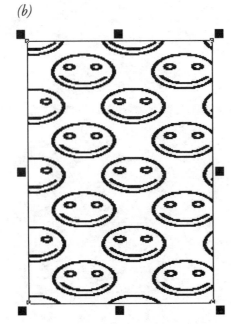

Figure 99. Moving the right square with the mouse changes the alignment of the two adjacent tiles (a). You can keep moving the right square down and under the left square to affect the horizontal alignment of the tiles (b).

Change the tiling by clicking on the *Apply* button. After you have selected the *Two-Color Pattern* fill button, click on the *Edit* button to open the *Two-Color Pattern* dialog box.

You can also open this dialog box from the Fill Tool fly-out menu. You can make more precise adjustments in the *Two-Color Pattern* dialog box than you can with the mouse.

(a)

(b)

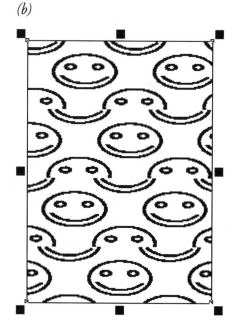

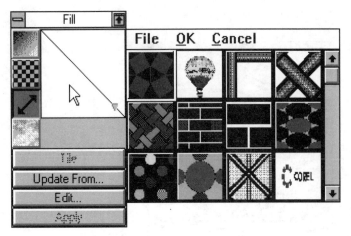

Figure 100. The next button in the *Fill* Roll-up is *Full-Color Pattern* (■). The patterns available in the associated pop-up palette are in full-color. The rest of the options in the Roll-up work as they do for two-color patterns, except you can't select a foreground and a background color for full-color patterns.

You open the *Full-Color Pattern* dialog box with the *Edit* button in the *Fill* Roll-up. You can also open this dialog box from the Fill Tool fly-out menu.

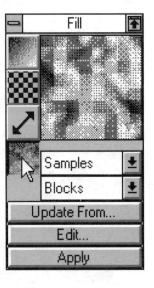

Figure 101. The bottom button in the *Fill* Roll-up is *Texture Fill*. From here you can select a *Texture Library* and a texture from the two drop-down lists. Click on the *Edit* button to open the *Texture Fill* dialog box.

Figure 102. The *Update From* button lets you copy a fill from one object on the screen to another.

Select the object you want to copy the fill to and click on the *Update From* button. With the arrow that appears (➡), click on the object that you want to copy the fill from.

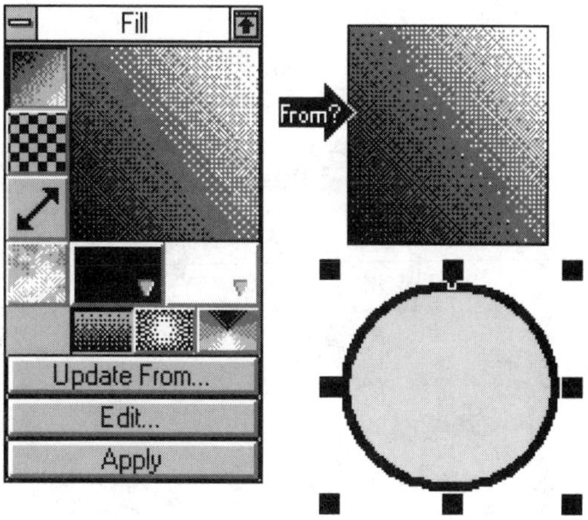

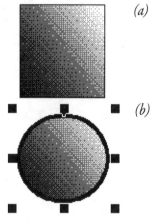

Figure 103. Next, click on the *Apply* button, and the object you originally selected with the Pick Tool (b) is given the same fill as the object you selected with the *From?* arrow (a).

(a)

(b)

NO FILL

Figure 104. The first option in the bottom row of the Fill Tool fly-out menu (⊠) applies a fill of *None* to a selected object(s).

The remaining options in the bottom row of the Fill Tool fly-out allow you to apply a color quickly, as a fill, from 0% (white) to 100% (in set percentages).

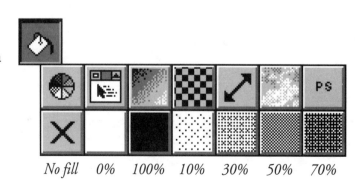

No fill   *0%*   *100%*   *10%*   *30%*   *50%*   *70%*

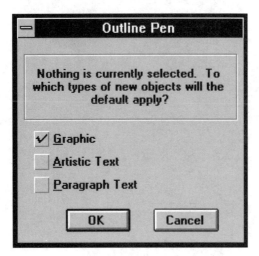

SETTING UP OUTLINE AND FILL DEFAULTS

Figure 105. To set up a default for an outline or fill, choose the relevant option with nothing selected on the page. This action displays a dialog box similar to this; make your selection and click on *OK*.

The new color or outline you choose is the new default setting for whichever option you select.

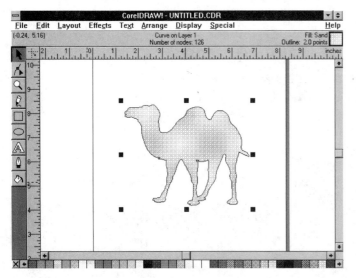

THE FILL INDICATOR

Figure 106. The *Fill Indicator* is displayed in the top right corner of the status line. This displays the outline and fill of any object selected with the Pick Tool.

Use this as your reference point to check the fill and outline details of any object. The *Fill Indicator* is active in both *full-color* and *wireframe* modes.

THE FILE MENU 4

THE FILE MENU COMMANDS

The commands contained in the **File** menu are common to most applications that run under Windows. These commands generally relate to a whole CorelDRAW file, whereas most of the other commands in the CorelDRAW menus relate only to certain objects on your page.

Figure 1. This figure displays the **File** menu with its associated commands.

File	
New	Ctrl+N
New From Template...	
Open...	Ctrl+O
Save	Ctrl+S
Save As...	
Import...	
Export...	
Insert Object...	
Print...	Ctrl+P
Print Merge...	
Print Setup...	
Exit	Alt+F4

NEW

Figure 2. Selecting the *New* command creates a new CorelDRAW file, and closes the CorelDRAW file currently open. If you haven't saved the current file, you are asked if you would like to now (see **Save** and **Save As** later).

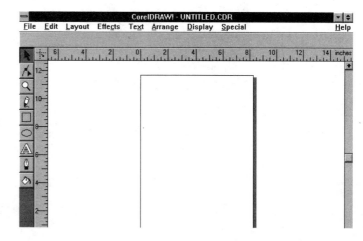

NEW FROM TEMPLATE

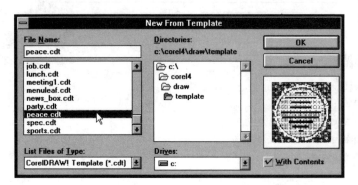

Figure 3. The *New From Template* command from the **File** menu opens the *New From Template* dialog box. If you have made any changes to the current file you have the opportunity to save these changes. In this dialog box you can select a template to open. Templates contain a collection of styles and graphics that you can use as a basis for one of your CorelDRAW documents.

Find the template file you want using the *Directories* and *Drives* drop-down lists and double-click on the template from the file list. CorelDRAW comes with a directory full of template files, which have a *cdt* extension.

Figure 4. When you double-click on a template file from the *New From Template* dialog box, it appears as though you have opened a CorelDRAW file. However, the title bar shows that this is a new file; you have, in effect, opened a copy of a CorelDRAW template ready to format in any way you like.

You can open a template as an untitled file and then make changes you want. The template files supplied with CorelDRAW are varied and you should be able to find a template to suit you.

For more information on creating, managing, and saving templates, see the *Styles Roll-up* command in Chapter 6.

OPEN

Figure 5. Selecting the *Open* command brings up the *Open Drawing* dialog box. If you have not saved the changes to the current file, CorelDRAW asks if you would like to now (see *Save* and *Save As*).

If the current directory includes any CorelDRAW (*.cdr*) files, the *Open Drawing* dialog box lists these files in a box below the *File Name* text box.

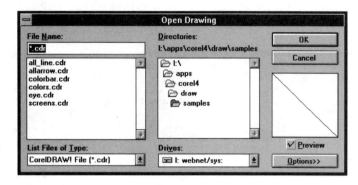

Figure 6. Clicking on a *cdr* file from this list usually displays the file's image header in the preview window. The image header is a bitmapped version of the file. You can set the resolution of this image when you save a file.

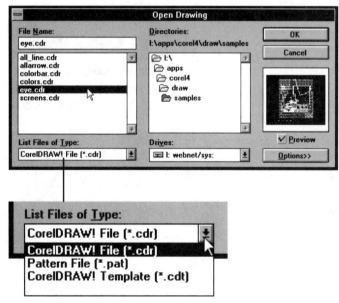

Figure 7. The *List Files of Type* drop-down list, at the bottom left of the *Open Drawing* dialog box, has three options. The default option is the *cdr* format. You can also open full-color pattern files by selecting the *Pattern File (*.pat)* option; these files display in the *Full-Color Pattern* dialog box available from the Fill Tool fly-out menu.

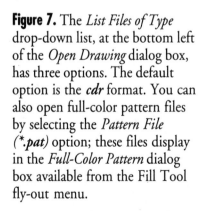

For more information on full-color patterns, see Chapter 3.

The third option is *CorelDRAW Template (*.cdt)*, so you can open a template file. For more information on creating, managing, and saving templates, see the *Styles Roll-up* command in Chapter 6.

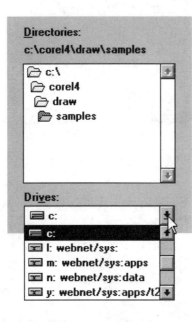

Figure 8. The *Directories* list box in the *Open Drawing* dialog box shows you all the directories and subdirectories on the current directory or drive.

Double-clicking on the drive letter (in this case c:) takes you back to the root directory. To open a specific directory, double-click on the directory name from this list.

The *Drives* list at the bottom of this figure gives you access to the computer's drives.

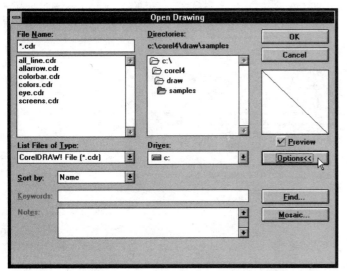

Figure 9. When you click on the *Options* button at the bottom right of the *Open Drawing* dialog box, it expands to include more options.

Figure 10. The first option in the newly enlarged *Open Drawing* dialog box is *Sort by*. Your choices here are whether you list the files alphabetically (*Name*) or in chronological order (*Date*).

So that you always display an image header for a selected *cdr* file in the preview window, click on the *Preview* checkbox.

Figure 11. Use the *Keywords* text box (also available in the *Save Drawing* dialog box) to insert words relating to the file you have selected from the list of files. You can use keywords to find files, or highlight files with the same keywords. You must separate keywords by a comma (,) or a + sign.

Use the *Notes* text box to insert any other information you want saved with the file.

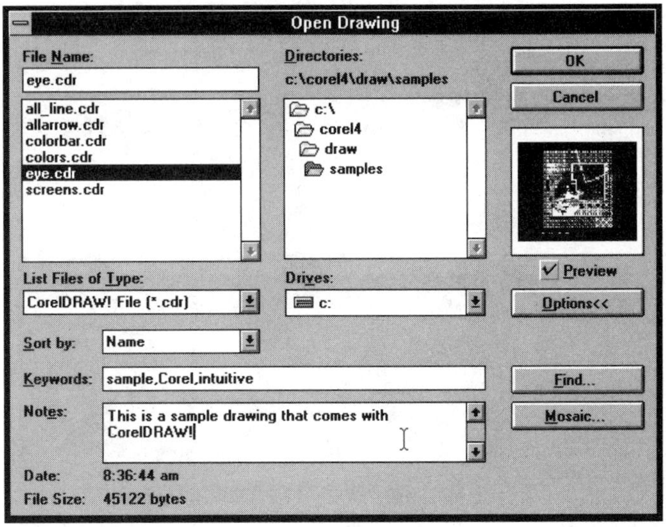

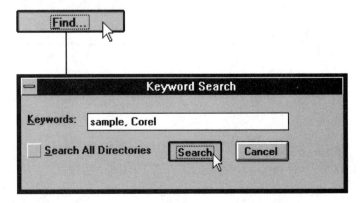

Figure 12. Clicking on the *Find* button in the *Open Drawing* dialog box opens the *Keyword Search* dialog box. Here you search the current (or all) directories for files with the same keywords. After inserting the keyword(s), click on the *Search* button. The file list in the *Open Drawing* dialog box then displays all the relevant files.

If you separate the keywords with a comma, the list shows all files with any of these keywords. If you separate the keywords with a +, it will display only the files including both words.

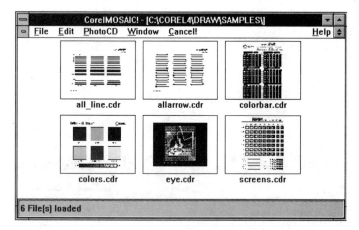

Figure 13. Clicking on the *Mosaic* button in the *Open Drawing* dialog box opens CorelMOSAIC. Corel-MOSAIC is a visual file selector and file management utility provided with CorelDRAW. See Chapter 14, for more information.

SAVE

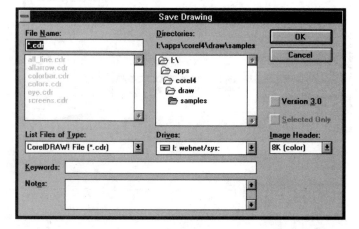

Figure 14. If you are currently in an *UNTITLED* CorelDRAW file, selecting the *Save* command opens the *Save Drawing* dialog box. Here you name the file and decide where you are going to save it. The names of the *cdr* files in the current directory appear in gray.

Type the name of the file in the *File Name* text box. CorelDRAW adds a *cdr* extension automatically to CorelDRAW files when you save them.

Figure 15. Use the *Directories* list box and *Drives* drop-down list to determine where you save the file.

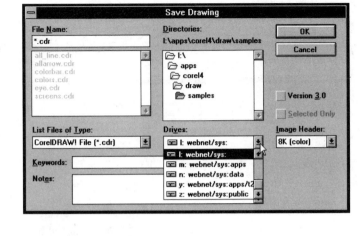

If you need to save the file in CorelDRAW 3 format, click on the *Version 3.0* option.

The *Selected Only* option lets you save only what you have selected.

Figure 16. The *List Files of Type*

option lets you save the file as a normal *CorelDRAW File*, as a *Pattern File*, or as a *CorelDRAW Template*. If you save the file as a *Pattern File*, you can then access this file through the *Full-Color Pattern* dialog box available from the Fill Tool fly-out menu, or from the *Open Drawing* dialog box.

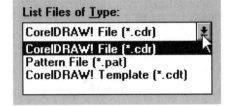

If you save the file as a template, you can open the file through the *New From Template* command in the **File** menu, the *Styles* Roll-up from the **Layout** menu, and the *Open Drawing* dialog box.

Figure 17. With the *Image Header* option in the *Save Drawing* dialog box, you can set the quality of the image in the preview window in the *Open Drawing* dialog box, and in CorelMOSAIC. The size of the saved file increases as the *Image Header* option does.

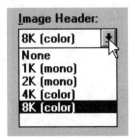

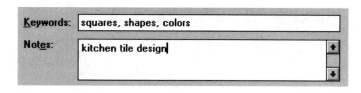

Figure 18. The *Keywords* text box in the *Save Drawing* dialog box is to insert words that relate to the file. In the *Open Drawing* dialog box, you can use keywords to find and highlight files with the same keywords (see Figure 11). You must separate keywords with a comma (,) or a + sign.

You use the *Notes* text box to put in any information you want saved with the file.

Choosing the *Save* command, after you have named a file, saves the changes made to the file since you last used the command, but does not open the *Save Drawing* dialog box.

SAVE AS

The *Save As* command opens the *Save Drawing* dialog box (Figure 14). If you have already saved the file, you can then make a copy of the file by giving it a new name, or saving it into a different directory. If you haven't saved the file, using the *Save As* command is the same as using the *Save* command.

IMPORT

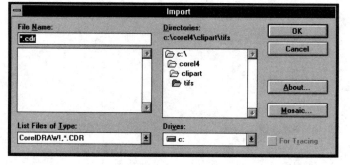

Figure 19. The *Import* command from the **File** menu brings up the *Import* dialog box. Use the *Directories* list box and *Drives* drop-down list to find the directory containing the files you need to import.

Figure 20. The options in the *List Files of Type* drop-down list show you which files you can import, including *cdr* (native Corel-DRAW format).

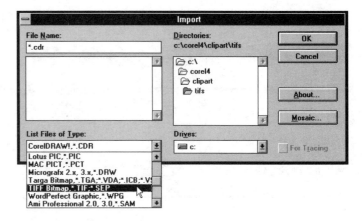

Figure 21. After you have selected the file type you want from the *List Files of Type* drop-down list, the file list displays all files in the current directory in the selected format. To import the file into CorelDRAW, select it from the list of files, and click on the *OK* button.

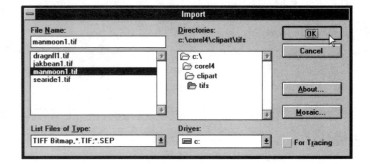

Clicking on the *Mosaic* button in the *Import* dialog box activates CorelMOSAIC. This is a visual file selector and file managing utility. For more information on CorelMOSAIC, see Chapter 14.

EXPORT

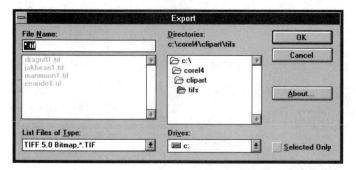

Figure 22. Selecting the *Export* command from the **File** menu opens the *Export* dialog box. Here you can save a file in various formats so you can import it into other programs that don't read the *cdr* format. You must have drawn an object before you can select the *Export* command.

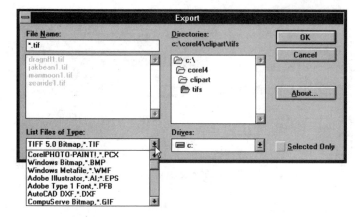

Figure 23. In the *Export* dialog box, select the format of your choice from the *List Files of Type* drop-down list. You might also need to change the drive and directory, otherwise the currently active drive and directory is where you will save the exported file.

The *Selected Only* option exports only the section of your drawing that you selected with the Pick Tool.

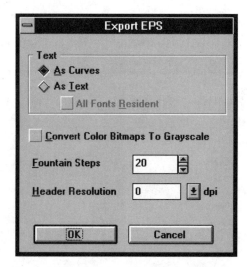

Figure 24. Certain file formats that you can export open a second export dialog box. The *Encapsulated PostScript* option opens the *Export EPS* dialog box.

Figure 25. Exporting to any of the *Bitmap* formats opens this dialog box.

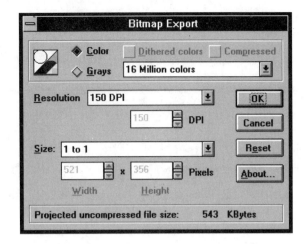

INSERT OBJECT

The *Insert Object* command takes advantage of the OLE capabilities of CorelDRAW running under Windows 3.1. OLE stands for *Object Linking and Embedding*, which lets you transfer information from one application to another. In the case of *Insert Object* in CorelDRAW, this embeds an object from another application (source document) into CorelDRAW (destination document). For information on linking, see the *Paste Special* command in Chapter 5.

Figure 26. Selecting *Insert Object* opens the *Insert Object* dialog box. From the list in this dialog box, you can choose the application in which you want to create the source document. The programs you have installed determine the list of available applications. This dialog box displays only applications with OLE capabilities. In this example, we selected the *Paintbrush Picture* option and clicked on *OK*.

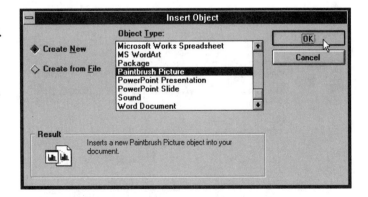

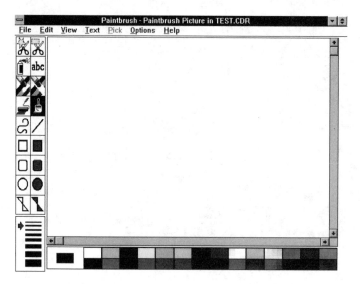

Figure 27. Clicking on *OK* in the *Insert Object* dialog box opens the *Paintbrush* application.

You can work with the *Paintbrush* window as it appears, or you can maximize it as we did in this example. The title bar of *Paintbrush* displays the title of your CorelDRAW file.

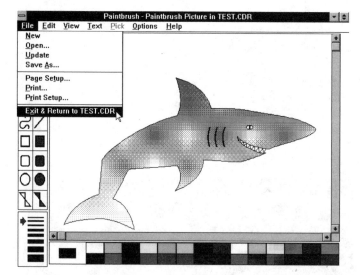

Figure 28. Once you have created the source document, you then embed the object into the CorelDRAW file. The way you do this differs depending on what application you are using. In *Paintbrush,* for example, you can use either the *Update* or the *Exit & Return to...* command from the **File** menu.

Using the *Update* command inserts the object into Corel-DRAW and still keeps *Paintbrush* open.

You can then continue to make changes to the *Paintbrush* document and update the object in CorelDRAW when necessary by choosing *Update* again. We are selecting *Exit & Return to...* in this example.

Figure 29. Using the *Exit & Return to...* command brings up this warning. Click on the *Yes* button to embed the object into your CorelDRAW file.

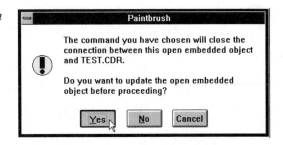

Figure 30. Once you have placed the object in CorelDRAW, you can move it around with the Pick Tool, just as you would with any object.

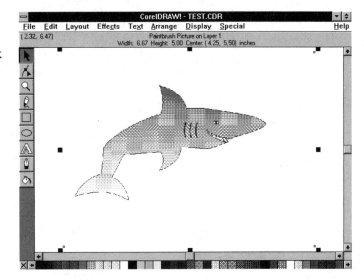

Figure 31. Because you have embedded the object, you can select it and choose *Edit Paintbrush Picture Object* from the **Edit** menu to open the original application to make any changes. Again, you can use the *Update* or *Exit* command in Paintbrush to update the destination file.

Alternatively, double-click on the embedded object to open the source program.

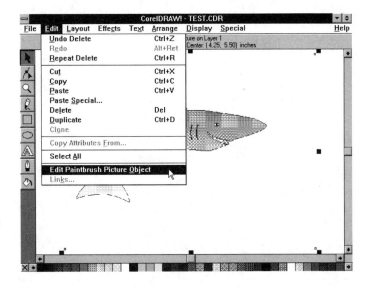

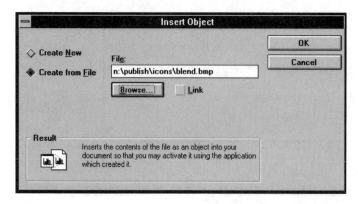

Figure 32. The *Create from File* option lets you insert an existing file as an embedded object. Type the path and name of the file into the *File* text box after you click on the *Create from File* option.

Alternatively, click on the *Browse* button to open a dialog box where you can choose the required file. Clicking on *OK* after doing this embeds the file into the current CorelDRAW drawing.

If you check the *Link* option, the file you select is linked to the CorelDRAW file. For more information on linking, see the *Paste Special* command in Chapter 5.

PRINT

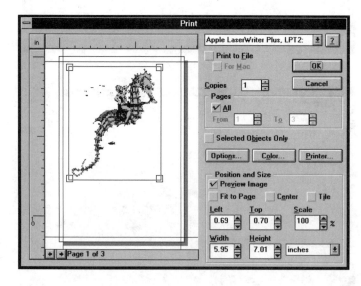

Figure 33. Selecting the *Print* command from the **File** menu opens the *Print* dialog box. The dialog box in this example displays the options for a PostScript printer. If you do not have a PostScript printer, you won't be able to choose some of the options discussed.

The first thing you will notice when you open this dialog box is the preview window that displays the document.

Figure 34. At the top of this dialog box you can select your required printer. From the drop-down list, choose the printer that you plan to output the Corel-DRAW file from. Clicking on the 🔲 icon next to this drop-down list opens a dialog box that describes the current printer's capabilities.

When you select a different printer, you may see the lines move in the display window; these lines indicate the margins on the printer you've selected. Each printer will have slightly different margin settings and these lines show where the printing cuts off.

Figure 35. Check the *Print to File* option in the *Print* dialog box, and click on *OK* in the *Print* dialog box to open the *Print To File* dialog box. Here you decide where you wish to save the print file. You must also give the print file a title, which you type into the *File Name* text box.

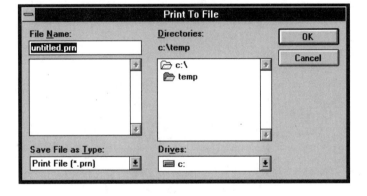

CorelDRAW uses the standard industry extension of *.prn* for print files. Before creating the print file, there may be other options in the *Print* dialog box you may want to select.

You create print files if you plan to send the file to a service bureau or want to print the file from a computer that does not have CorelDRAW. Before you create a print file, you should select the printer you plan to output the print file from.

When you select the *Print to File* option, you can select the *For Mac* check box. Selecting this option allows you to create a print file that will print from an Apple Macintosh printer. You create the print file in exactly the same way.

The *Copies* option in the *Print* dialog box lets you specify the number of copies you want to print.

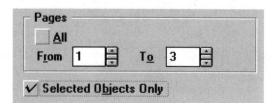

Figure 36. You can specify the page range to print (if you are working with multiple pages) in the *Pages* section of the *Print* dialog box. Checking the *All* option prints the entire document. If you deselect this option, you can select the page range that prints in the *From* and *To* edit boxes.

If you select any objects with the Pick Tool before you activate the *Print* dialog box, you can choose the *Selected Objects Only* option, prompting CorelDRAW to print only what you have selected.

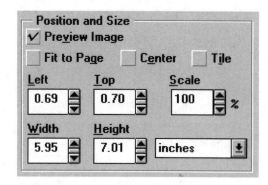

Figure 37. The first option in the *Position and Size* section is the *Preview Image* option. By default, this option is on, showing the drawing in the display window in the *Print* dialog box. If you deselect this option it will not display.

Figure 38. You have the option to decide at what size the drawing prints, regardless of the size of the actual drawing. Click on the *Fit to Page* option to fit everything in the drawing automatically to the page size. This affects the printed output only, not the actual drawing. Choosing the *Center* option moves the drawing to the center of the page. The *Center* option is the default for the *Fit to Page* option.

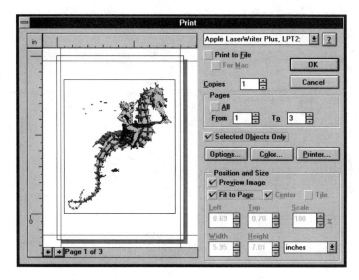

Use the *Tile* option to print files that are larger than the printer's page size. You can print different sections of the file on separate pages, and then paste them together to create posters or banners.

If you deselect the *Fit to Page* and the *Center* options, you can use the *Left* and *Top* options to change the position of the image in the display window. The *Left* option represents the top-left corner of the graphic, while the *Top* value represents the top of the graphic.

Figure 39. As an alternative to moving the image in the display window with the *Left* and *Top* options, you can hold the mouse button down with the cursor on the image and drag it to a new position.

The *Scale* option in the *Print* dialog box lets you scale the image for printing. With 100% as the original drawing size, you can resize according to what you want.

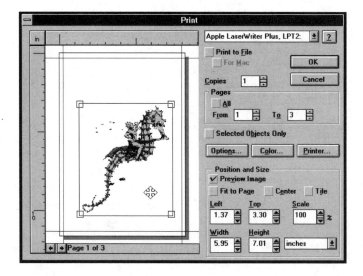

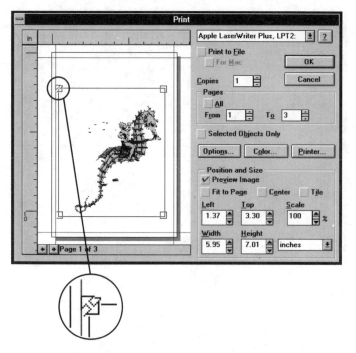

Figure 40. You can use the *Width* and *Height* options to change the size of the printout. Alternatively, drag one of the four corner nodes toward the center of the drawing to reduce the size, and away from the center to increase the size.

You can change the unit of measurement for all the options in this dialog box through the measurement drop-down list at the bottom right of the dialog box.

OPTIONS

Figure 41. Below the *Pages* section of the *Print* dialog box are three buttons: *Options, Color,* and *Printer.* Clicking on the *Options* button opens this dialog box.

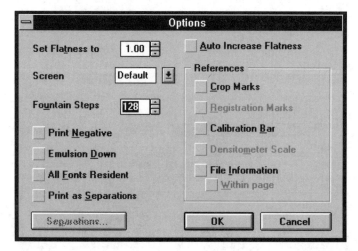

You can use the *Set Flatness to* feature of the *Options* dialog box to decrease the complexity of a drawing, which in turn speeds printing time. This option simplifies complex images when printing.

When you increase the number in the *Set Flatness to* box, it reduces the smoothness of your curves, as CorelDRAW decreases the number of segments in a curve. This affects the printed image only.

If you have trouble printing a graphic, use the *Auto Increase Flatness* option and CorelDRAW will increase the flatness value by increments of two each time you print. If this value ever exceeds the *Set Flatness to* value by ten, the printer will not print the offending object.

The *Screen Default* setting in the *Options* dialog box ensures CorelDRAW determines the screen frequency in relation to your printer, which may differ depending on the output device. You can also enter your own screen frequency. The lower the number you choose, the coarser the image. The *Default* setting will usually suffice, unless you need to create a special effect.

When creating color separations, the screen frequencies set in the *Separations* dialog box (see Figure 42) override the *Screen* setting in the *Options* dialog box.

You use the *Fountain Steps* option to determine the number of stripes a PostScript printer uses to create a fountain fill. The smaller the value, the quicker the printing time, but the transition between the two colors is not as smooth. The higher the value, the smoother is the fill, but the slower the printing time. When you output the file to a Linotronic typesetter, the *128* default setting is recommended for 1270 dpi, and *200* for 2540 dpi. If you alter the *Steps* value in the *Fountain Fill* dialog box (see Chapter 3), the *Fountain Steps* value in this options dialog box is ignored.

Choosing the *Print Negative* option prints your image as a negative. This is sometimes necessary if you are printing to film, and the commercial printer needs negative film.

The *Emulsion Down* option also relates to the printing of film. The emulsion of film is the light-sensitive coating and is usually printed facing up. In some cases your commercial printer may require the emulsion down. If this is the case, check this option.

When you select the *All Fonts Resident* option, CorelDRAW assumes the printer contains all the fonts you have specified in the document. It then uses the printer-resident fonts instead of the CorelDRAW fonts. If you have checked this option, and not downloaded the appropriate font to the printer, it prints in Courier, or not at all. Use this option if you are sending the file to a service bureau that has PostScript Type 1 versions of the fonts, or you have the corresponding Type 1 fonts and are able to download them to your printer. If you choose this option and the fonts are not in the printer, they will print as Courier or not at all.

Check the *Print As Separations* option if you plan to print color separations of the file. When you print the file as separations, you get a different page printed for each color specified. If you used the four process colors (*Cyan, Magenta, Yellow,* and *Black*) in your document, you will get a maximum of four printouts, one for each of the four process colors. If you choose only two of the process colors, you will get two printouts.

If your document is made up of spot colors, you will get a separate printout for every Pantone color you selected. You determine the maximum number of separations by the number of Pantone colors you use. You can print color separations to film or to paper. When you want to output color separations to film, you could create a print file and send this file to a bureau that outputs the file to film.

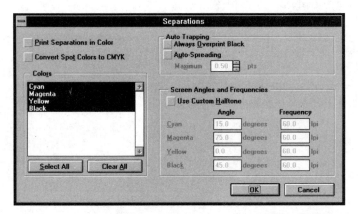

Figure 42. After checking the *Print as separations* option, click on the *Separations* button to activate the *Separations* dialog box. The first option in this dialog box is the *Print Separations in Color* option. If you are printing separations to a color printer, you can use this option to print each separation using its true color rather than printing in shades of gray.

If you have spot (Pantone) colors in your drawing, you can select the *Convert Spot Colors to CMYK* option. With this option, CorelDRAW temporarily converts the spot colors to the closest equivalent process colors. This is sometimes necessary if you have a large number of spot colors, yet you only want a maximum of four color separations. This affects the printout only, not the colors in the drawing.

The *Colors* section of the *Separations* dialog box lists all the colors used in your drawing. Select the colors you want to print as separations from this list. Click on the *Select All* button to highlight them all, or on the *Clear All* button, to deselect them all.

The first option in the *Auto Trapping* section in the *Separations* dialog box is the *Always Overprint Black* option. Checking this option ensures that any object with a greater than 95% black fill will overprint when it overlaps another color. Normally, when different colors overlap, the area underneath is knocked out.

Choose the *Always Overprint Black* option to ensure these knockouts do not occur with colored objects below black objects. This is known as trapping. CorelDRAW achieves *Auto Trapping* by applying an outline to the object the same color as its fill. When you select the *Auto-Spreading* option, CorelDRAW spreads the foreground color into the background to all objects in the drawing that have no outline, have a uniform fill, and have not been assigned the *Overprint Fill* option from the *Object Menu*. You can determine the amount of trapping by changing the *Maximum* value after checking the *Auto-Spreading* option. The amount of trapping applied is also determined by the object's color.

The main reason for overprinting is to avoid gaps that sometimes occur when printing from separations. If you overprint colors other than black, the two colors will mix and you may get a result you don't want.

You also have the ability to trap objects yourself manually. See the *CorelDRAW 4 Users Manual* from page 304.

Trapping objects and printing color separations is a complex process. You should talk to your bureau or commercial printer when creating color separations to find out exactly what options to choose.

The *Screen Angles and Frequencies* options determine the angle and frequency that each color appears in each separation. The settings in the *Separations* dialog box are the default settings. CorelDRAW may change these settings automatically according to the output device you have selected. The *coreldrw.ini* file includes optimized settings relating to the resolution and output device you have selected. Click on the *Use Custom Halftone* option to change the *Angle* and *Frequency* settings. In most cases you would leave these settings at their default, unless the commercial printer or bureau tells you to change a setting.

The *Frequency* settings that you use in the *Separations* dialog box overrides the *Screen* setting in the *Options* dialog box.

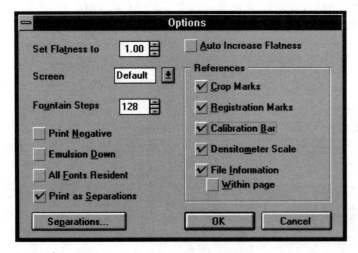

Figure 43. The *References* options back in the *Options* dialog box let you add certain items to your printout. These items will appear only if the drawing page size is smaller than the printer paper size.

Choosing the *Crop Marks* option prints crop marks to indicate the page size. This works if you are printing a page smaller than the printer's paper size. They are used as the final trim size for the printed document.

The *Registration Marks* option is available only if you are printing separations. Registration marks are lines that appear on each separation which the printer uses when aligning film separations.

Checking the *Calibration Bar* option tells CorelDRAW to add a strip of colors and grayscales to the printout. Doing this lets you calibrate the *Preview* in the *Color* dialog box (Figure 44) so it matches the printout.

The *Densitometer Scale References* option is available only when you are printing color separations. It adds a scale to each separation that shows the intensity of the CMYK inks for each separation.

Choosing the *File Information* option prints the file name, date, and time, on the page. When you are printing separations, it also includes the separation information. The program displays this information outside the crop marks, so if you are printing a page the same size as the printer paper, you would check the *Within Page* option to ensure the information appears on the page when printing proofs only.

Figure 44. Click on the *Color* button in the *Print* dialog box to open the *Color* dialog box. You use the options in this dialog box to prepare your CorelDRAW file for color separations. The tools in this dialog box are very complex and require a solid understanding of colors and printing separations.

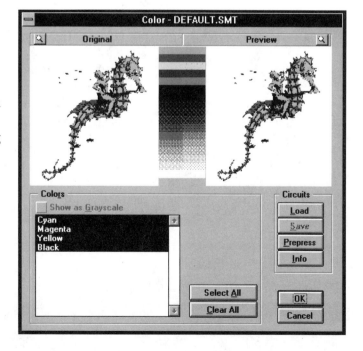

Speak to your bureau and read the *CorelDRAW Users Manual* for more information. Generally, if you plan on creating color separations the default settings will suffice. This means you can set up the separations without having to worry too much about changing the options in the *Color* dialog box.

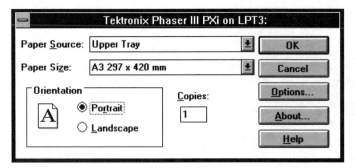

Figure 45. Clicking on the *Printer* button in the *Print* dialog box opens this dialog box. Here you set up the *Paper Size* you are printing to and the *Orientation* (*Portrait* or *Landscape*). Your *Orientation* option should match the orientation on the page you are printing.

Once you have set up your *Print Options* dialog box as you need, click on the *OK* button to start the printing process.

PRINT MERGE

Use the *Print Merge* option in the **File** menu to combine a word processing document with a CorelDRAW file. This feature is useful for things such as mailing lists, where you keep the image constant, and change the name and address for each printout.

CorelDRAW inserts the merged text in the appropriate places in the document and sends this to the printer; this prints multiple copies of the file with newly merged text in each one.

PRINT SETUP

Figure 46. Select *Print Setup* to open the *Print Setup* dialog box. The first option in this dialog box lets you override the current default printer (which is set up through the Windows Control Panel). After selecting the specific printer option, choose a printer from the drop-down list of printer names.

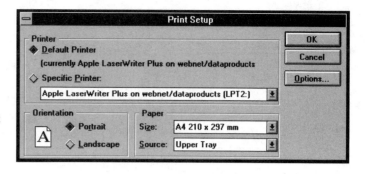

In the *Orientation* section, you can select *Portrait* or *Landscape*. This should match the orientation option you have selected in the *Page Setup* dialog box (see Chapter 6). Select the paper size of the printer in the *Paper* section of the dialog box.

EXIT

Figure 47. Use this command when you have finished working with CorelDRAW. If you have made any changes since last saving the current file, you are given the choice of whether or not to save these changes.

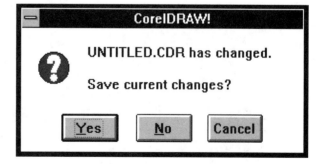

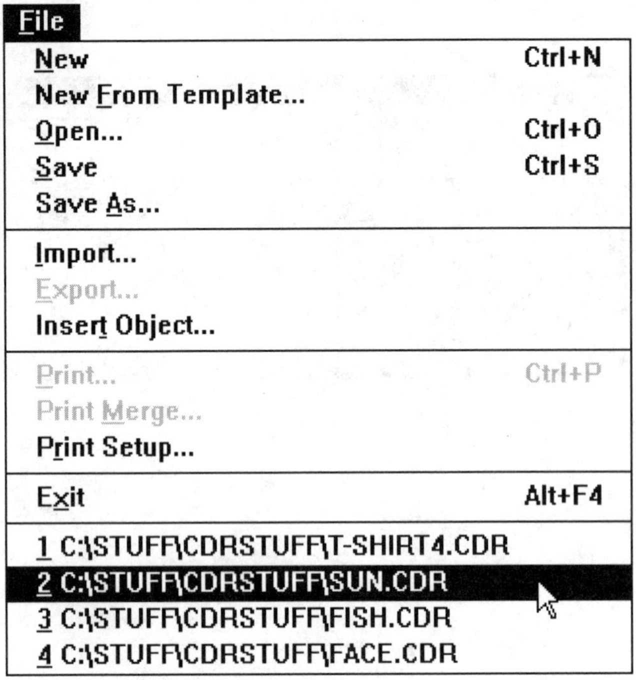

File	
New	**Ctrl+N**
New From Template...	
Open...	**Ctrl+O**
Save	**Ctrl+S**
Save As...	
Import...	
Export...	
Insert Object...	
Print...	Ctrl+P
Print Merge...	
Print Setup...	
Exit	**Alt+F4**
1 C:\STUFF\CDRSTUFF\T-SHIRT4.CDR	
2 C:\STUFF\CDRSTUFF\SUN.CDR	
3 C:\STUFF\CDRSTUFF\FISH.CDR	
4 C:\STUFF\CDRSTUFF\FACE.CDR	

Figure 48. The last four CorelDRAW files you opened and saved appear at the bottom of the File menu. You can select a file name from the **File** menu to open the file.

THE EDIT MENU COMMANDS

You use the commands in the **Edit** menu for basic editing options. Some of these commands, such as *Undo, Cut, Copy, Paste, Delete,* and *Select All* are common to most Windows applications. You also use this menu for managing linked or embedded files.

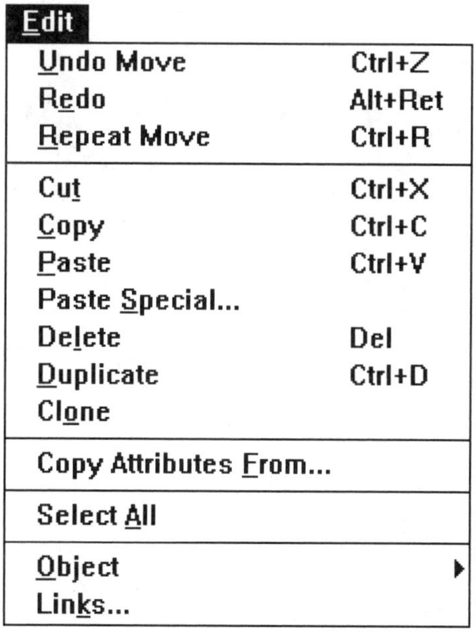

Figure 1. This figure displays the **Edit** menu with its associated commands.

```
Edit
    Undo Move              Ctrl+Z
    Redo                   Alt+Ret
    Repeat Move            Ctrl+R

    Cut                    Ctrl+X
    Copy                   Ctrl+C
    Paste                  Ctrl+V
    Paste Special...
    Delete                 Del
    Duplicate              Ctrl+D
    Clone

    Copy Attributes From...

    Select All

    Object                        ▶
    Links...
```

UNDO

The *Undo* command lets you return the graphic to the previous state it was in before you performed the last process. The number of previous actions you can undo is determined by the *Undo Levels* value you set in the *Preferences* dialog box (for more information, see the *Preferences* command in Chapter 11). You cannot undo a change of view, any command in the **File** menu, or any selection process.

REDO

You can access the *Redo* command only after you have used the *Undo* command. It reinstates whatever you changed with the *Undo* command.

REPEAT

You use this command to apply the very last process performed on an object to the currently selected object. In the example of Figure 2, we used the *Repeat* command after rotating an object.

(a) *(b)*

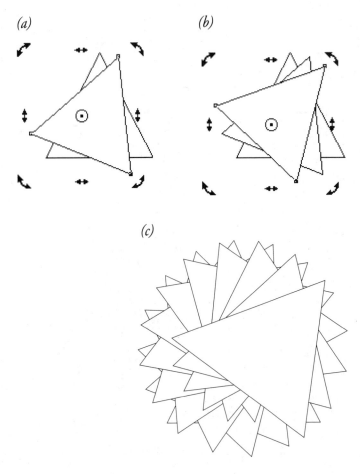

(c)

Figure 2. You can rotate and duplicate an object using the Pick Tool (a). (Press the + key on the numeric keypad, or the right mouse button, to duplicate the object while rotating it.)

When you select the *Repeat* command after rotating and duplicating the object, you repeat the rotation and duplication (b).

If you keep selecting the *Repeat* command before doing anything else, you can continue this process (c).

CUT

Use the *Cut* command to delete any selected object or objects from the page. *Cut* also transfers a copy of the deleted object to the Windows Clipboard. It remains there only until you use the *Cut* or *Copy* command again.

COPY

Choosing the *Copy* command copies any selected object or objects to the Windows Clipboard, leaving the original object behind. The copy remains in the Clipboard only until you use the *Cut* or *Copy* command again.

PASTE

The *Paste* command lets you re-insert the last object or objects that you cut or copied.

PASTE SPECIAL

You use the *Paste Special* command for linking documents. Linking connects a source document with CorelDRAW (in the destination document). Any changes you make in the source document appear automatically in the destination document.

Figure 3. Before copying the information you intend to paste into CorelDRAW, make sure you have saved the source document (in this case *Paintbrush*). Then, select the information you want, and choose *Copy* from the **Edit** menu. You can now either close the source document or switch to CorelDRAW.

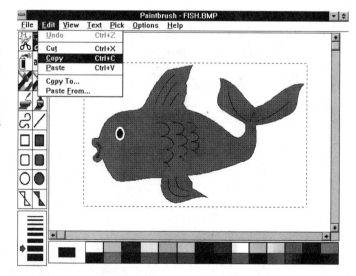

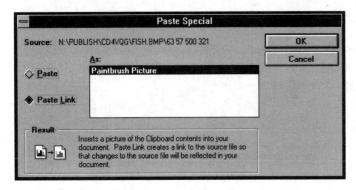

Figure 4. In CorelDRAW, select *Paste Special* from the **Edit** menu to open the *Paste Special* dialog box. Select the appropriate option from the list (in this case select the *Paintbrush Picture* option) and click on the *Paste Link* option.

Alternatively, choosing the *Paste* option will also insert the copied information into CorelDRAW; however, this does not create a link between the two programs.

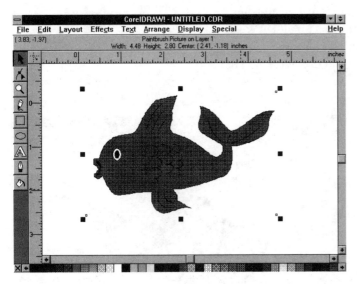

Figure 5. The information you copied from *Paintbrush* is now in CorelDRAW. Any changes you now make in the source document are automatically updated in the CorelDRAW file, unless you change the *Update* option in the *Links* dialog box. See the **Links** section later in this chapter for more information.

DELETE

To remove a selected object from the screen, select the *Delete* command. You can reverse this command by using the *Undo* command immediately after using *Delete*.

DUPLICATE

When you use the *Duplicate* command, it places a copy of the selected object on the screen. You can alter where CorelDRAW displays the duplicate with the *Preferences* command in the **Special** menu (see Chapter 11).

Figure 6. Select the object you want to duplicate, and choose *Duplicate* from the **Edit** menu. After selecting this command, CorelDRAW places the duplicate on top of the original object according to the *Place Duplicates and Clones* option in the *Preferences* dialog box.

In this example, we moved the bottom object down and to the left slightly, and gave it a black fill. We then gave the object on top a white fill. We did this to create a drop shadow effect.

You can also duplicate an object if you click on the right mouse button while in the process of moving, resizing, rotating, or skewing an object. Or, if you press the + key on the numeric keypad, a duplicate of the selected object appears directly on top of the original object.

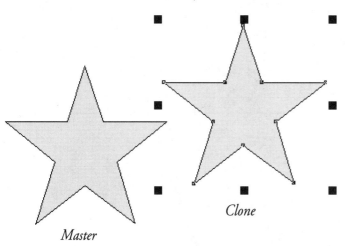

Master

Clone

CLONE

Figure 7. The *Clone* command from the **Edit** menu is similar to the *Duplicate* command, in that selecting it makes a copy of the selected object. The *Clone* command, however, takes this one step further by applying most changes made to the original object (the master object) to the clone object.

After selecting this command, CorelDRAW places the clone on top of the original object, governed by the *Place Duplicates and Clones* option in the *Preferences* dialog box.

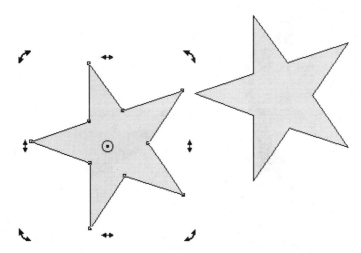

Figure 8. If you rotate the master object for example, the cloned object also rotates.

If you change a certain attribute of the cloned object, this attribute is no longer affected by the changes made to the master object. For example, if you rotate the clone, it will remain unaffected if you rotate the master object.

Figure 9. To determine which object is the master and which object is the clone, put the mouse cursor over the object and hold the right mouse button down. When the **Object Menu** appears, you will see either the *Select Master* or the *Select Clones* command at the bottom. The master object will have the *Select Clones* command and the clone, *Select Master*.

In this example, we held the right mouse button down on the master object. For more information on the **Object** menu, see Chapter 12.

You cannot clone an already existing clone. You can, however, duplicate a clone, and the changes made to the master object will also apply to the duplicate of the clone.

If you apply an envelope or change the perspective of the master object, this will also affect the clone, although the other special effects commands in the **Effects** menu will not.

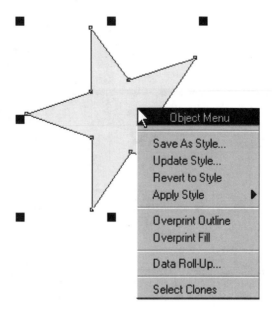

COPY ATTRIBUTES FROM

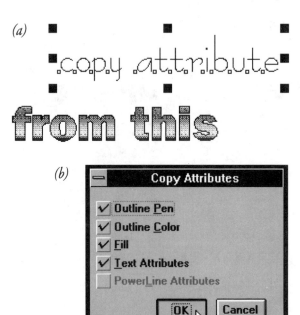

Figure 10. The *Copy Attributes From* command allows you to copy the *Outline Pen, Outline Color, Fill, Text Attributes,* and/or the *Powerline Attributes* from one object to another quickly. Select the object to which you want to copy the attribute (in this case (a), the top line of text), and choose the *Copy Attributes From* command.

Select the options you want in the *Copy Attributes* dialog box, and click on *OK* (b). We selected all the options except for the *Powerline Attributes.*

With the (➡) arrow, click on the object from which you want to copy the attribute (in this case (c), the bottom line of text).

The top text string now has the same attributes as the bottom text string (d).

SELECT ALL

Figure 11. The *Select All* command selects every object on your screen and automatically activates the Pick Tool, if you have not already selected it.

The status line in this example indicates that this command has selected all three objects on the page.

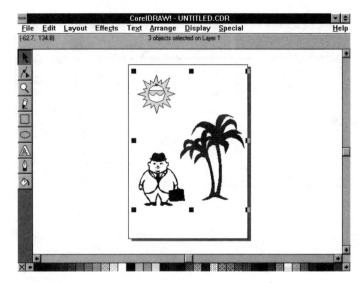

OBJECT

Figure 12. You can access the *Object* command only when you have selected a linked or embedded item on the CorelDRAW screen. The command changes according to the type of item you select.

Choosing this command after selecting a linked or embedded item opens the program that you created your selected item in. You can now edit this item in its original program and update the changes in the CorelDRAW file.

For more information, see the **Paste Special** section in this chapter, and the *Insert Object* command in Chapter 4.

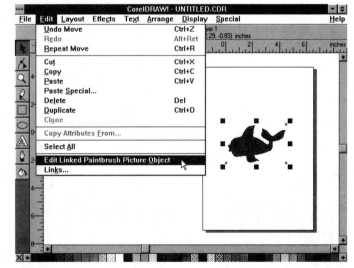

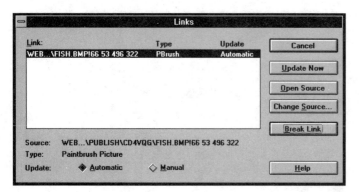

LINKS

Figure 13. When you select the *Links* command, the *Links* dialog box appears. You can access this dialog box only when you have linked items in the current Corel-DRAW file. This dialog box lists all the items that you have linked to the CorelDRAW file.

The information in this dialog box contains the source path, the source type (what program it was created in) and whether CorelDRAW updates the file automatically or manually.

Checking the *Update Automatic* option ensures that Corel-DRAW automatically updates any changes you made to a linked file in the source program. With the *Manual* option selected, you must click on the *Update Now* button in the *Links* dialog box to update any changes to source files. You must select the link option from the list in this dialog box before updating.

Choosing the *Open Source* button in the *Links* dialog box opens the source program and file that you have selected from the *Links* list.

Choosing the *Break Link* option cancels the link between the source file selected in the *Link* list and CorelDRAW.

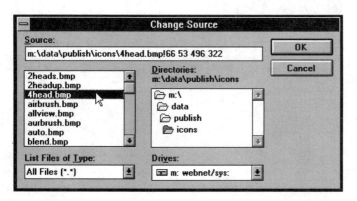

Figure 14. Click on the *Change Source* button in the *Links* dialog box to open the *Change Source* dialog box. From the list in this box, you can select a file to become the new source file. CorelDRAW then starts receiving the OLE information from the newly selected file. This can change the file significantly if the new source file is very different to the original one.

THE LAYOUT MENU

THE LAYOUT MENU COMMANDS

The commands in the **Layout** menu generally relate to the whole document. These commands include page, layer, style, grid, and guideline options.

Figure 1. This figure displays the **Layout** menu with its associated commands.

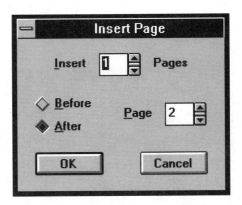

Layout	
Insert Page...	
Delete Page...	
Go To Page...	
Page Setup...	
Layers Roll-Up...	Ctrl+F3
Styles Roll-Up...	Ctrl+F5
Grid Setup...	
Guidelines Setup...	
Snap To	▶

INSERT PAGE

Figure 2. The first command in the **Layout** menu is the *Insert Page* command. This opens the *Insert Page* dialog box.

Change the number in the *Insert # Pages* option to the amount you want to include in your Corel-DRAW file. You can have up to 999 pages.

You then must decide where to put the page or pages. Click on the *Before* or *After* option and then choose which page you want to insert the pages before or after. Click on *OK* to insert the new pages.

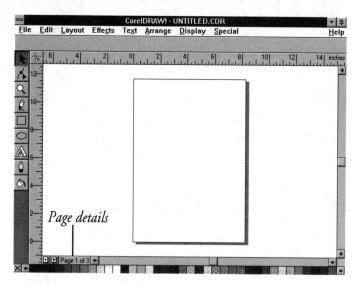

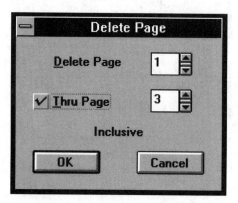

Figure 3. After you insert some pages, depending on where and how many you inserted, you will see a page add icon (⊞) or a page forward icon (▶) and a page back icon (◀). Also displayed, as shown in this figure, are the number of pages and which page you are on.

A page add icon (⊞) appears when you are on the last or first page of the document. Clicking on it brings up the *Insert Page* dialog box so you can add more pages.

The page forward (▶) and page back (◀) icons move you from one page to the next. If you have more than five pages in your document, clicking on one of these icons with the right mouse button moves you five pages at a time. If you click on the page back icon with the Ctrl key held down, you will move to the first page of the document. Using the page forward icon and the Ctrl key produces the opposite effect.

DELETE PAGE

Figure 4. If you need to delete a page, choose *Delete Page* to open the *Delete Page* dialog box. Here you can choose the page number which you want to delete. If you click on the *Thru Page* option, you can delete a number of pages ranging from the number you have in the top edit box to the number you have in the one below.

GO TO PAGE

Figure 5. To add a page, choose *Go To Page*, which opens the *Go To Page* dialog box. Key in the number of the desired page, and click on *OK*. CorelDRAW then moves you to this page.

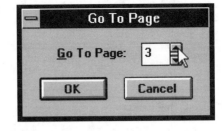

Figure 6. You can also open the *Go To Page* dialog box by clicking once on the page number indicator.

PAGE SETUP

Figure 7. Selecting the *Page Setup* command opens the *Page Setup* dialog box. The first option, *Paper Size*, determines the size of the page you are working on.

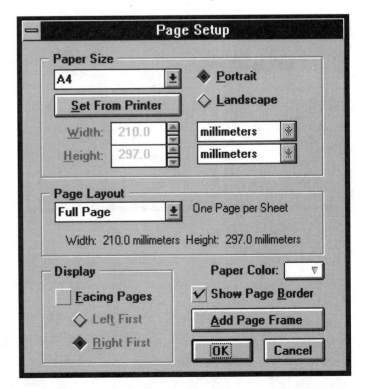

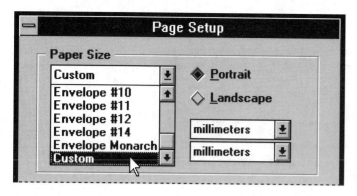

Figure 8. You can choose one of the preset page size options from the drop-down list. If you select the *Custom* option from the bottom of this list, you can change the values in the *Width* and *Height* edit boxes to determine your own page size.

If you click on the *Set From Printer* option underneath the *Paper Size* text box, CorelDRAW automatically assigns the paper size and orientation to match the current paper size you've set for printing.

You also have the option of choosing either *Portrait* (vertical) or *Landscape* (horizontal) layouts.

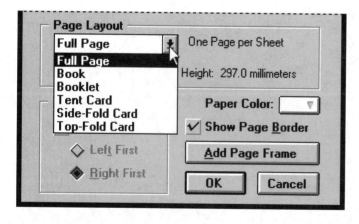

Figure 9. The *Page Layout* drop-down list contains a number of preset page layouts you can select from. The *Full Page* option is the normal, default setting. If you choose one of the other options, CorelDRAW arranges the pages so they are in the correct order for publication, even though each page appears separately in Corel-DRAW.

In the case of an even page book, for example, the last and the first pages are printed on the one page, the second and the second last pages are printed on the one page, and so on. When the book is bound, the pages will then appear in the correct order.

Figure 10. In the *Display* section of the *Page Setup* dialog box, you can choose to display the pages side by side (if you have multiple pages in the document). If you do select the *Facing Pages* option, you can choose whether the pages start to face each other on an odd or an even page.

Figure 11. In this example, we chose the *Facing Pages* and *Right First* options, and pages 1 and 2 are displaying together.

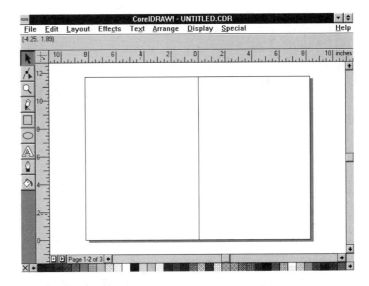

Figure 12. The *Paper Color* quick-pick palette lets you apply a color to the page when you are working in *full-color* mode or viewing the preview screen. This affects the page only on the screen and does not print with this color.

Click on the *More* button at the bottom of the quick-pick palette to access all the color methods. You must select white from the quick-pick palette if you want the page to return to normal.

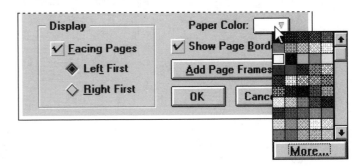

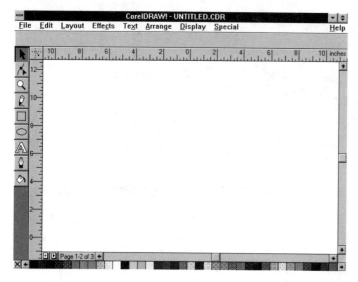

Figure 13. If you deselect the *Show Page Border* option in the *Page Setup* dialog box, the page border on the screen disappears.

Clicking on the *Add Page Frame* option in the *Page Setup* dialog box puts a rectangle on the page that is the same size as the current page. You can fill, outline, or resize this rectangle as you would any other rectangle.

Click on the *OK* button in the *Page Setup* dialog box to return to the drawing with any changes you have made. Changing any of the *Page Setup* options affects all pages in the document.

LAYERS ROLL-UP

Figure 14. Selecting the *Layers Roll-up* command brings up the *Layers* Roll-up. CorelDRAW lets you create several layers in a document. You can then place objects on different layers. The advantages of layers are discussed in this section.

The *Layers* Roll-up contains four layers that appear in each new file. When you begin drawing objects in a new file, CorelDRAW places them on *Layer 1*. Selecting a layer from the list in the Roll-up switches to that layer.

GRID LAYER

You cannot draw or place objects on the *Grid* layer. It contains only the grid, which you access through the **Layout** menu. Having a separate layer for the grid lets you disable the grid quickly and easily.

GUIDES LAYER

Any guides you place on the page are automatically placed on the *Guides* layer. Objects on all layers will snap to the guidelines if you select *Guidelines* from the *Snap To* submenu in the **Layout** menu. You can put objects on the *Guides* layer; these are known as guide objects and are dashed like guidelines. Any objects on the *Guides* layer act as normal guides and objects snap to them.

DESKTOP LAYER

Figure 15. Objects are automatically placed on the *Desktop* layer if you drag them off the page onto the pasteboard area.

When you are working with multiple page documents, you can see the *Desktop* layer (objects not on the page) on any page you are viewing. This lets you drag objects from the *Desktop* layer onto any page in the document without having to copy and paste them through the Windows Clipboard.

The status line in this example indicates the selected object off the page is on the *Desktop* layer.

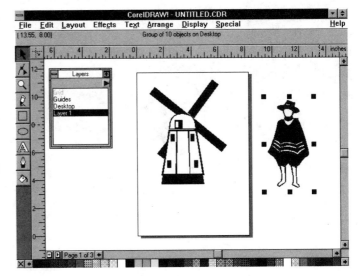

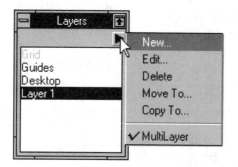

LAYERS FLY-OUT MENU

Figure 16. Clicking on the ▶ icon in the *Layers* Roll-up opens the *Layers* fly-out menu.

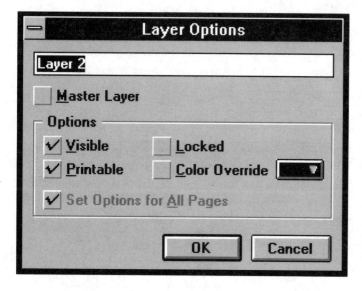

Figure 17. Selecting *New* from the *Layers* fly-out menu brings up the *Layer Options* dialog box. This box automatically displays a name for the *Layer* you are about to create.

CorelDRAW assumes you are going to name the layers in order (e.g. the next layer after *Layer 1* will be *Layer 2*). You can keep this name or create your own, a maximum of 32 characters. After clicking on *OK*, the *Layers* Roll-up window displays the new layer name in its layers list.

Selecting *Edit* from the *Layers* fly-out menu also opens the *Layer Options* dialog box of Figure 17. The name of the active layer appears in the text box at the top of the dialog box.

For more information on the *Master Layer* option, see **Master Layer** later in this chapter.

Deselecting the *Visible* option lets you temporarily hide the objects on the current layer. This does not affect the printing of these objects. Hiding layers also lets you speed up screen redrawing time.

Selecting the *Locked* option from the *Layers Options* dialog box locks the objects on the current layer. You can't select or edit the objects on the locked layer. You can add and edit objects on a locked layer, but as soon as you deselect the object, you can't select it again. The *Locked* option in the *Grid* layer is constantly on; you can't deselect it.

The *Printable* option lets you print only the layers that you have checked this option for. If you don't want to print a layer, deselect this option. Selecting this option in the *Guides* and *Grid* layers lets you print the guidelines and the grid.

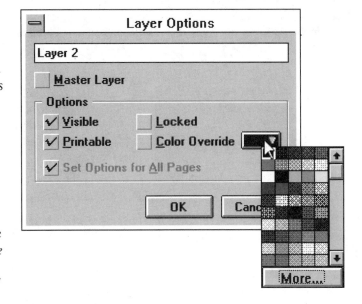

Figure 18. *Color Override* gives you the option of assigning an outline color to all objects in the layer. This doesn't affect the true fill and outline of the objects, it simply lets you see through them if you are working on the objects underneath. Select the color from the quick-pick palette that appears when you click on the color swatch.

CorelDRAW assigns this color to the objects only when you place a check mark in the *Color Override* option. The *Color Override* option is a default in the *Guides* and *Grid* layers and you can't deactivate it.

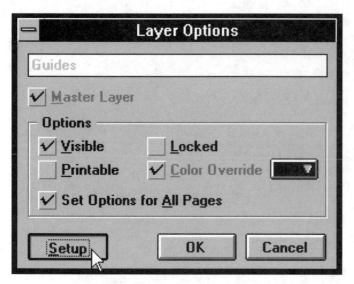

Figure 19. The *Layer Options* dialog box for the *Guides* and *Grid* layers also includes a *Setup* button. Clicking on this button opens the *Guidelines* or *Grid Setup* dialog box—depending on which layer is active.

Selecting *Delete* from the *Layers* fly-out menu removes the active layer and all the objects on it. CorelDRAW warns you before it does this; you then confirm whether or not you want to delete the layer.

Figure 20. The *Move To* command from the *Layers* fly-out menu lets you move selected objects to another layer. Select *Move To* to display the ( ) arrow. With this arrow, click on the layer in the list where you want to move the selected objects.

The *Copy To* command from the *Layers* fly-out menu works as does the *Move To* command, except it places a copy of the selected object on the selected layer. The object remains on its original layer.

The *MultiLayer* command is active when you check it in the *Layers* fly-out menu. You can now select any object on any layer. If you deselect this option, you can select only the objects on the current layer. You can't select objects on locked layers even with the *MultiLayer* option selected.

Figure 21. Changing the order of the layers in the Roll-up list also changes the order of the layers in the drawing. The top layer in the list is the top layer in the drawing.

Using the mouse, you can drag a layer name into a new position in the *Layers* Roll-up. This changes the order of the layers in the drawing. In this example we have moved *Layer 1* to the top of the list.

Figure 22. This may cause some objects to cover other objects that previously covered them. The stacking order commands in the *Order* submenu of the **Arrange** menu (*To Front, To Back, Forward One, Back One,* and *Reverse Order*) change the order of the selected objects in the layer only. Choosing *To Back,* for example, moves a selected object behind all other objects in that layer, but it will still be on top of any objects in lower layers.

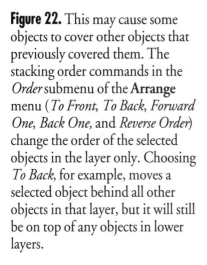

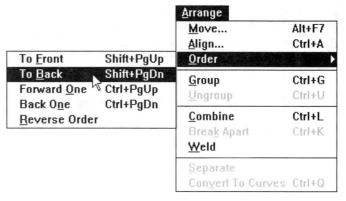

You can select objects from different layers simultaneously. You can also group and combine them. When you group or combine objects from different layers, the objects move to the current layer.

When combining objects, CorelDRAW assigns the fill and color of the last object selected, or the most recently selected object if marquee selecting. The status line always tells you which layer a selected object is on.

MASTER LAYER

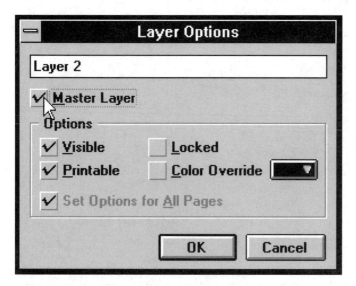

Figure 23. Check the *Master Layer* option in the *Layer Options* dialog box, and all the objects in the current layer will appear on every page. In this example we applied the *Master Layer* option to *Layer 2*. All our *Layer 2* options will now appear on every page.

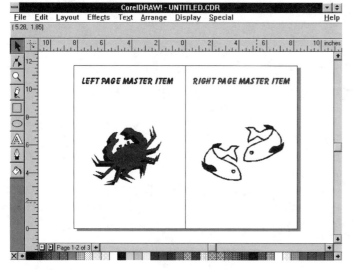

Figure 24. If you have facing pages, all left page items will appear on the left pages in the document, while all right page items will appear on the right pages in the document.

If you do not want a *Master Layer* item to appear on a certain page, deselect the *Set Options for All Pages* on that page.

If you delete or move a *Master Layer* item on any page, this affects all corresponding *Master Layer* items on other pages.

STYLES ROLL-UP

Figure 25. The *Styles Roll-up* command brings up the *Styles* Roll-up. This Roll-up lets you apply styles to items on the page. Styles are a group of saved attributes that you can use to format Artistic Text, Paragraph Text, and graphics quickly and easily.

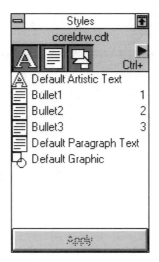

If you have experience with a word processing or a page layout program, you will be familiar with styles.

When you first open the *Styles* Roll-up (and you have no objects selected) you will see a number of styles already listed. The styles listed in Figure 25 are the default template styles. If you have another template file loaded, the styles will be different. These styles include the default settings for Artistic Text, Paragraph Text and graphics, as well as three extra Paragraph Text styles.

Figure 26. The three icons at the top of the *Styles* Roll-up let you show/hide some or all of the style types, including Artistic Text styles (A), Paragraph Text styles (目), and graphics styles (a). In this example, we clicked on all three buttons to hide all the styles.

STYLES FLY-OUT MENU

Figure 27. Clicking on the ► icon in the *Styles* Roll-up pops-up the **Styles** fly-out menu.

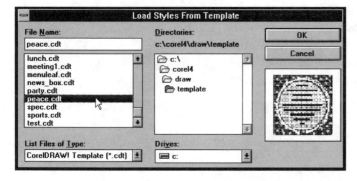

Figure 28. The *Load Styles* command in the **Styles** menu opens the *Load Styles From Template* dialog box.

In the *corel4\draw\template* directory you will see a list of files with a *cdt* extension. These are the template files that come with CorelDRAW, and they all contain different styles.

You can load new styles into your *Styles* Roll-up by selecting a new template from the list in this dialog box and clicking on *OK*. A template is a special kind of document that you save to include all your style details.

For more information on templates, see the *New From Template* command in Chapter 4.

Figure 29. After selecting a template from the *Load Styles From Template* dialog box and clicking on *OK*, the styles in the *Styles* Roll-up change to include the styles contained in the selected template.

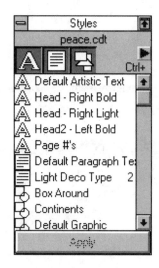

CREATING AND SAVING A STYLE TEMPLATE

You can create and save your own template of styles and then open this template to create documents later. You can also load the styles from this template into any Corel-DRAW document.

After creating all the necessary styles, you can save them in a template file. This does not affect naming or saving the current CorelDRAW file.

For more information on creating styles, see Chapter 12.

Figure 30. To save a template, choose *Save Template* from the **Styles** (▶) menu in the *Styles* Roll-up. This opens the *Save Template* dialog box. This dialog box works like the *Save Drawing* dialog box in that you must name the file and choose where you want to save it.

CorelDRAW automatically applies a *cdt* extension to the file name.

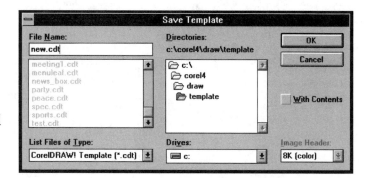

The *With Contents* option saves the file with any objects you have on the page when you save the template. You can choose the *Image Header* option if you save the template with any objects on the page; you can then view the template file in the preview box of the *Load Styles From Template* dialog box (Figure 28).

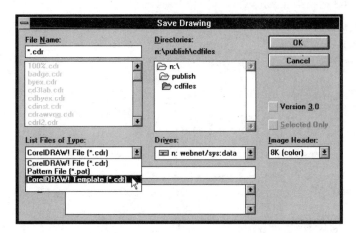

Figure 31. You can also save a template through the *Save Drawing* dialog box. Choose the *Corel-DRAW Template (*.cdt)* option from the *List Files of Type* drop-down list. However, when you save a template this way, the name of the file takes on the name of the template.

Figure 32. If you make changes to the current template (like adding or deleting a style), you are warned whenever you go to load new styles or exit CorelDRAW.

If you click on the *Save As* option from the screen prompt of the above figure, you activate the *Save Template* dialog box where you can save the amended template file under a new name. The changes you made to the template will then not affect the original template file.

Figure 33. You can choose the *Set Hotkeys* option in the **Styles** menu (Figure 27) only if you have one of the Paragraph Text styles selected in the *Styles* Roll-up. Choosing this option opens the *Set Hotkeys* dialog box.

Here you can assign keystrokes to your Paragraph Text styles. You can then apply these styles to selected Paragraph Text quickly and easily by pressing a key combination.

The Paragraph Text styles of the current template appear in the list in this dialog box. Listed under the *Ctrl+* heading are the current hotkeys assigned to a style. The number here is the key you press in conjunction with the Ctrl key to apply the style.

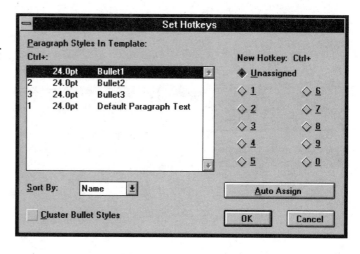

Figure 34. To assign a hotkey to any of the styles not already assigned, select the style from the list and click on a number (one that is not already used in a key combination). In this example, we selected the *Default Paragraph Text* style and clicked on the number *4*. This number then appears next to the style in this dialog box.

If you choose a number that is already assigned to a style, this key combination is then removed from the original style and is assigned to the new style.

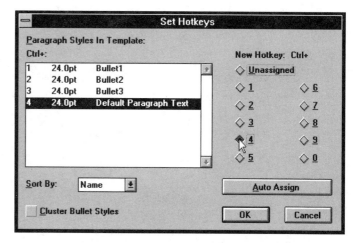

You can change the keystroke for a style by choosing the style from the list in this dialog box and clicking on a different number.

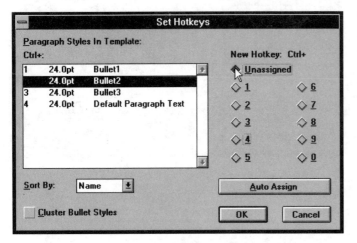

Figure 35. If you do not want a style to have a key combination assigned to it, select the style from the list in the *Set Hotkeys* dialog box and click on the *Unassigned* option.

You can use the *Auto Assign* button in the *Set Hotkeys* dialog box to have CorelDRAW automatically assign keystrokes to any listed Paragraph Text styles that are unassigned.

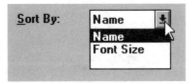

Figure 36. The *Sort By* drop-down list in the *Set Hotkeys* dialog box gives you two options for listing the styles in this dialog box. You can list them either by *Name* (alphabetically) or by *Font Size* (from largest to smallest).

The *Cluster Bullet Styles* option lets you group all the styles in the *Set Hotkeys* dialog box that include bullets. For more information on bullets, see Chapter 8.

Figure 37. The *Delete Style* option in the *Styles* menu lets you delete the style currently selected in the *Styles* Roll-up. You cannot delete a default style.

If you choose the *Find* option, this automatically selects an object (text or graphic) in your drawing that is using the currently highlighted style in the *Styles* Roll-up. This command then changes to *Find Next*, letting you find the next object with this style.

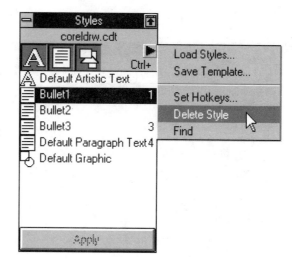

APPLYING STYLES

Figure 38. To apply a style to an object (text or graphic), first select the object with the pointer tool, choose the required style from the *Styles* Roll-up and click on the *Apply* button (a). The result in this example is shown in (b).

If you are applying styles to Paragraph Text, you can use Hotkeys to apply the style. See Figures 33 through 36 earlier in this chapter for more information.

(a)

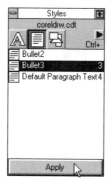

(b)

- To apply a style to an object (text or graphic), first select the object with the pointer tool, choose the required style from the Styles roll-up and click on the Apply button.
- If you are applying styles to paragraph text you may be able to use Hotkeys to apply the style.

GRID SETUP

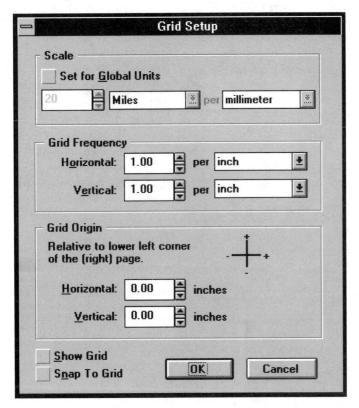

Figure 39. The *Grid Setup* command opens the *Grid Setup* dialog box, which you can also open by double-clicking anywhere on the vertical or horizontal ruler.

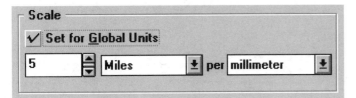

Figure 40. Check the *Set for Global Units* option when you want to set a particular scale in your drawing with one unit of measurement equaling another unit of measurement in the rulers.

The options in the first drop-down list in this section of the dialog box let you set the global unit of measurement in relation to the unit of measurement in the second drop-down list.

The *Grid Frequency* settings in the *Grid Setup* dialog box determine the spacing of the grid. For example, if you have 1 per inch for both the *Horizontal* and *Vertical* settings, your grid will consist of 1 inch squares. When you change the unit of measurement in this dialog box, the *Horizontal* and *Vertical* settings do not change to match, so you need to convert them manually every time you change the measurement system.

Changing the *Grid Origin* settings determines where the zero point of the rulers is on your page. The default *Grid Origin* is the bottom left of the current page. If, for example, you are working in inches, and you change the *Horizontal* and *Vertical Grid Origin* settings to 5 and 5, the zero point moves up and across the page 5 inches.

Figure 41. You can also change the zero point of the rulers with the mouse. To do this, drag the icon in the corner where the two rulers meet down and across. Wherever you release the mouse button is the new zero point.

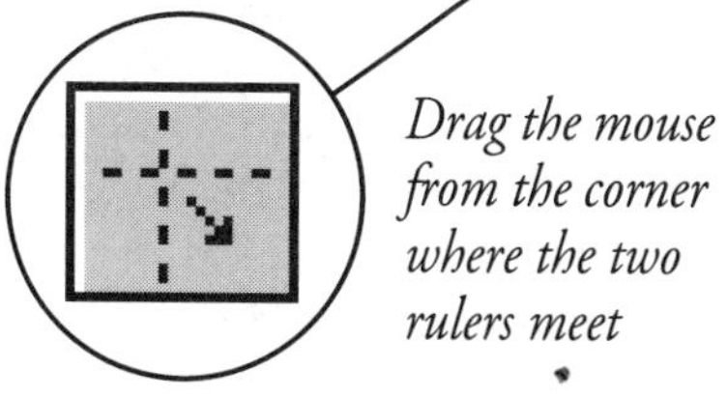

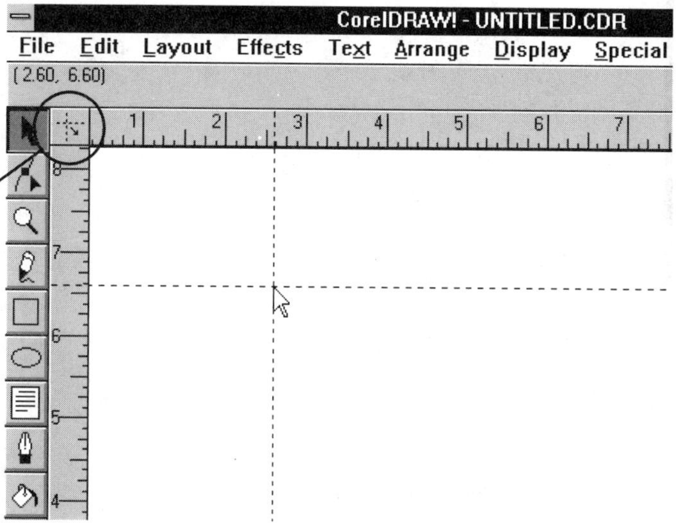

Drag the mouse from the corner where the two rulers meet

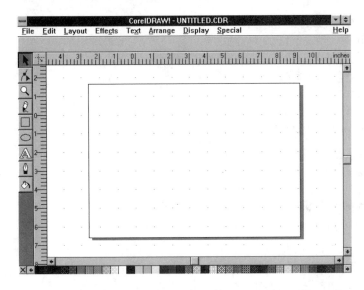

Figure 42. The *Show Grid* option, at the bottom left of the *Grid Setup* dialog box, gives you the option of displaying the grid on the screen. Checking this option covers the screen in dots representing the grid.

The *Snap To Grid* option at the bottom left of the *Grid Setup* dialog box is the same as the *Snap To Grid* command at the bottom of the **Layout** menu (discussed below).

GUIDELINES SETUP

Figure 43. The *Guidelines Setup* command brings up the *Guidelines* dialog box. The options available in this dialog box let you place horizontal and vertical guidelines on the page. The first option is *Guideline type*. You are given the choice of placing a *Horizontal* or *Vertical* guideline. The *Ruler Position* section specifies where this horizontal or vertical guideline goes on the page. The setting is in relation to the zero point of the rulers. °

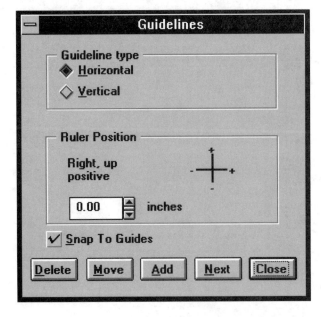

Click on the *Add* button once you have positioned the guide.

The *Delete* option in the *Guidelines* dialog box removes a guideline from the page. The *Move* option changes the position of a guideline. If you have multiple guidelines on the page, the *Next* option displays the position of each guideline, one by one. Once you have found the guideline for which you are looking, you can then move or delete it.

Figure 44. You can also add guidelines to your page by holding the mouse button down when the cursor is on the vertical or horizontal ruler and dragging out onto the page. Release the mouse button where you want the guideline.

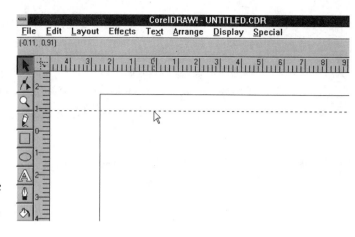

You can move guidelines by dragging them to a new position. Dragging a guideline back into the ruler removes it from the page. Double-clicking on a guideline brings up the *Guidelines* dialog box.

SNAP TO

Figure 45. The *Snap To* submenu in the **Layout** menu contains three snap options.

GRID

When you select the *Snap To Grid* command, it forces the mouse to stay on the grid you specified in the *Grid Setup* dialog box when you are creating, moving, and resizing objects (see **Grid Setup** above). There are some exceptions to this rule: selecting objects; drawing curves with the Pencil Tool and autotracing; rotating and skewing objects; manipulating ellipses with the Shape Tool; and using the Zoom Tool.

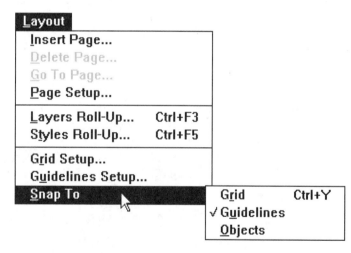

The status line always shows if the *Snap To Grid* option is on. Activating or deactivating this command is the same as selecting or deselecting the same option in the *Grid Setup* dialog box (Figure 39).

GUIDELINES

If you have placed any guidelines on your page (see **Guidelines Setup** above), any objects you move or draw near a guideline snap to it. The *Snap To Guidelines* command takes precedence over the *Snap To Grid* command.

OBJECTS

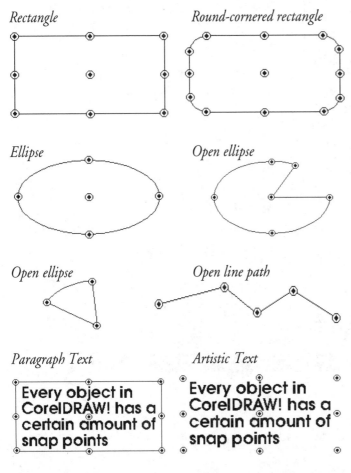

Rectangle

Round-cornered rectangle

Ellipse

Open ellipse

Open ellipse

Open line path

Paragraph Text

Every object in
CorelDRAW! has a
certain amount of
snap points

Artistic Text

Every object in
CorelDRAW! has a
certain amount of
snap points

Figure 46. CorelDRAW provides every object with a certain number of snap points. Each one of these snap points has a restricted gravity range similar to the gravity range of a guideline. The type of object determines the position of these snap points. In this example, we have indicated the snap points of objects with a ⊛.

The *Snap To Objects* command lets you snap an object you are moving to another object that is anchored. The snap point of the object you are moving is where you selected it. If you selected the object within the gravity range of one of its snap points, it uses this snap point for the two objects.

When you move an object within the gravity range of one of the snap points on the anchored object, they will snap together like magnets.

You can add snap points to an object simply by adding a node where you want to put the snap point. In the case of rectangles, ellipses, and text, you must convert them to curves before you can add a node.

Bitmap   *Rotated bitmap*

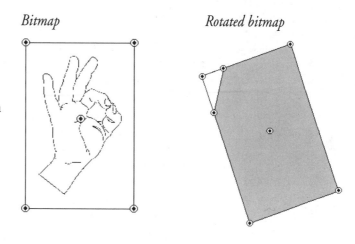

Figure 47. In this example we are moving the white rectangle with the mouse in the top right corner of the rectangle. (This means that the top right snap point of the rectangle is the active snap point.) As we move it closer to the black rectangle, it snaps to the bottom left snap point of the black rectangle.

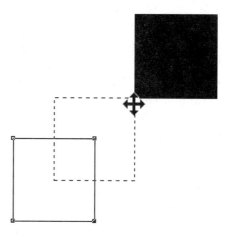

THE EFFECTS MENU

THE EFFECTS MENU COMMANDS

The commands in the **Effects** menu directly relate to the manipulation and applying of special effects to objects.

Figure 1. This figure displays the **Effects** menu with its associated commands.

Effects	
Rotate & Skew...	Alt+F8
Stretch & Mirror...	Alt+F9
Add Perspective	
Envelope Roll-Up...	Ctrl+F7
Blend Roll-Up...	Ctrl+B
E**x**trude Roll-Up...	Ctrl+E
Co**n**tour Roll-Up...	Ctrl+F9
PowerLine Roll-Up...	Ctrl+F8
Clear Perspective	
Copy Effect **F**rom...	▶
C**l**ear Transformations	

ROTATE & SKEW

Figure 2. Choosing the *Rotate & Skew* command brings up the *Rotate & Skew* dialog box. Here you can enter specific values to adjust the angle of rotation and skew of the selected object. To make a copy of the original object, check the *Leave Original* option.

This command gives you an alternative to the rotate and skew handles that appear when you click the mouse twice on an unselected object (see the Pick Tool in Chapter 2).

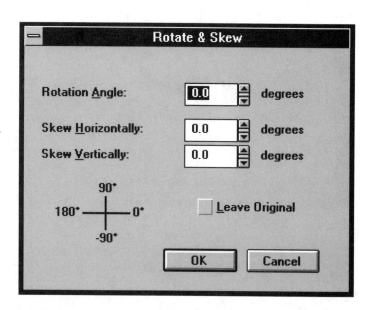

185

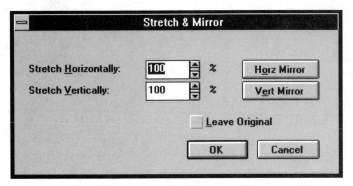

STRETCH & MIRROR

Figure 3. You use the *Stretch & Mirror* command to open the *Stretch & Mirror* dialog box, which offers an alternative method of stretching and mirroring with the mouse. Changing the setting in either the *Stretch Horizontally* or *Stretch Vertically* option stretches selected objects according to the percentage in the text box.

The *Horiz Mirror* and *Vert Mirror* options mirror selected objects in the direction you specify (either horizontal or vertical). Checking the *Leave Original* option leaves a copy of the original object.

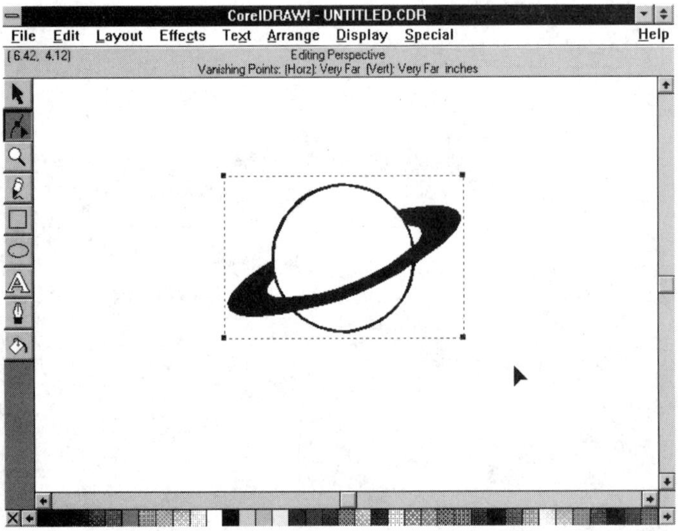

ADD PERSPECTIVE

Figure 4. You use the *Add Perspective* command with the Shape Tool to change the depth of an object. Applying the *Add Perspective* command to a selected object displays a perspective frame around the object.

The Shape Tool is automatically selected when you apply a perspective to an object.

Figure 5. Use the Shape Tool to move one of the four corner nodes to alter the perspective of the object.

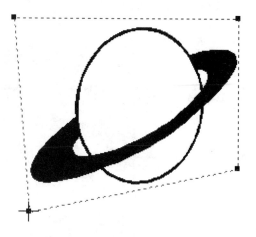

Figure 6. Continue to move the perspective box until you are satisfied with the results. Watch the status line to see the position of the vanishing points.

Shortening two sides of the object lets you create a two-point perspective. Using the Ctrl and Shift keys while dragging a handle forces the opposite handle to move an equal distance but in the opposite direction.

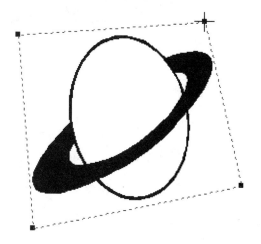

Figure 7. The × symbol that sometimes appears when you are altering an object's perspective shows the vanishing point. Move this symbol to alter the object's vanishing point.

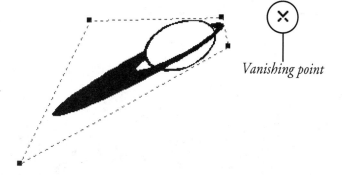

Vanishing point

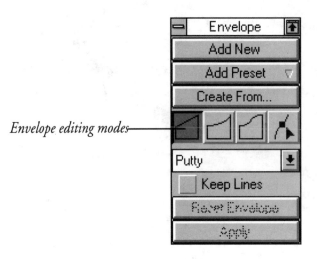

ENVELOPE ROLL-UP

Figure 8. Selecting the *Envelope Roll-Up* command opens the *Envelope* Roll-up. You use the options in the *Envelope* Roll-up in conjunction with the Shape Tool to change the shape of an object.

Envelope editing modes

ENVELOPE EDITING MODES

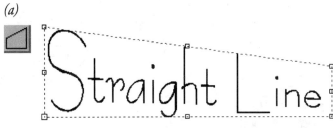

(a)

Figure 9. There are four envelope editing modes (see Figure 8) corresponding to the four edit options in the *Envelope* Roll-up. The editing modes are: (a) *Straight Line*, (b) *Single Arc*, (c) *Two Curves*, and (d) *Unconstrained*.

The first three envelope editing modes let you move one handle at a time horizontally or vertically.

(b)

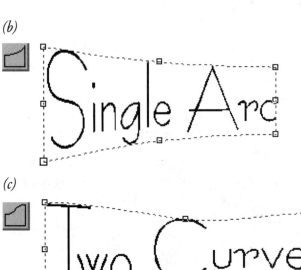

The *Unconstrained* mode (see top of next page) gives you more flexibility when you alter the shape of an object. This option has two control points attached to each handle so you can alter it further. It also lets you select more than one handle at a time by holding the Shift key down and clicking on the handles. Alternatively, you can marquee select the required handles.

(c)

The active mode in the Roll-up affects all objects on the page that you have applied envelopes to. Note that you can switch modes at any time.

(d)

Figure 10. You can apply an envelope to any selected object (except bitmaps). Clicking on the *Add New* option at the top of the *Envelope* Roll-up adds an envelope frame around the object. This frame has eight handles around it so you can change the shape of the object with the Shape Tool.

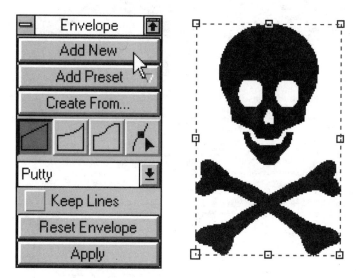

Figure 11. Once you have added a new envelope frame to the object, CorelDRAW automatically selects the Shape Tool. Hold the Shape Tool on any one of the handles around the envelope frame and drag it to a new position.

Figure 12. Once you have changed the position of one, some, or all of the handles, click on the *Apply* button at the bottom of the *Envelope* Roll-up to apply the envelope changes to the object.

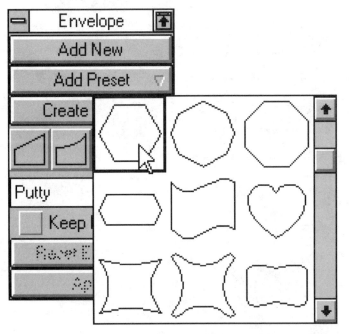

Figure 13. The *Add Preset* pop-up palette contains a range of envelope frames that you can apply to an object. Use the scroll bar to the right of this list to gain access to the preset options not in view; click on one of the preset options to attach that envelope frame to your object.

Figure 14. After selecting a preset envelope, click on the *Apply* button to affect the object. You can edit a preset envelope frame with the Shape Tool as you can any envelope frame, although not all envelope editing modes are available with all the preset envelope frames.

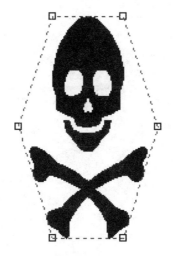

You use the *Create From* option in the *Envelope* Roll-up to copy the shape of one enveloped object to that of another. The object you are creating the envelope from must be a single curved object.

Figure 15. With the Pick Tool, select the object that you want to copy the envelope to (in this case the square) and click on the *Create From* button. This displays the ▰➡ arrow (a).

Now click on the object which you want to copy the envelope from (b). CorelDRAW then applies an envelope frame to the object you selected with the Pick Tool (c). Click on the *Apply* button to complete the procedure (d).

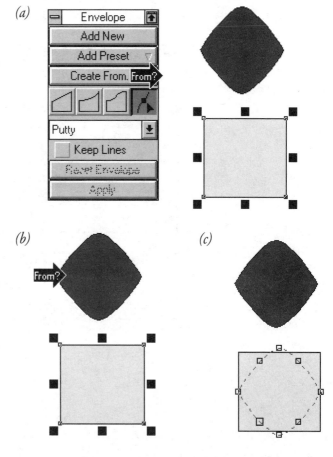

(d)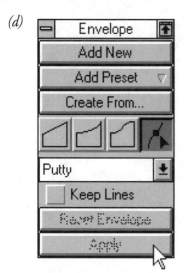

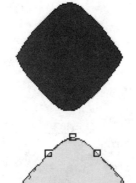

If you click on an inappropriate object with the arrow or you miss the object, you are warned and then given the option of trying again.

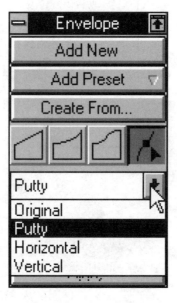

Figure 16. This drop-down list in the *Envelope* Roll-up contains the Mapping Modes. These options have a direct effect on how the object fits to the envelope frame.

Selecting the *Keep Lines* option below this drop-down list in the *Envelope* Roll-up ensures that straight lines in the object are not converted to curves when you apply an envelope to them.

The *Reset Envelope* option in the *Envelope* Roll-up returns the envelope frame to what it was before you applied the envelope.

Figure 17. If you apply an envelope to Paragraph Text, the text is not enveloped but the Paragraph Text frame is. The text will flow inside the shape of the text frame so you can create interesting text wraps. In this example, we added a preset envelope frame to a block of Paragraph Text.

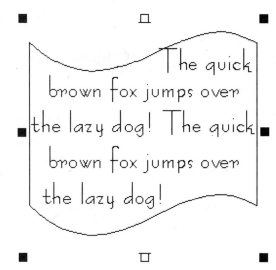

CTRL AND SHIFT KEYS

Holding the Ctrl and Shift keys down while using the envelope option lets you create mirrored and identical sides of the enveloped object. You can use these keys only with the first three envelope modes.

Figure 18. Using the Ctrl key while enveloping forces the handle opposite the one you are manipulating to move in the same direction (a).

Using the Shift key while enveloping forces the handle opposite the one you are manipulating to move in the opposite direction (b).

Holding the Ctrl and Shift keys down together when enveloping forces all other handles to move in opposite directions (c).

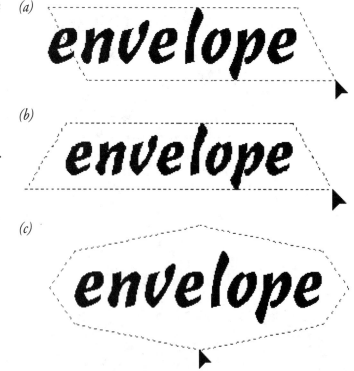

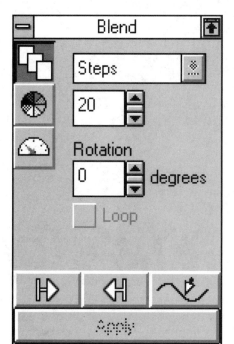

Figure 19. You can add a new envelope to an object that you have already enveloped. To do this, make sure the object is selected and click on the *Add New* button in the *Envelope* Roll-up.

BLEND ROLL-UP

Figure 20. Clicking on the *Blend Roll-Up* command opens the *Blend* Roll-up. The options in this window let you blend two objects into the one blend group.

Along the left of the *Blend* Roll-up window there are three icons. CorelDRAW selects the top icon (🗗) by default when you first open this Roll-up.

The drop-down list at the top of the *Blend* Roll-up has two options. The *Steps* option lets you set how many blend steps there are between the two objects. The *Spacing* option lets you set how much space there is between each step in the blend.

These two options are mutually dependent—changing one affects the other. You can use the *Spacing* option only when you have blended two objects along a path.

BLENDING OBJECTS

Figure 21. In this example we have blended two objects with 10 steps.

To achieve this simple blend, make sure your *Blend* Roll-up is open. Then, with the Pick Tool, select the two objects you want to blend. In this example we created and selected an ellipse and a rectangle as our blend objects. Change the *Steps* value to 10 and click on the *Apply* button.

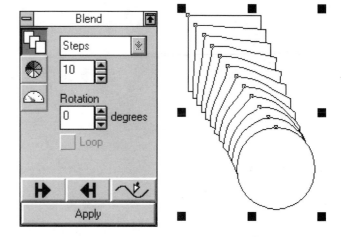

Figure 22. Once you have blended two objects together, they are all part of the one blend group. You can however select the start or end objects of the blend individually. You do this by deselecting the entire blend group and clicking on either the start or end object (the original objects you blended). These objects are known as the Control objects and the status line tells you when you have selected a Control object.

If you click on one of the objects that make up the blend, you select the entire blend group.

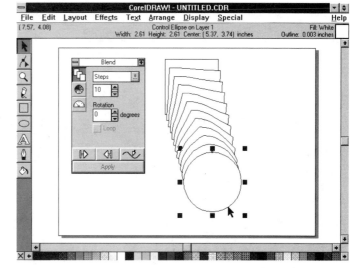

(a)

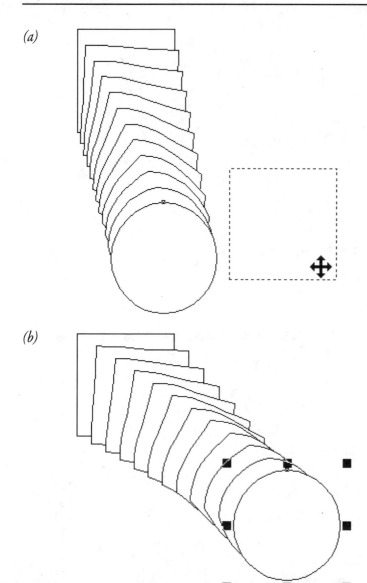

(b)

Figure 23. You can move either the start or the end object (a) and have the blend update immediately (b).

You can also resize, rotate, skew, change the perspective, add an envelope, and edit the start or end objects as you would normally edit them; most changes are updated automatically in the blend.

Figure 24. You can change the color of either the start or the end object (or both) and the changes are updated automatically.

Figure 25. If you use the *Rotation* option in the *Blend* Roll-up you can rotate the blend steps. In this example, we have shown two objects blended together with 10 steps with 360 degrees rotation.

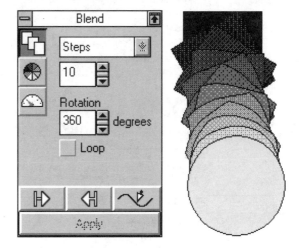

Figure 26. If you check the *Loop* option, the blend steps rotate around a point that is halfway between the start and end objects of the blend.

You can access the *Loop* option only when the *Rotation* value is greater than zero.

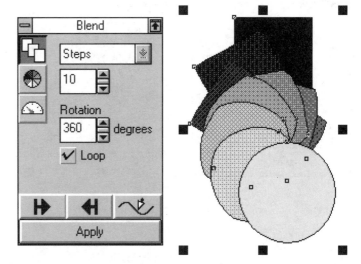

CHANGING BLEND COLORS

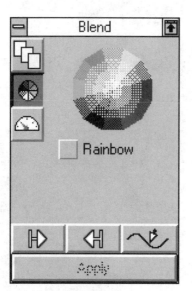

Figure 27. Clicking on the ⊛ icon displays the *HSB* color wheel. The options here change the color of the blend steps.

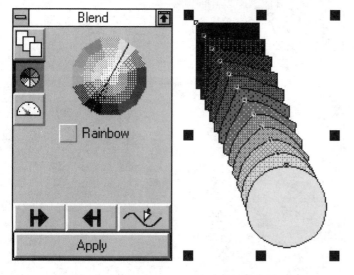

Figure 28. Initially, there is no check mark in the *Rainbow* option. This means that when you select the blend group, a straight line appears on the color wheel, lying between the two colors of the start and end objects. This line determines the color of the blend steps.

Figure 29. If you change the color of one of the Control objects, the color changes in the blend steps automatically.

In this example, we selected the start object (the rectangle) and changed its color by clicking on a different color from the color palette. The line in the color wheel changes to indicate the new color used when we reselected the whole blend group.

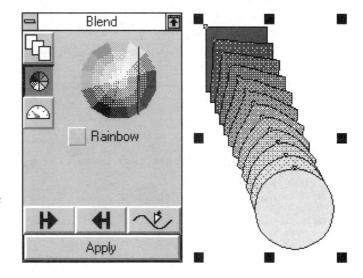

Figure 30. When you check the *Rainbow* option, the straight line on the color wheel in the previous figure moves to the perimeter of the wheel. If you now click on the *Apply* button, the blend steps change color. Compare this figure to the previous one.

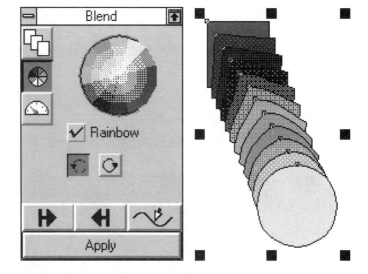

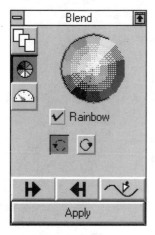

Counterclockwise ↺

Clockwise ↻

Figure 31. The two options immediately below the *Rainbow* check box determine the direction this line takes around the color wheel; they represent clockwise and counterclockwise. The line around the perimeter of the color wheel changes direction (which changes the color blend) when you select the two different options.

If your blend group has no fill but only colored outlines, the *Rainbow* option applies to the object's outline.

MAP NODES/SPLIT/FUSE

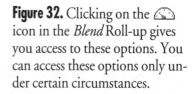

Figure 32. Clicking on the icon in the *Blend* Roll-up gives you access to these options. You can access these options only under certain circumstances.

The *Map Nodes* option blends two objects according to the nodes you select. You can do this when blending the objects for the first time, or after you have blended them already.

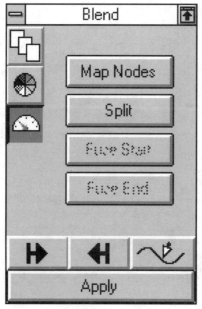

Figure 33. Click on the *Map Nodes* button after selecting the two objects you want to blend (a). An arrow icon appears and highlights one of the object's nodes. With this arrow, click on the node you want as the blend point.

With the second arrow that then appears, click on one of the other object's nodes (b).

Lastly, click on the *Apply* button to blend the objects. You have now blended the two objects according to the nodes you selected (c).

Figure 34. Clicking on the *Split* option splits the blend group at the object you click on with the arrow ($\swarrow$) (a).

The blend group is now split into two, with the object you clicked on becoming the start object of one blend and the end object of the other blend that makes up this formation. This object is now also a Control object. In this example, we changed the formation of the blend by moving the new Control object (b).

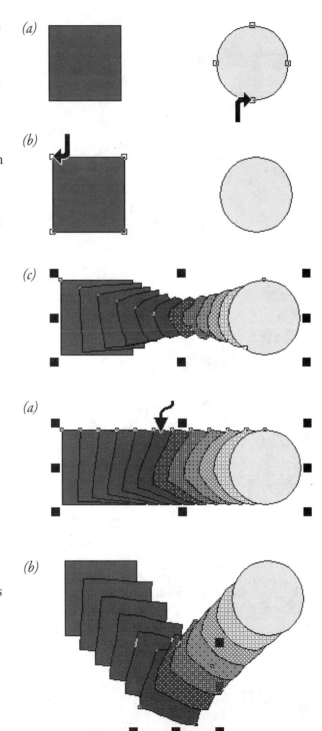

(a)

(b)

(c)

(a)

(b)

You can select the start and end objects in a blend group individually. If you click on any of the objects that make up the blend steps, you select the entire blend group including the start and end objects. If you have split a blend group into two blend groups, you must hold down the Ctrl key to select one blend group individually, otherwise you select both blend groups. When you select an entire blend group, you change the (➡️ ⬅️) icons in the *Blend* Roll-up to black, otherwise they are white.

You can use *Separate* in the **Arrange** menu to separate the blend steps from the start and end objects. You can then use *Ungroup* in the **Arrange** menu to separate the steps that make up the blend, so you can select them individually.

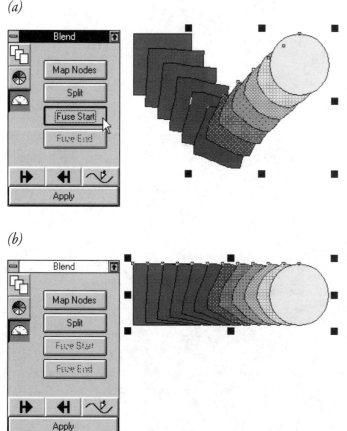

(a)

(b)

Figure 35. The *Fuse Start* and *Fuse End* options recombine split blends. Hold the Ctrl key down and select one of the split blend groups; either the *Fuse Start* or *Fuse End* button becomes active (depending on which blend group you selected). Click the appropriate fuse button (a) and the original start and end objects are fused, rejoining the two split blend groups (b).

If your Control object is the start or end object for more than one blend group, hold the Ctrl key down and select the blend group you want to fuse. Then click on the *Fuse Start/Fuse End* button, and with the special pointer that appears, click on an intermediate object at least one object away from the Control object you are using in the fuse.

START AND END OBJECTS OF A BLEND

Figure 36. Choosing *Show Start* from the ⇨ menu in the bottom section of the *Blend* Roll-up (a) highlights the start object in a selected blend (b). This is useful if you have a complex drawing and cannot find the start of the blend.

Selecting *Show End* from the ⇦ menu finds the end of the blend group.

After finding the start or end of a blend group, you can drag it to a new position. When you release the mouse button, the entire blend group adjusts accordingly.

(a)

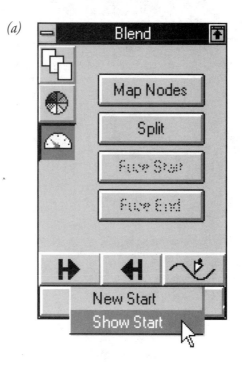

The *New Start* and *New End* commands from these menus let you change the start and end objects of a blend respectively (see Figure 37).

(b)

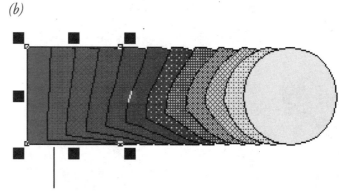

The start object in this blend group is currently selected

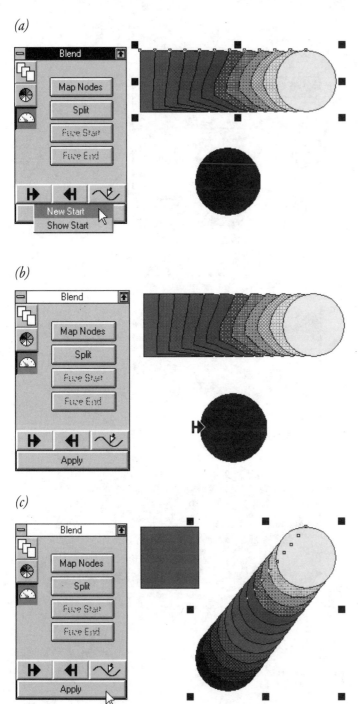

(a)

(b)

(c)

Figure 37. The first step in changing the start object in a blend is to select the entire blend group (a). To do this, click on any one of the blend steps with the Pick Tool. Then choose *New Start* from the ▸ menu.

With the arrow that appears, click on your new start object (b). (The new start object must be behind the end object.)

After clicking on the *Apply* button, the object you have clicked becomes the new start object for the blend group (c).

To create a new end object, follow the steps above, but select *New End* from the ◂ menu.

CHANGING THE BLEND PATH

Figure 38. To change the blend path with the Pick Tool, select the blend group that you want to affect. Then select *New Path* from the ⤳ menu which adds the 𝆏 arrow (a). This deselects the blend group and you select the path for the blend steps to follow with the 𝆏 arrow (b).

Click on the *Apply* button to flow the blend along the path (c).

Selecting *Show Path* from the ⤳ menu selects the path the blend is attached to. This is useful if you have a complex drawing and are having trouble finding the path.

Selecting *Detach From Path* separates the path and the blend group. The blend group remains where it was when it was fitted to the path.

If you attach a blend group to a path, the ⤳ icon becomes black when you select the blend group.

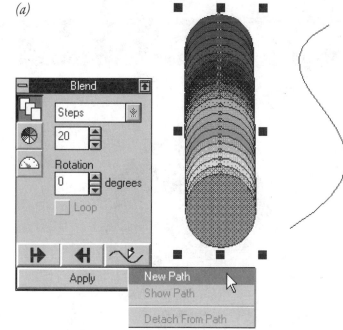

(a)

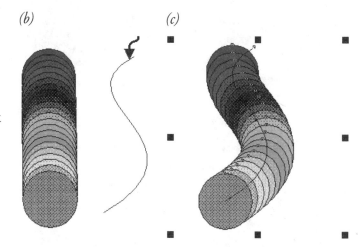

(b)

(c)

OTHER BLEND FEATURES

Figure 39. You can use grouped objects as the start and end objects of a blend. Make sure you have grouped the objects before you blend them.

Figure 40. You can use a single object in more than one blend group. In this example, we have blended the circle at the top with both circles below it.

CREATING HIGHLIGHTS

Figure 41. You can use the *Blend* feature for creating highlights in objects. In this example, we have placed a small tear drop on top of a larger tear drop object.

Make sure you place the lighter colored object on the top, or the effect does not work (a).

You can see the highlight after you have done the blending (b).

If you have checked the Rainbow option, the highlight effect can look even more interesting (c).

You cannot blend across different layers. If you try to do this, CorelDRAW moves the objects to the same layer. See Chapter 6 for more information on layers.

(a)

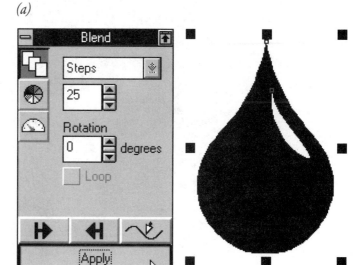

(b)   (c)

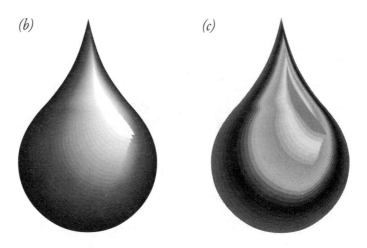

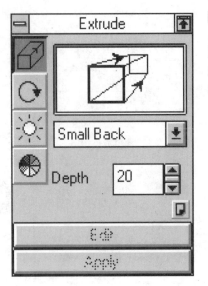

EXTRUDE ROLL-UP

Figure 42. Using the *Extrude Roll-Up* command opens the *Extrude* Roll-up. You use this option to make an object appear three dimensional.

APPLYING AND EDITING AN EXTRUSION

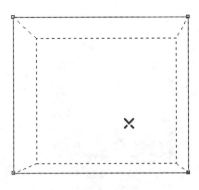

Figure 43. If you open the *Extrude* Roll-up with an object selected, CorelDRAW automatically applies a wireframe extrusion to it. As you make changes in the *Extrude* Roll-up, they are reflected in the wireframe extrusion.

You can also alter the wireframe extrusion by moving the × icon (the vanishing point) with the mouse. You can open the *Extrude* Roll-up before you select your object; select the object, then click on the *Edit* button to apply the wireframe extrusion to this object. You are then free to make any changes to the object in the *Extrude* Roll-up.

Figure 44. Clicking on the *Apply* button after you have made changes in the *Extrude* Roll-up applies these changes to the object. As long as you keep the object selected, the wireframe extrusion remains and you can still edit it.

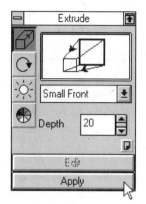

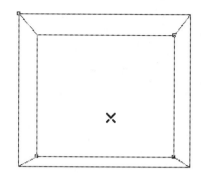

When you deselect the object after using the *Apply* button, the wireframe extrusion disappears leaving the extrusion as it was when you clicked on *Apply*.

To edit the extrusion again, select the object and click on the *Edit* button in the *Extrude* Roll-up.

Figure 45. The first icon in the *Extrude* Roll-up window (☐) is the *Depth* icon. The options in the drop-down list shown here determine the effect of the extrusion. You can choose either a perspective or a parallel extrusion through these options.

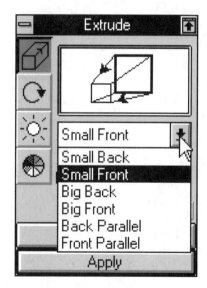

With a perspective extrusion, the extrusion always looks as though it is heading toward or away from the vanishing point. The first four options in this drop-down list are perspective extrusions. The front and back choices indicate whether the extrusion will appear in front of or behind the object you are extruding.

With a parallel extrusion, the extrusion face is the same size as the original object, and the vanishing point is always in the center of the extrusion face. The last two options in this drop-down list are the parallel extrusion options.

As you select a different option from this drop-down list, you will see how it affects the selected object.

The higher the value in the *Depth* option below the drop-down list, the closer the extrusion is to the vanishing point. You can change the *Depth* option only when you are working with perspective extrusions.

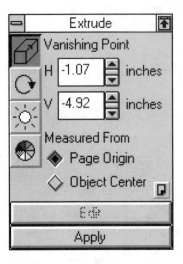

Figure 46. Click on the 🢓 icon in the bottom right of the *Extrude* Roll-up for the options shown here. These options let you position the vanishing point (✕) of the extrusion precisely. You do this by typing in a horizontal (*H*) and vertical (*V*) value.

You can adjust these values in relation to either the zero point of the ruler (*Page Origin*), or the middle of the object's highlight box (*Object Center*).

ROTATING EXTRUSIONS

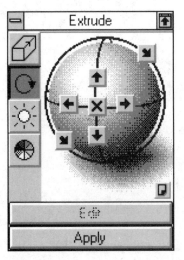

Figure 47. The second icon in the *Extrude* Roll-up (⟳) is the *3-D Rotation* icon. Clicking on this option brings up the *Extrude rotator*. The *Extrude rotator* does not work with parallel extrusions, only perspective.

Figure 48. The two arrows around the outside of the *rotator* circle (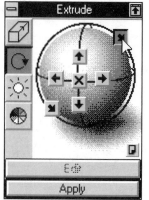) rotate the object five degrees clockwise or anti-clockwise when you click on them. The extrusion wireframe moves as you click on these arrows.

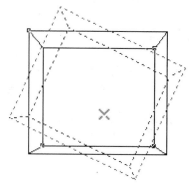

Figure 49. The four arrows on the *rotator* spin the object five degrees in the direction of the arrow you click. This example displays the spinning option using the right arrow (➡).

The up and down arrows tumble the object, end over end, either forwards or backwards.

The ✕ button at the center of the sphere removes any rotations you have applied to an object.

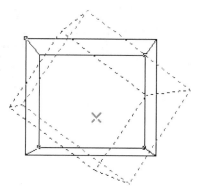

Figure 50. Clicking on the ▣ icon at the bottom right of the *Extrude rotator* gives you these options (for perspective extrusion only). Selecting these options makes the same changes that you make with the *rotator*, except that you key in a value instead of selecting it visually as in the previous two figures.

Click on the ▣ icon to return to the *Extrude rotator*.

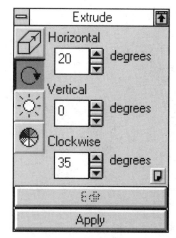

Once you have rotated the object the way you want, click on the *Apply* button.

CHANGING THE LIGHT SOURCE

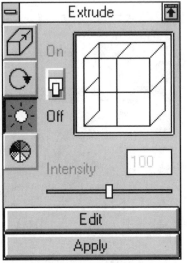

Figure 51. The *Light Source Direction* icon (☼) determines the direction of the light source shining on the object.

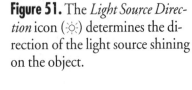

Figure 52. Click on the ⏻ switch to turn on the light. This displays a sphere, representing your object, inside a wireframe arc. The ✗ represents the light source.

Figure 53. Click anywhere in the cube where two or more lines connect to change the position of the light source ✕. You can, of course, see this effectively only when you have applied a fill to your object.

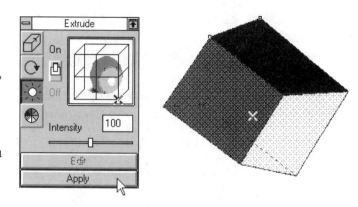

The *Intensity* option changes the strength of the light source. As you increase the number above 100, you move the object's color to white. As you decrease the value below 100, you move the object's color to black.

The light source remains in the same place, even if you later rotate or spin the object.

CHANGING THE EXTRUDE COLOR

Figure 54. The *Extrusion Coloring* icon (⊛) determines the color of the extrusion. Clicking on the *Use Object Fill* option gives the extrusion the same fill as the original object.

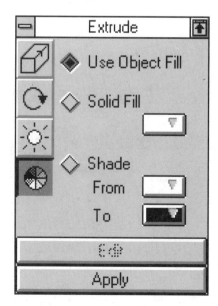

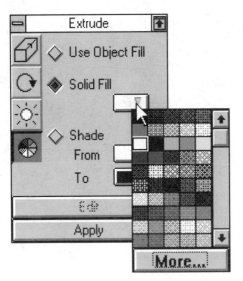

Figure 55. The *Solid Fill* option lets you choose a separate color for the extruded surfaces. Click on the color swatch to display a color quick-pick palette where you can select the color you want.

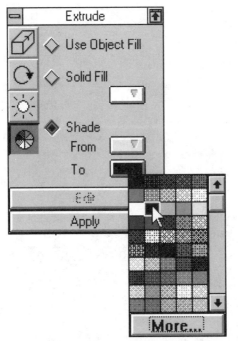

Figure 56. The *Shade* option lets you apply a linear fountain fill to the extruded surfaces. Use the *From* and *To* options to select the two colors that make up the shading.

Use the *Apply* button to apply the colors to the selected object's extrusion.

Regardless of the way you color your extrusion, the choices you make in the light source direction and intensity will influence the object's final appearance.

CONTOUR ROLL-UP

Figure 57. The *Contour Roll-Up* command from the **Effects** menu brings up the *Contour* Roll-up. The options in this Roll-up let you create a series of contour lines on the inside or outside of a selected object.

You can apply contours to all objects except grouped, linked, or embedded objects, and bitmaps.

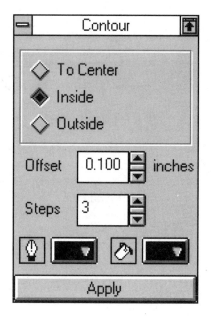

CONTOUR DIRECTION

Figure 58. The first choice in the *Contour* Roll-up determines whether the contour lines appear inside or outside the object. The *To Center* option creates contour lines that go towards the center of the object (a). The *Inside* option also creates contours toward the center of the option, but you decide how many progressive shapes are included by changing the number of steps (b). The *Outside* option creates contours that appear on the outside and each shape moves further away than the previous contour shape (c). The *Outside* option can dramatically increase the size of the object, depending on the number of steps.

(a)

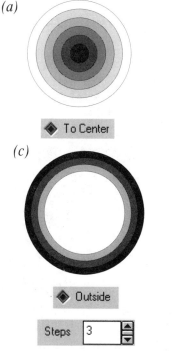

The object in all these examples is the white circle

(b)

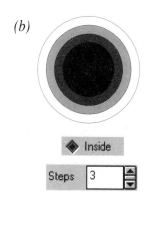

(c)

CONTOUR OFFSET AND STEPS

The *Offset* value in the *Contour* Roll-up determines the amount of space between each contour shape. You can enter any value between 0 and 10 inches.

The *Steps* option sets the number of contour steps. If you have the *To Center* contour direction selected, you can't select the *Steps* option.

If you have the *Inside* option selected, and all the contour steps will not fit, the contours continue to the center of the object and stop when there is no more room. The reason for this is that the *Offset* option takes precedence over the *Steps* value. You may have to reduce the *Offset* to fit all the contours inside your object.

CONTOUR COLOR

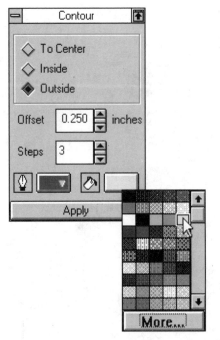

Figure 59. Clicking on the 🖉 and 🖎 quick-pick palettes at the bottom of the *Contour* Roll-up lets you select an outline and fill color that your object will blend to.

Click on the *More* button at the bottom of the palettes to see all color models.

Figure 60. The original object you are contouring must have at least a fill for the contour effect to work. The fill and outline color of the original object will then blend with the fill and outline colors you have selected in the quick-pick palettes of the *Contour* Roll-up.

If the original object has no fill, the contour steps will also be empty regardless of the fill color you have selected in the *Contour* Roll-up.

You can change the color of both the original object and the contour fill once you have applied the contour.

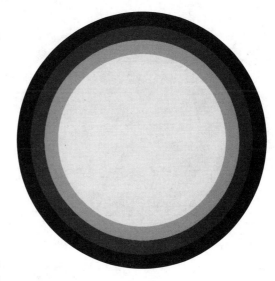

Figure 61. If you choose *Separate* from the **Arrange** menu when you have the *Contour Group* selected (the status line indicates when you do), you can then select each shape in the contour separately.

Do this by holding the Ctrl key down and clicking on the contour shape you want to select. The status line then shows you have a *Child Curve* selected, and the selection handles are more circular than normal.

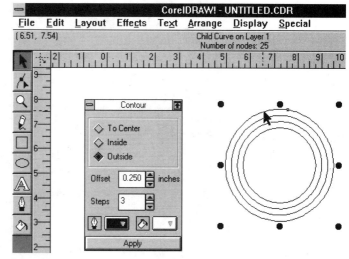

Figure 62. Following the steps in the previous figure lets you change the fill and outline of each shape in the contour individually.

The *Apply* button at the bottom of the *Contour* Roll-up applies any changes you have made to the selected object.

POWERLINE ROLL-UP

Figure 63. Choosing the *PowerLine Roll-up* command opens the *PowerLine* Roll-up. You can use PowerLines to give your objects a hand-drawn look.

You can apply PowerLines to existing drawings, or you can add them later.

PRESET POWERLINES

Figure 64. The first option in the *PowerLine* Roll-up ( ) is the *Preset* option. The list here contains 24 preset PowerLine options for you to choose from.

When you select a preset option from the list in the *PowerLine* Roll-up, an example of how the PowerLine will look is displayed at the top of the Roll-up.

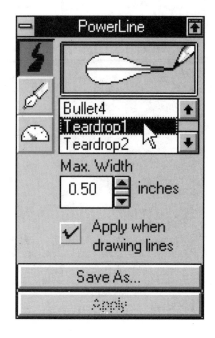

Figure 65. These preset options work in conjunction with the *Max. Width* value below the list. If you have the *Apply when drawing lines* option checked, all lines you draw with the Pencil Tool will automatically look like the preset PowerLine with the maximum width applied to them. The *Max. Width* value can be anything from 0.01 to 16 inches.

To apply a PowerLine to an existing object, first select the object with the Pick Tool, then choose the preset option you want. Change the *Max. Width* value (if necessary) and click on the *Apply* button.

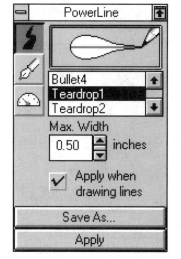
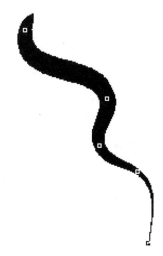

NIB SHAPE

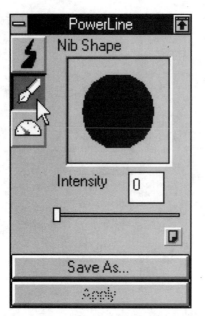

Figure 66. Click on the ✎ button in the *PowerLine* Roll-up to adjust the *Nib Shape* of the PowerLines. Adjusting these options changes the shape and thickness of the PowerLine.

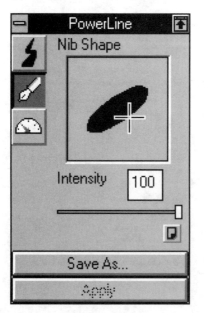

Figure 67. Hold the mouse down on the nib shape representation and drag it around to change the shape of the nib.

The *Intensity* setting affects the width of the line along its entire length, with 100 ensuring the line (at a 90° angle) is at its maximum width. Click anywhere along the *Intensity* gauge or move the gauge marker (□) to change this setting.

Figure 68. Clicking on the ▣ icon in the *PowerLine* Roll-up of the previous figure changes to these settings which let you make precise changes to the *Nib Shape*.

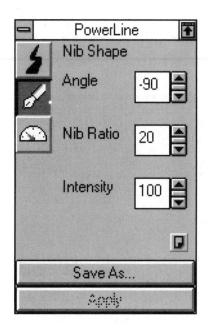

SPEED/SPREAD/INK FLOW

Figure 69. Click on the ⌂ button in the *PowerLine* Roll-up to show these settings.

The *Speed* option affects the curves and changes in direction of a PowerLine. The higher the *Speed* value, the wider the PowerLine appears at a change of direction.

The *Spread* option determines the smoothness of the PowerLine. The higher the *Spread* value, the smoother the line. If the *Speed* setting is on 0, you can't change the *Spread* option.

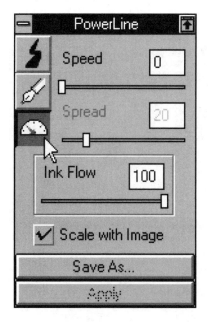

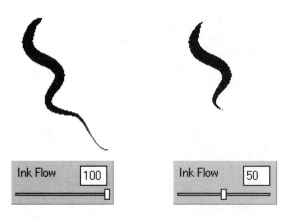

Figure 70. Decreasing the *Ink Flow* value decreases the amount of "ink" in the PowerLine. Compare the two lines in this example. One has an *Ink Flow* of *100* while the other has an *Ink Flow* of *50*.

When you check the *Scale with Image* option, the PowerLine width increases or decreases when you resize the PowerLine.

SAVING POWERLINE EFFECTS

When you make changes to the *Nib Shape, Speed, Spread,* and *Ink Flow* options, this automatically selects the *Custom* setting in the *Preset* list. You can save and name your custom Power-Line effects by clicking on the *Save As* button at the bottom of the *PowerLine* Roll-up.

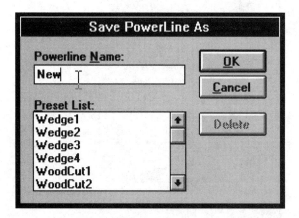

Figure 71. In the *Save PowerLine As* dialog box, type the name of your custom PowerLine in the *Power-line Name* text box and click on the *OK* button.

Figure 72. The name of your custom PowerLine now appears in the list of preset PowerLine effects.

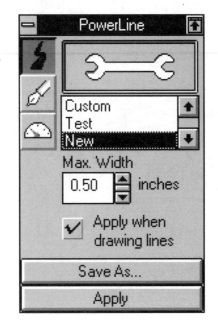

You can access the *Delete* option in the *Save PowerLine As* dialog box only for custom PowerLines. To delete a custom PowerLine, select it from the *Preset List* in the *Save PowerLine As* dialog box and click on *Delete*.

The *Apply* button at the bottom of the *PowerLine* Roll-up applies the PowerLine settings to the selected object.

EDITING POWERLINES WITH THE SHAPE TOOL

Figure 73. You can edit PowerLines with the Shape Tool just like any curved objects in CorelDRAW. The line running through the middle of the PowerLine (the core line) holds the nodes. You can see the core line and the nodes much easier in wireframe mode.

However, the *Node Edit* Roll-up contains a further option that you can access only when editing PowerLines. To open the *Node Edit* Roll-up, double-click on the node of a PowerLine or anywhere along the core line.

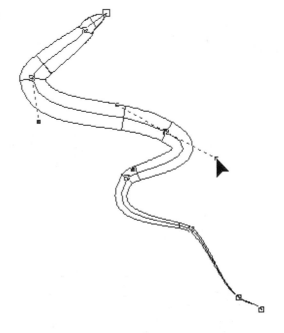

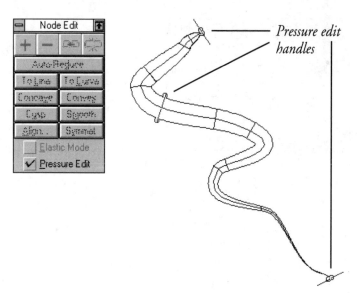

Pressure edit
handles

Figure 74. Once the *Node Edit* Roll-up is open, choose the *Pressure Edit* option at the bottom of the Roll-up. When you select this option, sets of pressure edit handles appear at both ends of the PowerLine and sometimes at intervals along the line.

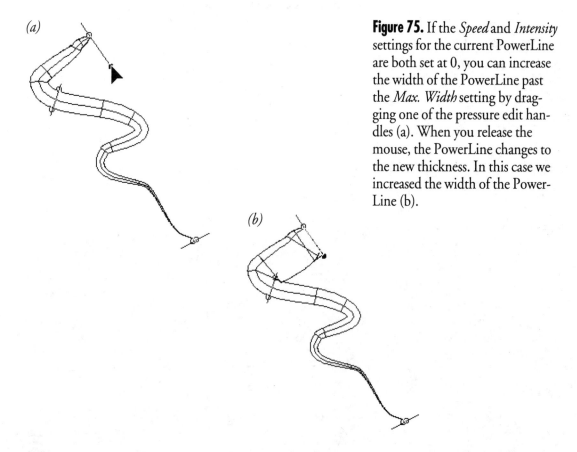

(a)

(b)

Figure 75. If the *Speed* and *Intensity* settings for the current PowerLine are both set at 0, you can increase the width of the PowerLine past the *Max. Width* setting by dragging one of the pressure edit handles (a). When you release the mouse, the PowerLine changes to the new thickness. In this case we increased the width of the Power-Line (b).

Figure 76. If the *Speed* or *Intensity* settings are greater than 0 and you want to pressure edit the Power-Line, you can't increase the width of the PowerLine past the *Max. Width* that is currently in the *PowerLine* Roll-up. If this is the case, indicators appear on the pressure edit handles showing how far you can drag them (⊢━◉━⊣).

Figure 77. You can add pressure handles along the core line of the PowerLine by clicking wherever you want the pressure handles (this adds a ● to the line) and then choosing the + symbol from the *Node Edit* Roll-up.

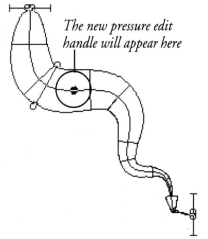

The new pressure edit handle will appear here

Figure 78. If you deselect the *Pressure Edit* option in the *Node Edit* Roll-up, you can add nodes to the core line of the PowerLine.

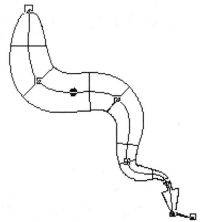

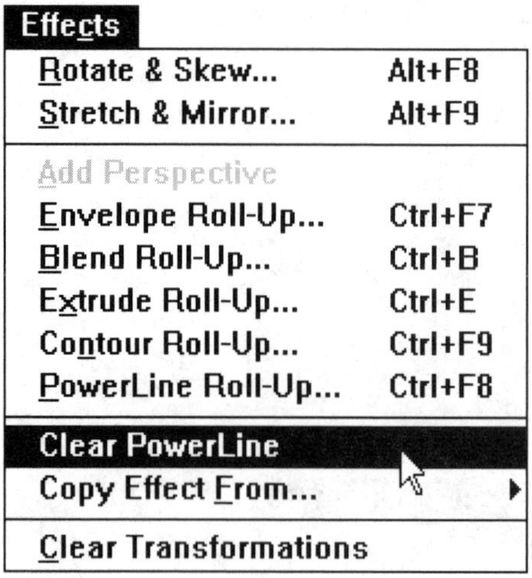

Clear (Effect)

Effects	
Rotate & Skew...	Alt+F8
Stretch & Mirror...	Alt+F9
Add Perspective	
Envelope Roll-Up...	Ctrl+F7
Blend Roll-Up...	Ctrl+B
Extrude Roll-Up...	Ctrl+E
Contour Roll-Up...	Ctrl+F9
PowerLine Roll-Up...	Ctrl+F8
Clear PowerLine	
Copy Effect From...	▶
Clear Transformations	

Figure 79. Using *Clear (Effect)* from the **Effects** menu removes the last effect you applied to the selected object.

This command changes depending on which effect you applied to the object.

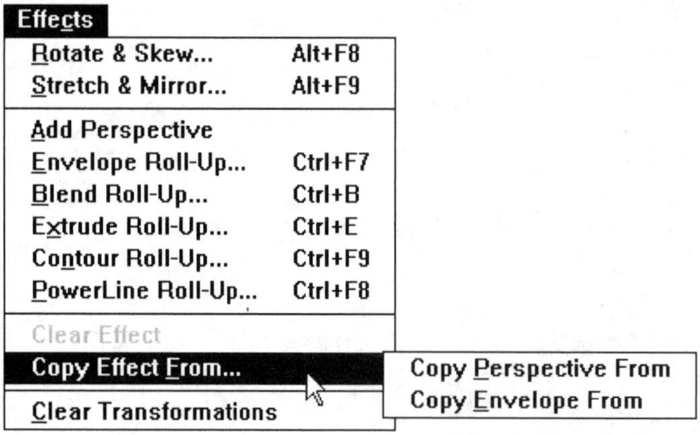

Copy Effect From

Effects	
Rotate & Skew...	Alt+F8
Stretch & Mirror...	Alt+F9
Add Perspective	
Envelope Roll-Up...	Ctrl+F7
Blend Roll-Up...	Ctrl+B
Extrude Roll-Up...	Ctrl+E
Contour Roll-Up...	Ctrl+F9
PowerLine Roll-Up...	Ctrl+F8
Clear Effect	
Copy Effect From...	
Clear Transformations	

Copy **P**erspective From
Copy **E**nvelope From

Figure 80. The *Copy Effect From* command lets you copy either a *Perspective* effect or an *Envelope* effect from one object to another.

See Figure 81 for an example of copying effects from one object to another.

Figure 81. The first thing to do is use the Pick Tool to select the object that you want to copy the effect to.

Figure 82. Then, choose either *Copy Perspective From* or *Copy Envelope From*, depending on the effect you are about to copy.

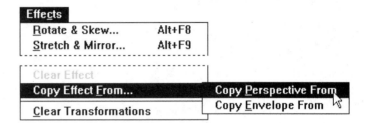

Figure 83. With the From? arrow that appears, click on the object that has the effect you want to copy (a).

The object you selected in Figure 81 now has the effect applied to it (b).

If you click on an inappropriate object with the From? arrow, or you miss the object, you are warned and then given the option of trying again.

If you choose *Copy Perspective From*, you must click on an object that you have applied a perspective to. Likewise, if you select *Copy Envelope From*, you must click on an object with an envelope.

(a)

(b)

CLEAR TRANSFORMATIONS

Use the *Clear Transformations* command in the **Effects** menu to return selected objects to their original state. Transformations are stretching, mirroring, resizing, rotating, moving the objects center of rotation, skewing, enveloping, and changing perspective.

If the objects are part of a group, choosing the *Clear Transformations* command clears only the transformations you applied to the group, not to any transformation you made to the individual objects before grouping them.

THE TEXT MENU COMMANDS

The commands in the **Text** menu help you edit text in your CorelDRAW document.

Figure 1. This figure displays the **Text** menu with its associated commands.

Te<u>x</u>t	
Text <u>R</u>oll-Up...	Ctrl+F2
<u>C</u>haracter...	
<u>F</u>rame...	
<u>P</u>aragraph...	
Fit <u>T</u>ext To Path...	Ctrl+F
Align To Bas<u>e</u>line	Alt+F10
<u>S</u>traighten Text	
Sp<u>e</u>ll Checker...	
Thesa<u>u</u>rus...	
F<u>i</u>nd...	
Rep<u>l</u>ace...	
Edit Te<u>x</u>t...	Ctrl+T

TEXT ROLL-UP

Figure 2. Clicking on the *Text Roll-up* command opens the *Text* Roll-up. The *Text* dialog boxes discussed in Chapter 2 also have these options.

The top five buttons in the *Text* Roll-up govern the justification of text. The options available are *left, centered, right, full* (available for Paragraph Text only), and *none*.

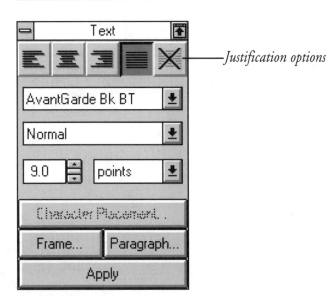

Justification options

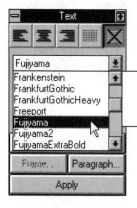

Figure 3. The first drop-down list below the justification buttons lets you select a different font. As you drag the mouse down the list of fonts, a preview box appears to give you an indication of what the typeface looks like.

Use the scroll bar to the right of the list to access the fonts not currently in view.

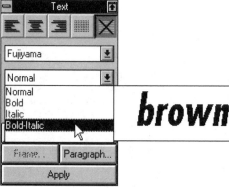

Figure 4. The next drop-down list contains the style options. Not all styles (*Normal, Bold, Italic, Bold-Italic*) are available for all typefaces. Again, a preview box lets you see what the style change looks like before you apply it.

Size is the next option in the *Text* Roll-up. You can also change the unit of size, if you select a different option from the appropriate drop-down list.

Figure 5. You can select the *Character Placement* button only if you have one or more text nodes selected with the Shape Tool. Clicking on this button opens the *Character Placement* dialog box (Figure 6).

You have to select one or more text nodes with the Shape Tool before you can open the Character Placement dialog box.

Figure 6. The options available in the *Character Placement* dialog box determine the *Horizontal* and *Vertical* placement of text characters, and their *Angle*. You can also choose to create *Superscript* and *Subscript* characters through this dialog box.

See the *Character* command later in this chapter for more information on these options.

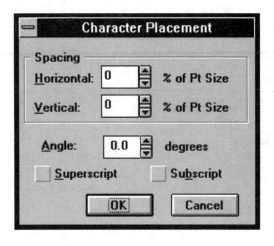

Figure 7. You can click on the *Frame* button in the *Text* Roll-up only if you have selected Paragraph Text with the Pick Tool. (You do not get it for Artistic Text.) The *Frame* button opens the *Frame Attributes* dialog box.

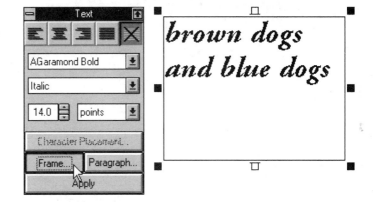

Figure 8. The *Frame Attributes* dialog box lets you apply columns to Paragraph Text. See the *Frame* command later in this chapter for more information on this dialog box.

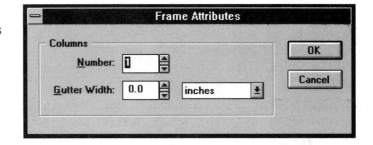

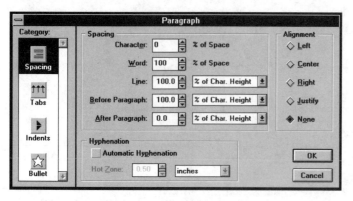

Figure 9. You can click on the *Paragraph* button in the *Text* Roll-up with either Paragraph or Artistic Text selected. Clicking on this button opens the *Paragraph* dialog box.

See the *Paragraph* command later in this chapter for more information on the options in this dialog box.

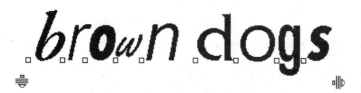

Figure 10. You can also change text characters (Paragraph or Artistic) individually through the *Text* Roll-up. Select one or more text characters with the Shape Tool and choose a new font, style or size to achieve this effect.

Click on the *Apply* button at the bottom of the *Text* Roll-up window to apply any changes you made in the Roll-up to selected text.

CHARACTER

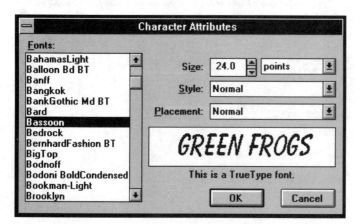

Figure 11. Choosing the *Character* command from the **Text** menu, when your text is selected with the Pick Tool, brings up this *Character Attributes* dialog box. Here you can change the *Font, Size, Style,* and *Placement* of the selected text.

The *Placement* option includes *Normal, Superscript*, and *Subscript*.

Figure 12. You can also choose the *Character* command from the **Text** menu, if your text is selected with the Shape Tool. You must select one or more of the text block's nodes with the Shape Tool to use this command. In this example, we have selected the node of the letter "f" with the Shape Tool.

Figure 13. The *Character Attributes* dialog box is now different from the one in Figure 11. You can still change the *Font, Size, Style,* and *Placement* of text, but there are now three new options in this dialog box. These are *Horizontal Shift, Vertical Shift,* and *Character Angle.*

You change the *Font, Size,* and *Style* in the same way as described earlier for the *Text* Roll-up window.

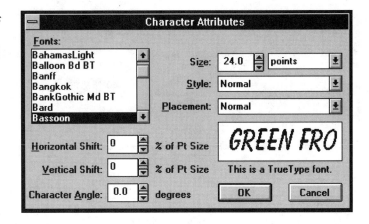

Figure 14. The *Horizontal Shift* option moves the selected text characters, along the baseline, by whatever percentage you insert. In this case we moved the letter "f" -15%.

Figure 15. The *Vertical Shift* option moves the selected text characters vertically by whatever percentage you insert. We moved the letter "f," in this example, vertically 25%.

The letter f was shifted horizontally -15%

Figure 16. The *Character Angle* option shifts the angle of the selected text characters by the degrees you insert. We have shifted the letter "f", in this example, 10 degrees.

FRAME

Figure 17. Choosing *Frame* from the **Text** menu opens the *Frame Attributes* dialog box. Here you can insert the number of required columns for your selected Paragraph Text. The *Gutter Width* determines the amount of space between each column.

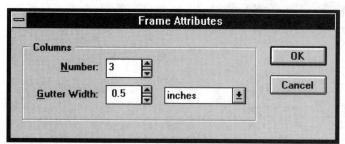

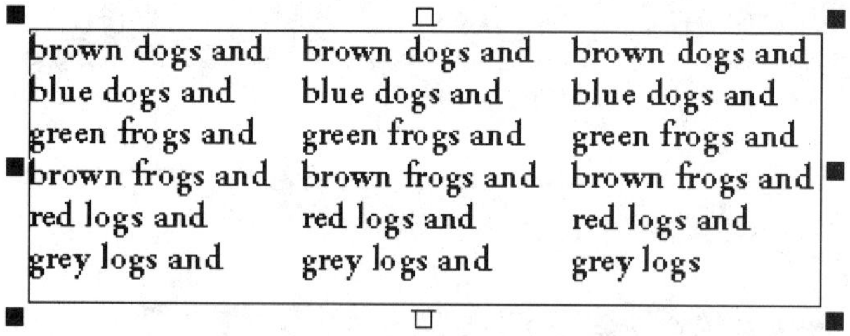

Figure 18. In this example we applied three columns to our paragraph of text with a gutter width of half an inch.

PARAGRAPH

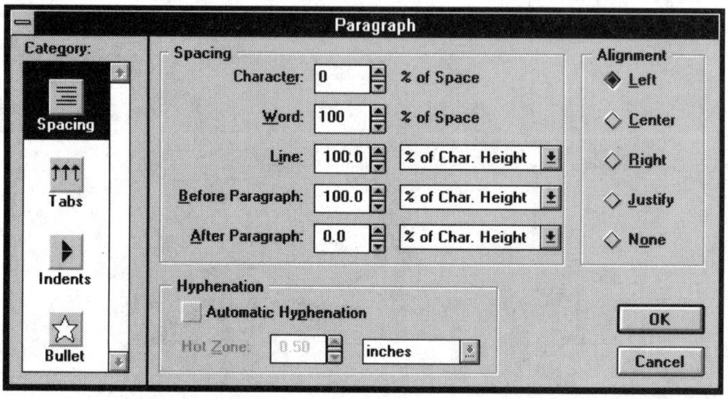

Figure 19. The *Paragraph* command in the **Text** menu brings up the *Paragraph* dialog box. You cannot access all the options in this dialog box for Artistic Text.

SPACING

The first *Category* option available in the *Paragraph* dialog box is the *Spacing* (▦) option.

Figure 20. The *Character* option in the *Spacing* section of the *Paragraph* dialog box lets you select the amount of space between characters in a text block.

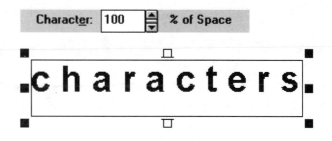

Figure 21. The *Word* option in the *Spacing* section of the *Paragraph* dialog box determines the amount of space between words in a text block.

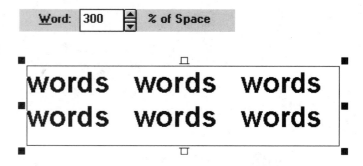

Figure 22. The *Line* option in the *Spacing* section of the *Paragraph* dialog box sets the amount of space between lines of text in a text block.

You can only access the *Before Paragraph* and *After Paragraph* options when you are working with Paragraph Text. These options let you insert space before and after paragraphs of text.

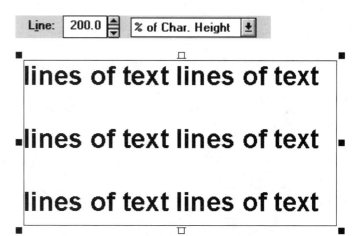

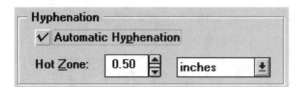

Figure 23. Clicking on the *Automatic Hyphenation* option in the *Paragraph* dialog box turns on hyphenation for the selected Paragraph Text. The *Hot Zone* determines where the program hyphenates a word.

This zone extends to the right of the text frame by whatever amount you insert. CorelDRAW hyphenates a word if a valid hyphenation point falls inside the *Hot Zone*. If not, it pushes the word onto the next line. You can only use hyphenation with Paragraph Text.

The *Alignment* options in the *Paragraph* dialog box are to change the alignment of selected text.

TABS

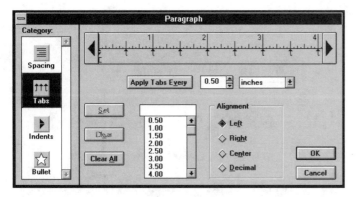

Figure 24. Click on the *Tabs Category* (↑↑↑) option to access the options shown here. Tab options let you apply tab stops to your Paragraph Text (not available for Artistic Text).

Those of you who are familiar with word processing and page layout programs will be familiar with tabs.

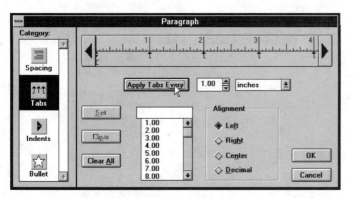

Figure 25. The *Apply Tabs Every* button adds evenly spaced tabs along the ruler in the position indicated in the adjacent box. Change this amount, then click on the button to apply the tab stops.

In this example we cleared all the tabs and applied tabs at every inch.

In some cases you may need to click on the *Clear All* button before you apply tabs stops along the ruler in this dialog box.

Figure 26. The *Set* button adds a tab stop to the ruler in the position indicated in the adjacent box. The position is then added to the list of tab positions below. In this case we cleared all the tab stops (by clicking on the *Clear All* button) and then added at tab at 0.39 of an inch.

Immediately after you add a tab to the ruler it is highlighted. A highlighted tab is clear (⇧), rather than black (⬆).

Figure 27. You can highlight tabs in two ways. The first way is to select the tab position number from the list by clicking on it with the mouse (a).

The second way is to click on the tab marker in the ruler in this dialog box (b).

Clicking on the *Clear* button removes the currently highlighted tab.

The *Clear All* button removes all the current tab stops from the ruler.

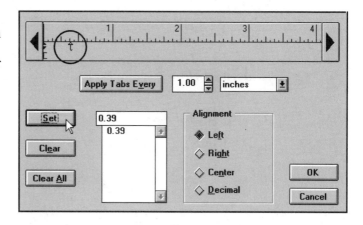

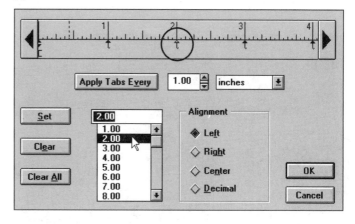

(a)

(b)

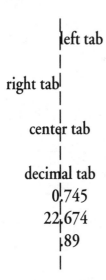

left tab

right tab

center tab

decimal tab
0.745
22.674
.89

Figure 28. The *Alignment* options affect how the text sits in relation to the tab. The dashed line in this example shows the tab stop.

To apply an *Alignment* option to a tab, choose the required *Alignment* option before applying the tab. You can also change the *Alignment* of a tab by highlighting the tab and clicking on the new alignment option.

Figure 29. You can also add tabs by clicking directly on the ruler with the mouse.

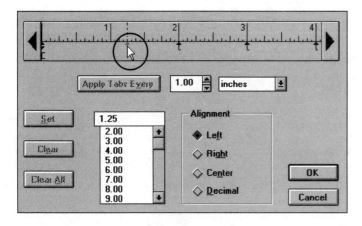

Figure 30. You can also move tab stops by holding the mouse down on them in the ruler and dragging to a new spot. The text box adjacent to the *Set* button shows where the current tab stop is, so as you move the tab stop you can see where it is on the ruler numerically.

Figure 31. The right (▶) and left (◀)facing arrows at opposing ends of the ruler let you scroll to parts of the ruler not currently on screen.

INDENTS

Figure 32. Click on the *Indents Category* (▣)button to access these options. These options let you apply certain indents to Paragraph Text.

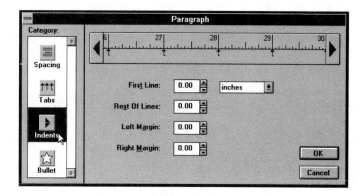

Figure 33. The *First Line* indent option indents the first line of the text whatever number you insert. The ◣ marker on the ruler in this dialog box moves as you change the *First Line* indent setting.

The *Rest of Lines* option will indent all the remaining lines (other than the first line). The ◤ marker on the ruler in this dialog box moves as you change the *Rest of Lines* indent setting.

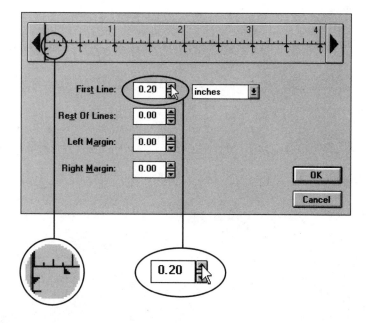

(a)

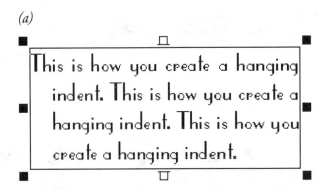

This is how you create a hanging indent. This is how you create a hanging indent. This is how you create a hanging indent.

Figure 34. You can create a hanging indent (a) by making the *Rest of Lines* indent option larger than the *First Line* option (b). Note the position of the *First Line* and *Rest of Lines* indent markers on the ruler when you have created a hanging indent.

(b)

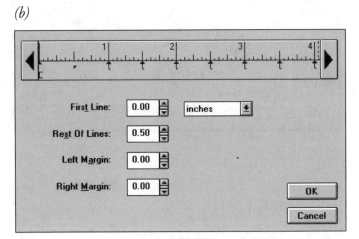

Figure 35. The *Left Margin* option lets you indent the entire text block from the left side of the text frame. All the markers on the ruler in this dialog box move as you change the *Left Margin* setting.

The *Right Margin* option is to indent the entire text block from the right side of the text frame.

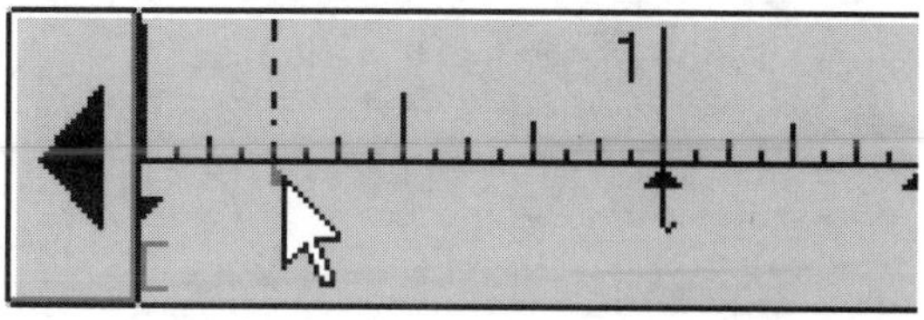

Figure 36. You can also alter the indent settings directly through the ruler in this dialog box. By dragging the ⬉ marker in the ruler, you change the *First Line* indent setting. Release the mouse on the ruler in the position you want to indent the first line of your text.

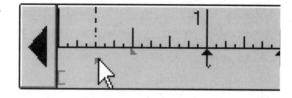

Figure 37. By dragging the ⬎ marker, you change the *Rest of Lines* indent setting. As you drag this marker, the *First Line* indent marker moves as well so that the First Line indent remains.

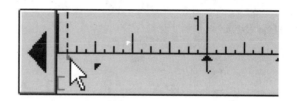

Figure 38. You can create a hanging indent by dragging the *Rest of Lines* marker further to the right than the *First Line* marker.

If you drag the ⌐ marker, you change the *Left Margin* setting.

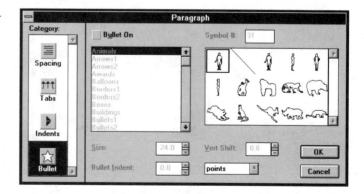

BULLETS

Figure 39. Click on the *Bullet Category* (☆) option in the *Paragraph* dialog box to access these options. The options here let you add bullets to your Paragraph Text.

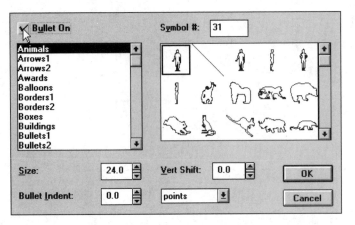

Figure 40. You must check the *Bullet On* option if you want to apply bullets to your text. You can now display a bullet at the beginning of each paragraph in your text.

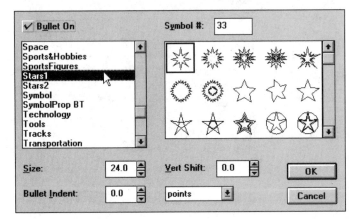

Figure 41. Below the *Bullet On* option is a list of symbol categories. These are the same symbol categories that appear in the *Symbols* Roll-up. From this list you can select the symbol category that contains the symbol you want to use as a paragraph bullet.

Use the scroll bar at the right of this list to see the categories not currently in view.

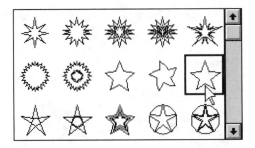

Figure 42. Once you have chosen the symbol category, click on the symbol from the preview window to the right of the list. You may need to use the scroll bar to the right of this preview window to see the symbols that aren't on screen.

The *Size* option lets you set the size of the bullet. However, CorelDRAW automatically resizes the symbol in proportion to its accompanying text.

The *Vert Shift* option shifts the bullet up or down in relation to the text.

The *Bullet Indent* option indents the bullet from the left side of the text frame. This, of course, also affects the indent of the text.

Figure 43. The bullet we chose in the previous figure looks like this when you apply it to paragraphs of text.

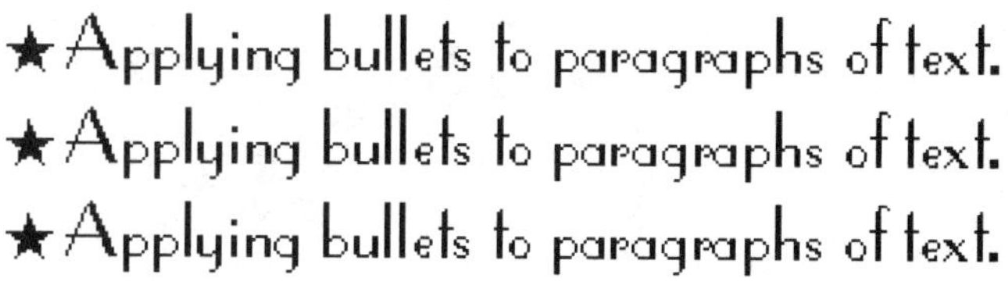

★Applying bullets to paragraphs of text.

★Applying bullets to paragraphs of text.

★Applying bullets to paragraphs of text.

Click on *OK* in the *Paragraph* dialog box to close it and apply any changes to your text.

FIT TEXT TO PATH

Figure 44. You use the *Fit Text To Path* command to open the *Fit Text To Path* Roll-up. You can use only Artistic Text to fit to a path.

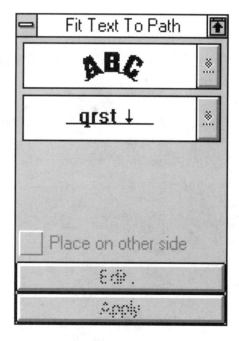

Before you can use most of the options in this Roll-up, you must select your text plus a curved object with the Pick Tool. A curved object includes anything created with the Pencil Tool, or any object you have applied the *Convert To Curves* command to. (See Chapter 9 for more information on this command.)

As with all Roll-ups, you must click the *Apply* button to apply the options you have selected in the Roll-up.

TEXT ORIENTATION

Figure 45. Selecting the first option in the top drop-down list rotates the letters to follow the curve of the path.

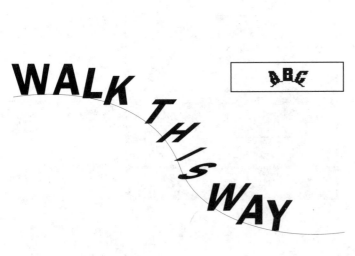

Figure 46. Selecting the second option vertically skews the text in relation to the tangential slope of the path. The more vertical the path, the more it skews the letters.

Figure 47. Selecting the third option skews the text horizontally according to the path. The more vertical the path, the more it flattens the text.

Figure 48. Selecting the last option causes the text to remain upright as it follows the path.

TEXT DISTANCE FROM PATH

Figure 49. Selecting the first option in the second drop-down list ensures that you place the baseline of the text directly on the path.

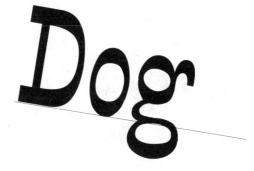

Figure 50. Selecting the second option aligns the ascender directly with the path.

Figure 51. Selecting the third option aligns the descender directly with the path.

Figure 52. Selecting the fourth option centers the text on the path.

Figure 53. Selecting the fifth option lets you put the text above or below the path. Use the mouse to move the text after choosing this option.

Hold the Ctrl key down to select the text independently from the Control Curve. An arrowhead guide tells you how far you are moving the text above or below the path. Release the mouse button to reformat the text in the new position.

TEXT ALIGNMENT ON A PATH

Figure 54. The third option in the *Fit Text To Path* Roll-up changes according to the type of path you have selected.

If the path is an object made up of curves, you use the drop-down list with the three options available as shown in (a).

If the object is a true ellipse or rectangle, an icon with four available selections replaces the drop-down list (b).

(a)

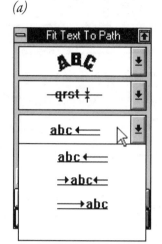

(b)

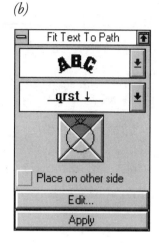

CURVED PATH

Figure 55. Selecting the first option in the drop-down list of Figure 54(a) (the default setting) places the first character of the text at the first node of the path.

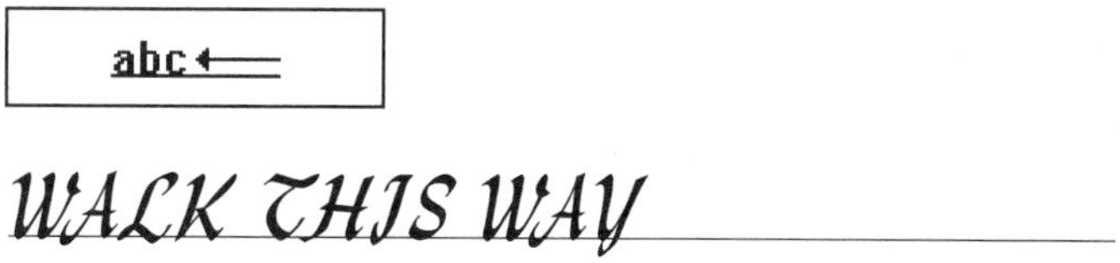

WALK THIS WAY

Figure 56. Selecting the second option centers the text between the start and end nodes of the path.

WALK THIS WAY

Figure 57. Selecting the third option aligns the last text character with the end node of the path.

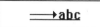

WALK THIS WAY

ELLIPSE OR RECTANGLE

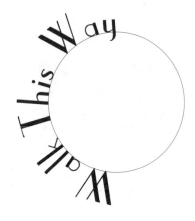

Figure 58. A square icon with four available selections replaces the third drop-down list if you want to fit your text to an ellipse or rectangle. From here you can select from one of four options to set which side of the object you center the text on.

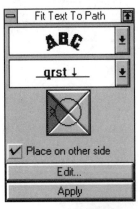

Figure 59. Choose the *Place on other side* option to place the text on the other side of the path. The text is mirrored horizontally and vertically.

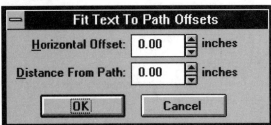

Figure 60. Clicking on the *Edit* button, in the *Fit Text To Path* Roll-up, opens the *Fit Text To Path Offsets* dialog box. Selecting the *Horizontal Offset* option shifts the text horizontally along the path.

If you have changed the alignment of the text in the alignment drop-down list, the horizontal offset is added to this. Altering the *Distance From Path* option moves the text either above or below the path. Entering a negative value moves the text below the path.

Remember, you use the *Apply* button at the bottom of the *Fit Text To Path* Roll-up to apply any changes you made to the text and path.

To edit the text on the path, hold down the Ctrl key and select it with the Pick Tool. This selects only the text. You can now select any text editing commands and apply them to the text.

For interactive kerning and character editing, select the text with the Shape Tool. You can now kern the text or select character nodes. You can also edit the path with the Shape Tool, which automatically reformats the text to the new path.

You can use the *Separate* command from the **Arrange** menu to separate the text and the path.

ALIGN TO BASELINE

Figure 61. Choosing the *Align To Baseline* command (a) shifts any text that you have moved vertically back to the original baseline as in (b). Using this command does not alter the horizontal position of text.

When you rotate text, you rotate the baseline with it. Therefore, you can return any rotated text characters that you have shifted vertically off the baseline to the rotated baseline. To do so, select the *Align To Baseline* command.

(a)

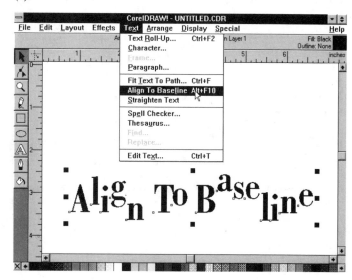

(b)

STRAIGHTEN TEXT

You use this command to straighten text that you have shifted off the baseline horizontally or vertically, altered the character angle of, or changed any individual characters in the *Character Attributes* dialog box. Using this command does not straighten text in which you have altered its inter-word, inter-character, or inter-line spacing, or text that you have rotated, skewed, or resized with the Pick Tool.

To straighten text after you have fitted it to a path, you must first separate the text and the path with the *Separate* command from the **Arrange** menu.

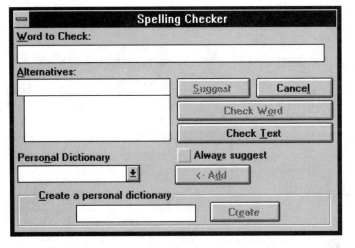

SPELL CHECKER

Figure 62. Using the *Spell Checker* command from the **Text** menu opens the *Spelling Checker* dialog box.

If you want to check the spelling for an entire text block (Artistic or Paragraph Text), select the text with the Pick Tool before opening this dialog box. If you want to check just a few words, highlight the words with the Text Tool before using the *Spelling Checker*.

Click on the *Check Text* button to begin spell checking.

Figure 63. When the spell checker comes across a word it does not recognize, it inserts this word into the *Word not found* field.

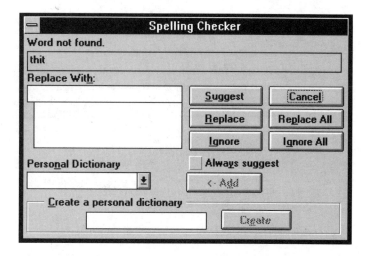

Figure 64. Clicking on the *Suggest* button displays similar words in the *Replace With* list. Selecting a word from this list puts it in the *Replace With* text box.

If there are no suggestions for the misspelled word, you can insert your own replacement in the *Replace With* box. Click on the *Replace* button to replace the word in the selected text with the word in the *Replace With* frame. Clicking on the *Replace All* button replaces all occurrences of the misspelled word with the one in the *Replace With* frame.

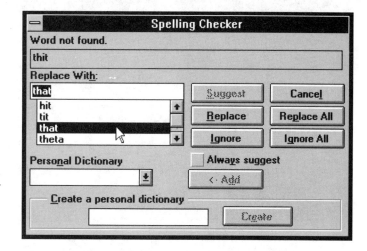

Use the *Ignore* button if the spell checker has highlighted a word that you have spelled correctly, but does not appear in the dictionary, such as a name. Clicking on the *Ignore All* button skips all occurrences of the word in the text.

Checking the *Always suggest* button ensures the spell checker always lists alternative words for each misspelled word.

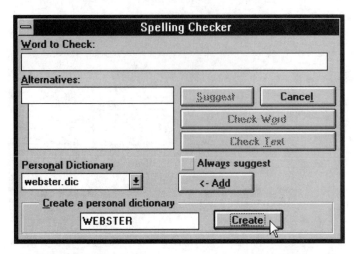

Figure 65. To create a personal dictionary, type the name of the dictionary in the *Create a personal dictionary* box and click on the *Create* button.

CorelDRAW then adds this name to the *Personal Dictionary* list with any others you may have created.

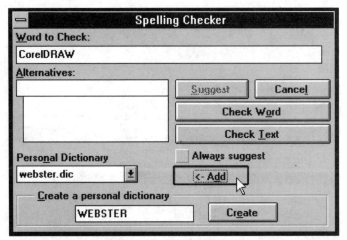

Figure 66. Click on the *Add* button, after selecting the *Personal Dictionary* from the drop-down list, to add words in the *Word to Check* field to the personal dictionary. A screen prompt then appears telling you the word has been added to the dictionary.

The spell checker will use your personal dictionary when spell checking your text.

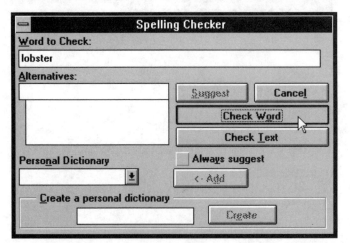

Figure 67. You can also type words directly into the *Word to Check* field for spell checking. Click on the *Check Word* button to spell check the word.

CorelDRAW tells you if the word is correct or if it has not found the word in the dictionary. Click on the *Suggest* button to display a list of alternatives.

THESAURUS

Figure 68. Choosing the *Thesaurus* command from the **Text** menu opens the *Thesaurus* dialog box. If you have selected a word with the Text Tool before selecting the *Thesaurus*, this dialog box displays the highlighted word in the *Synonym for* field, and the meaning of the word in the *Definition* field.

It also displays further definitions of the selected word (if any) and a list of alternative words in the *Synonyms* list in the two lists below.

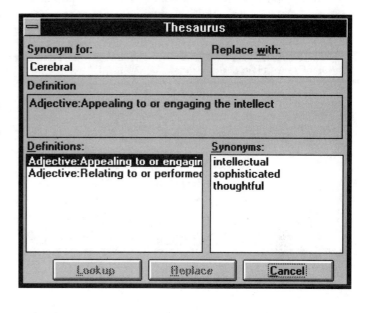

Figure 69. If there is more than one definition for the word, selecting a different one from the *Definitions* list displays a new list of synonyms.

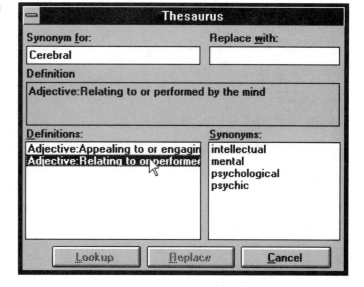

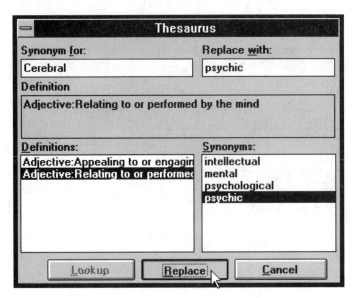

Figure 70. Selecting a new word from the *Synonyms* list adds this word to the *Replace with* text box. Clicking on the *Replace* button replaces the word in the text with this word and closes the *Thesaurus* dialog box.

If you choose the *Thesaurus* command with no text selected, nothing will appear in the *Synonyms for* field in the *Thesaurus* dialog box. Type your own word into this field, and click on the *Look up* button to display a list of synonyms for the word.

In this case, you cannot open the *Replace with* text box and the *Replace* button, because the word you typed directly into this dialog box does not exist in the text.

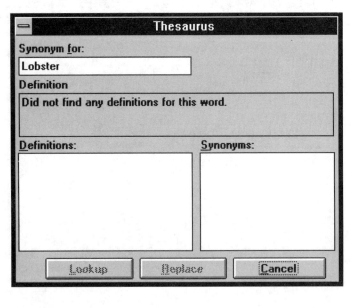

Figure 71. If the word in the *Synonyms for* field is not in the dictionary, a message appears in the *Definition* field telling you that it did not find any definitions for this word.

FIND

Figure 72. You use the *Find* command from the **Text** menu to find a word, sentence or certain characters in your Paragraph Text. The first thing to do is to insert the text cursor in the block from where you want to begin the search. To do this, select the Paragraph Text Tool (▤) and click the mouse once in the text block from where you want to begin the search. In this case we inserted the text cursor at the beginning of the text block.

Figure 73. Following on from the previous figure, choose the *Find* command to bring up the *Find* dialog box. (You cannot choose the *Find* command if you have the text block selected with the Pick Tool.)

You can hold the mouse button down when the cursor is on the title bar of this dialog box and drag it above or below the text you are searching. This lets you see Corel-DRAW select the word once it has found it.

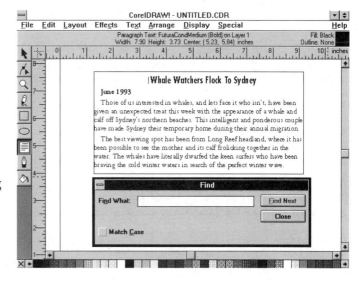

Figure 74. Type the word, sentence, or character in the *Find What* text box and click on the *Find Next* button. (You can type up to 100 characters in the *Find What* box.)

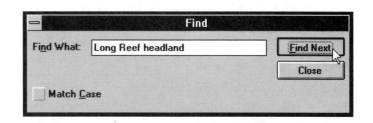

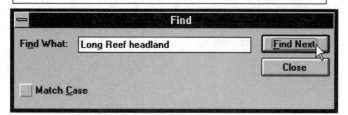

Whale Watchers Flock To Sydney

June 1993

Those of us interested in whales, and lets face it who isn't, have been given an unexpected treat this week with the appearance of a whale and calf off Sydney's northern beaches. This intelligent and ponderous couple have made Sydney their temporary home during their annual migration.

The best viewing spot has been from Long Reef headland, where it has been possible to see the mother and its calf frolicking together in the water. The whales have literally dwarfed the keen surfers who have been braving the cold winter waters in search of the perfect winter wave.

Find

Find What: | Long Reef headland | **Find Next**
Close

☐ Match Case

Figure 75. If the specified word (or phrase) is in the selected text, the *Find* command selects the first occurrence after the cursor. You can now click on the *Close* button to finish the process (with the relevant text still selected); or click on the *Find Next* button again to find the next occurrence of the word.

You can actually edit the text with the *Find* dialog box still on screen. You can make any necessary changes to the found text and still use the dialog box.

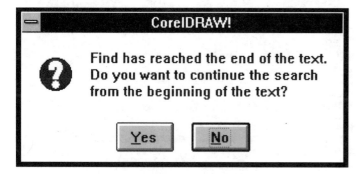

CorelDRAW!

❓ **Find has reached the end of the text. Do you want to continue the search from the beginning of the text?**

Yes   **No**

Figure 76. When the search has reached the end of the text block, CorelDRAW displays this screen prompt. You can either continue the search from the beginning of the document (*Yes*) or finish the search (*No*).

The *Match Case* option in the *Find* dialog box lets you find words that match the case (upper or lower) of whatever you insert in the *Find What* text box.

REPLACE

Selecting the *Replace* command opens the *Replace* dialog box. As with the *Find* command, you can only use *Replace* if you have the insertion point in the text you want to search.

Figure 77. As with the *Find* dialog box, you insert in the *Replace* dialog box the word you are looking for in the *Find What* text box. However, the options in this dialog box let you not only find this word, but replace it as well.

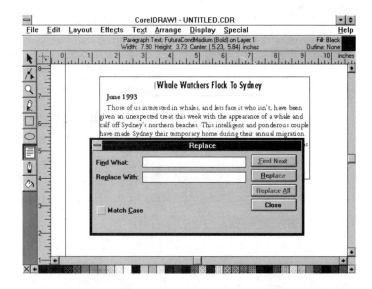

Figure 78. You can also enter in the *Replace With* text box the replacement word you've chosen.

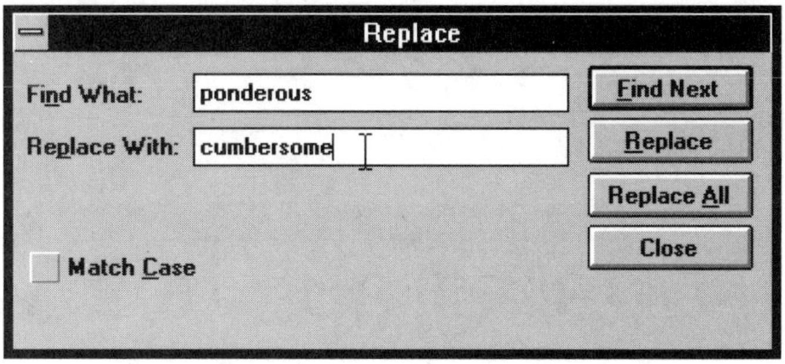

As with the *Find* dialog box, you can drag the title bar above or below the text you are searching. This lets you see CorelDRAW select and replace the word once it has found it.

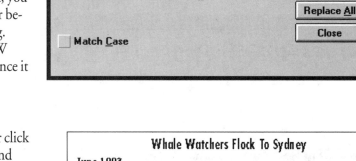

Figure 79. You can now either click on the *Find Next* button to find and select the first occurrence of the word after the insertion point; or you can click on the *Replace* button to find, select, and replace the first occurrence of the word after the insertion point.

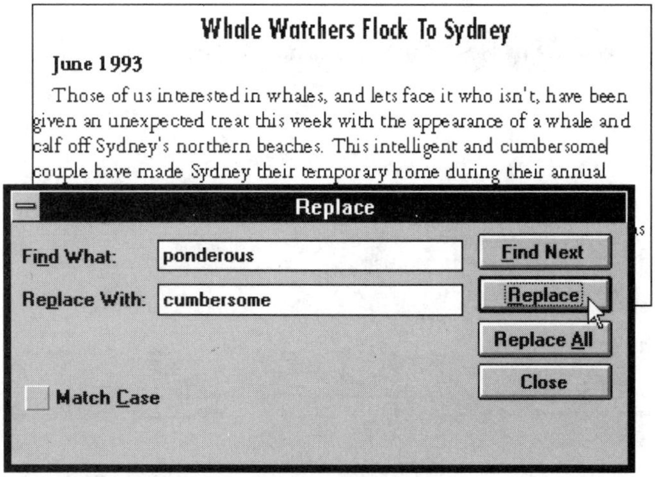

Use the *Find Next* button if you want to first find the word and then decide whether you want to replace it.

You may, however, like to keep some occurrences of the word in the text; in that case you would keep using the *Find Next* button until you find the occurrence of the word you want to change. Then click on the *Replace* button to change the text.

If you want to change all occurrences of the word in the text, click on the *Replace All* button.

The *Match Case* option in the *Replace* dialog box lets you find and replace words that match the case (upper or lower) of the word or sentence you insert in the *Find What* text box.

EDIT TEXT

Figure 80. The *Edit Text* command opens either the *Artistic Text* or the *Paragraph Text* dialog box. The dialog box that appears depends on what sort of text you have selected. If you have Artistic Text selected (a) when you choose the *Edit Text* command, you will activate the *Artistic Text* dialog box. Selecting Paragraph Text (b) activates the *Paragraph Text* dialog box.

(a)

:artistic text:

(b)

paragraph text

ARTISTIC TEXT

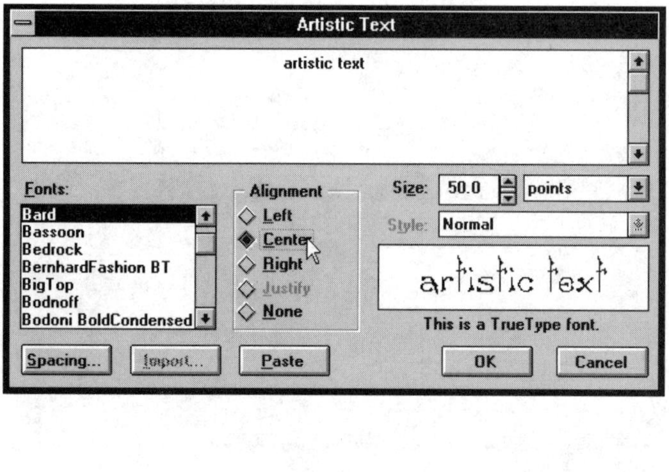

Figure 81. In the *Artistic Text* dialog box, you can change the *Font*, *Alignment*, *Size*, and *Style* of the selected Artistic Text. (You can access the *Justify Alignment* option only for Paragraph Text.)

The *Spacing* button lets you open a dialog box with the same spacing options as the *Paragraph* dialog box (explained earlier).

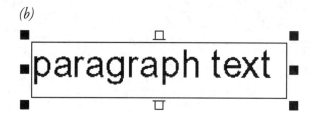

You can use the *Import* button only with Paragraph Text, and the *Paste* button pastes any text currently in the Windows Clipboard into this dialog box.

PARAGRAPH TEXT

Figure 82. The *Paragraph Text* dialog box contains all the options of the *Artistic Text* dialog box, and more.

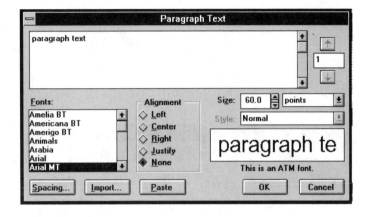

Figure 83. To the right of the preview window at the top of the *Paragraph Text* dialog box are up (▲) and down (▼) arrows and the number of the paragraph you are viewing.

If the selected text block contains more than one paragraph, you can use the up and down arrows to view each paragraph at a time. The number between the arrows always tells you which paragraph you are viewing.

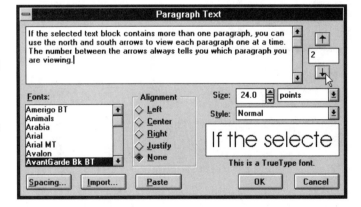

You can edit and change each paragraph separately without affecting any of the other paragraphs in the selected text. If you make any font, alignment, size, style, or spacing changes to text through the *Paragraph Text* dialog box, it will affect only the paragraph you were viewing when you made the changes.

If you want to affect the whole text block with font, alignment, size, style, and spacing options, you must do it through the *Text* Roll-up. (See the *Text* Roll-up earlier in this chapter for more information.)

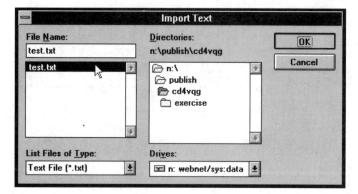

Figure 84. The *Import* button in the *Paragraph Text* dialog box opens the *Import Text* dialog box. Through here you can import an ASCII text file into the *Paragraph Text* dialog box. Using the *Directories* and *Drives* lists, you can find and select the text file and click on *OK* to import it.

You can import up to 4000 characters into each paragraph and each text block can contain an unlimited number of paragraphs. Each paragraph of text in the ASCII file is imported into a new paragraph in the CorelDRAW file.

When you import ASCII text into CorelDRAW, it is unformatted and any tabs in the original file come in as spaces.

You can also use the *Justify* option in the *Alignment* section of the *Paragraph Text* dialog box.

THE ARRANGE MENU

THE ARRANGE MENU COMMANDS

The commands in the **Arrange** menu affect the arrangement and position of objects in your current file, and determine whether the objects are independent or connected to other objects.

Figure 1. This figure displays the **Arrange** menu and its associated commands.

Arrange	
Move...	Alt+F7
Align...	Ctrl+A
Order	▶
Group	Ctrl+G
Ungroup	Ctrl+U
Combine	Ctrl+L
Break Apart	Ctrl+K
Weld	
Separate	
Convert To Curves	Ctrl+Q

MOVE

Figure 2. Use the *Move* command as an alternative to moving objects with the mouse. Select the object you want to move, and then choose *Move*. This opens the *Move* dialog box.

The *Horizontal* and *Vertical* values in the *Move* dialog box let you move an object by as little as one-thousandth of an inch. Selecting the *Leave Original* option makes a copy of the object, and moves it the specified distance.

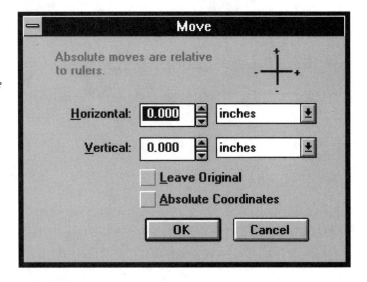

Move

Absolute moves are relative to rulers.

Horizontal: **0.000** inches

Vertical: **0.000** inches

☐ Leave Original
☐ Absolute Coordinates

OK   Cancel

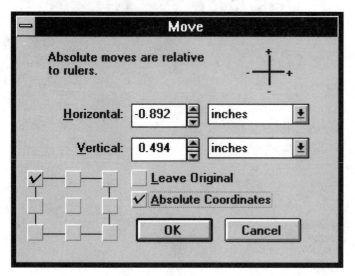

Figure 3. The *Absolute Coordinates* option lets you move a selected object to a precise location. When you check this option, a box representing the selected object appears at the bottom left of the *Move* dialog box.

After clicking on *OK* in the *Move* dialog box, CorelDRAW moves the node that was checked to the *Horizontal* and *Vertical* coordinates you specified. See Figure 4 for an example.

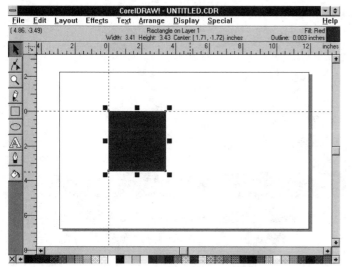

Figure 4. In this example, we set the top left node of the rectangle in the *Move* dialog box to align with the zero point of the rulers. This was done by changing both the *Horizontal* and *Vertical* options to 0.

See Chapter 10 for more information on how to change the zero points of the rulers.

ALIGN

Figure 5. The *Align* command activates the *Align* dialog box which lets you horizontally and vertically align objects. No matter what alignment options you choose, the last object you selected does not move—all other selected objects align around it. If you marquee select, the first object you created is the object around which all others align.

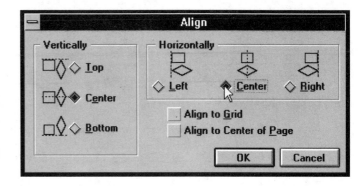

The *Align to Grid* option lets you align objects to the grid, while *Align to Center of Page* aligns objects to the center of the page. Choosing *Align to Center of Page* automatically selects the *Center* option for both horizontal and vertical. Selecting *Align to Center of Page* center aligns the objects in relation to each other and then moves them to the center of the page.

ORDER

Figure 6. The *Order* submenu from the **Arrange** menu contains these commands: *To Front, To Back, Forward One, Back One,* and *Reverse Order.* You use these commands on selected objects to change their drawing position.

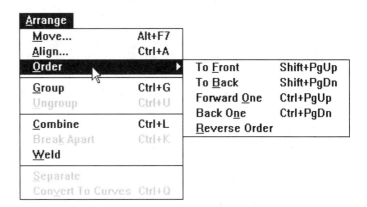

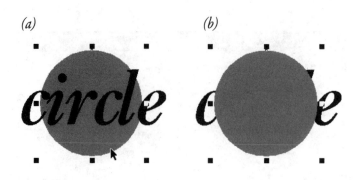

(a)   *(b)*

TO FRONT

Figure 7. By default, the last object you drew or placed on the page sits on top of all other objects.

If you want an object in front of all others on its layer, select it with the Pick Tool, then choose the *To Front* command (a).

In this example, we selected the circle and chose *To Front* (b).

TO BACK

To Back is the opposite of the *To Front* command. If you wish to send to the back any object that is on top of all other objects on its layer, select it with the Pick Tool, then choose *To Back*.

FORWARD ONE

Selecting *Forward One* moves the current object forward one place in its layer.

BACK ONE

Selecting *Back One* moves the selected object back one place in its layer.

REVERSE ORDER

Figure 8. Using the *Reverse Order* command reverses the places of two or more objects in the layer, either from front to back (a) or back to front (b).

(a)   *(b)*

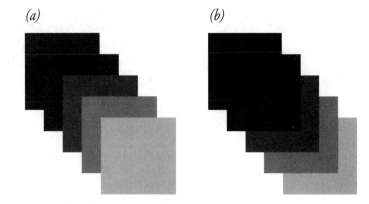

GROUP

Figure 9. The *Group* command lets you combine objects so that you can then treat them as a single object. You can color and manipulate the grouped objects as you would a single object, making this a quick way to apply attributes to more than one object at a time. In this example, the status line indicates that the five symbols are grouped.

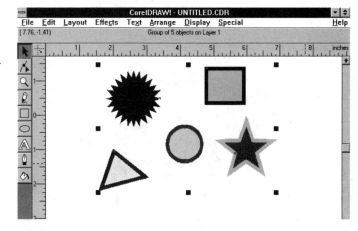

To group objects, select them all with the Pick Tool and choose the *Group* command. When you select any object from a group, CorelDRAW selects all objects automatically. You cannot use the Shape Tool on a grouped object, but you can use the Pick Tool to resize and move it.

You can apply most features to a grouped object, except for the following: *Combine, Break Apart, Edit Text, Fit Text To Path, Straighten Text, Align To Baseline,* and *Extrude.*

Note: You can group grouped objects with other objects or other groups. You can have up to 10 levels of grouping within a group.

Ungroup

Selecting *Ungroup* separates a group of objects, returning each object to its independent status, so that you can manipulate them as single objects. If you have levels of grouping, the *Ungroup* command separates what the last *Group* command combined. You must ungroup each set of objects you grouped.

Combine

The *Combine* command is a different type of grouping, which you can use for a number of effects and reasons. When you combine two or more objects, wherever they overlap will be a gap or window that you can see through. You can use this to create a mask effect, where you can see one object through parts of another. CorelDRAW automatically converts text, ellipses, and rectangles to curves when you group them with the *Combine* command. You can't edit them as you could before you combined them.

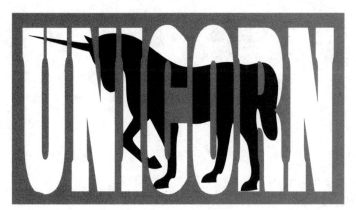

Figure 10. To create this image, we selected the text and the rectangle and combined them. This created a transparent area where the text and the rectangle overlapped. We then placed the image of the unicorn at the back. Because we placed the unicorn on the page last, we needed to use the *To Back* command.

Break Apart

You apply the *Break Apart* command to objects that you have combined previously.

WELD

The *Weld* command lets you join or "weld" objects that overlap so they become the one object. It differs from the *Combine* command in that it removes the parts of the object between the intersection points of the two objects.

Figure 11. Choose the overlapping objects with the Pick Tool before choosing the *Weld* command. Here we are working in *wireframe* mode so you can see what happens when you use this command.

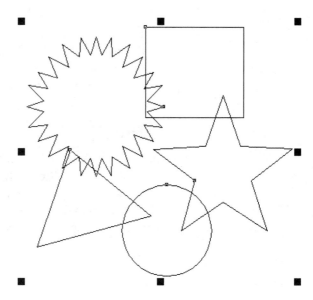

Figure 12. After you choose the *Weld* command, the objects become one, with only the outline of the objects remaining.

When you weld objects, they take on the fill and outline of the last object you selected before you welded them. If you marquee-select the objects, they take on the fill and outline of the object at the bottom.

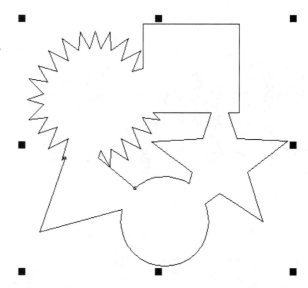

You can also weld single objects that have lines that cross. This breaks the object into several subpaths.

You can weld as many objects as you like at one time. If the objects are on different layers, you must have the *MultiLayer* option checked in the *Layers* submenu (see Figures 23 and 24 in Chapter 6). If the objects are on different layers, select them one by one (with the Shift key held down) to move them to the layer that contains the object you selected last.

If you marquee-select the objects, they will all move to the layer containing the object you created first when you weld them. For more information on *Layers*, see Chapter 6.

SEPARATE

You use the *Separate* command from the **Arrange** menu on objects that CorelDRAW dynamically links. It dynamically links, for example, the objects that make up the steps of a blend group to the start and end objects of a blend. Dynamic linking also applies between the original object and the objects that form an extrusion.

CONVERT TO CURVES

Figure 13. You apply *Convert To Curves* to text, ellipses, or rectangles so you can manipulate them with the Shape Tool, as you would any freehand line. In this example, we applied the command to a text string. You can now change the shape of any text character with the Shape Tool.

Figure 14. Whenever you break apart text that you have converted to curves, you should remember that some characters, such as an "A," are made up of two objects. You must combine both objects that make up the letter so that it displays correctly.

We converted to curves and then broke apart the letter "A." You cannot see the middle section of the letter, as it also has a black fill. Combining the two objects solves this problem.

THE DISPLAY MENU 10

THE DISPLAY MENU COMMANDS

The commands in the **Display** menu do not have a direct effect on any objects on your page. Rather they make changes to the screen and its components.

Figure 1. This figure shows the **Display** menu and its associated commands.

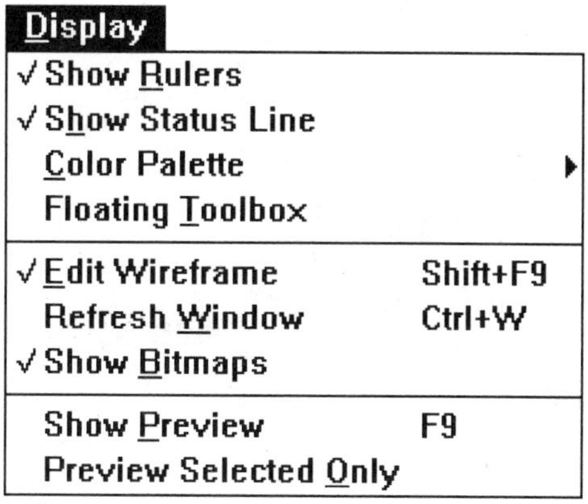

```
Display
√ Show Rulers
√ Show Status Line
  Color Palette                    ▶
  Floating Toolbox

√ Edit Wireframe           Shift+F9
  Refresh Window           Ctrl+W
√ Show Bitmaps

  Show Preview             F9
  Preview Selected Only
```

SHOW RULERS

Figure 2. The *Show Rulers* command from the **Display** menu displays or hides the horizontal and vertical rulers on the screen.

In this example we have disabled the rulers.

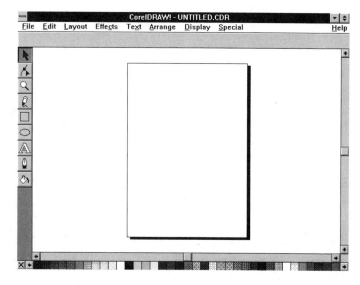

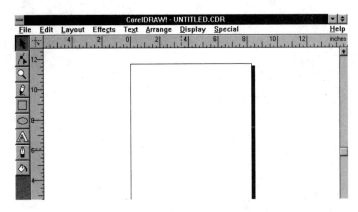

SHOW STATUS LINE

Figure 3. By default, CorelDRAW displays the status line on your screen. To deactivate it, select *Show Status Line.* To turn it on again, simply select the same command. It is good idea to keep the status line active, as it provides vital information about what you are creating. In this example, we have turned off the status line.

COLOR PALETTE

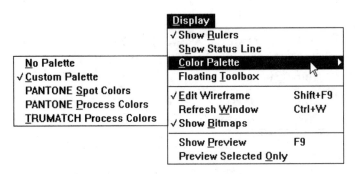

Figure 4. This command activates a submenu with five options. The *No Palette* option removes the color palette from the bottom of the screen. The *Custom Palette* option displays the current custom palette you have loaded. The next three options let you use Pantone spot or process colors or Trumatch Process colors. (See Chapter 3 for more information on color palettes.)

The color palette lets you apply a different fill or outline color to a selected object quickly and easily. Click on the color you want with the left mouse button and this applies a fill to the selected object. To change the outline color, click on the color you want with the right mouse button. Use the arrows at each end of the palette to scroll to colors you can't see.

The (✗) button at the very left of the palette lets you remove the fill and outline of a selected object. Clicking on it with the left mouse button removes the fill, and clicking on it with the right mouse button removes the outline.

FLOATING TOOLBOX

Figure 5. The *Floating Toolbox* command switches the Toolbox from its normal position at the extreme left side of the screen to where it is in this figure.

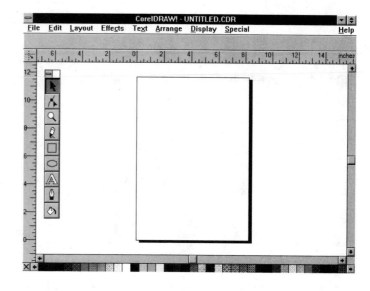

Figure 6. You can move the floating Toolbox around the screen by holding the mouse button down with the cursor on its title bar. Release the mouse button when the Toolbox is wherever you want it to be.

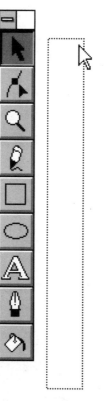

As an alternative to selecting the *Floating Toolbox* command, you can double-click on the gray area below the Toolbox.

To return the Toolbox to its original spot, choose the *Floating Toolbox* command again, or double-click on the control menu box (⊟).

(a)

(b)

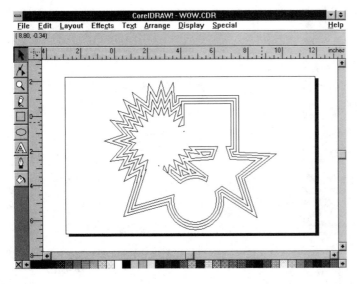

EDIT WIREFRAME

Figure 7. The *Edit Wireframe* command switches you back and forth between *full-color* mode (a), and *wireframe* mode (b). You may find it easier and faster to work in *wireframe* mode, and then move back to *full-color* mode to preview the drawing.

Use the Shift+F9 keys to move between the two views quickly.

REFRESH WINDOW

If you have interrupted a screen, you can redraw them by selecting the *Refresh Window* command. This also cleans up any remnants of previous CorelDRAW editing that may remain on the screen. Alternatively, clicking on either scroll button (▢) redraws the screen. This works in either *full-color* or *wireframe* modes.

SHOW BITMAPS

Deselecting the *Show Bitmaps* command hides any bitmaps on the *wireframe* screen only; they appear as empty rectangles. A bitmap that you have hidden on the *wireframe* screen still displays in *full-color* mode, or when previewing a drawing.

SHOW PREVIEW

The *Show Preview* command previews the drawing without any
page boundaries, Toolbox, status line, or menu bar. The F9 key
quickly moves you back and forth between the preview and
your artwork. You can also deactivate the preview screen by
pressing any key on the keyboard.

PREVIEW SELECTED ONLY

With the *Preview Selected Only* command, you have the option
of displaying in the full preview screen only objects that you
have selected.

THE SPECIAL MENU

THE SPECIAL MENU COMMANDS

The **Special** menu commands let you create patterns, arrows, and symbols, extract and merge text, as well as customize some of the features of CorelDRAW.

Figure 1. This figure displays the Special menu and its associated commands.

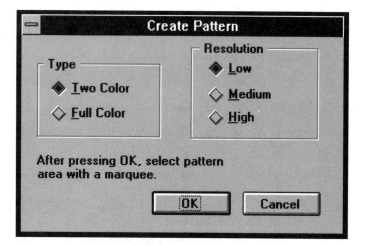

CREATE PATTERN

Figure 2. The *Create Pattern* command lets you create patterns from an image you have drawn on your page. This image or drawing then becomes part of the patterns in the *Two-Color Pattern* or *Full-Color Pattern* dialog boxes. Selecting this command brings up the *Create Pattern* dialog box.

Your first choice is whether you want the pattern to be a *Two Color* or a *Full Color* pattern. You can select the three *Resolution* options only if you are creating a *Two Color* pattern. Click on *OK* once you have made your choices.

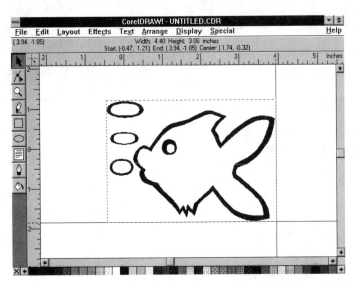

Figure 3. As suggested in the *Create Pattern* dialog box (Figure 2), you must now marquee-select the area you want to include in the pattern. The mouse pointer changes to a cross-hair that covers the whole screen. This makes it easier for you to select the area you want.

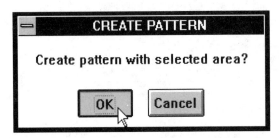

Figure 4. After selecting the area, release the mouse; this displays a screen prompt asking you to confirm that the area you selected with the cross-hair is the area you want in the pattern. Clicking on *OK* creates the pattern.

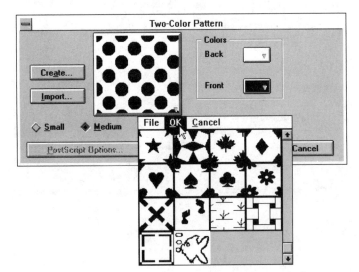

Figure 5. The *Two-Color Pattern* dialog box now shows the new graphic. If we had selected the *Full Color* option in the *Create Pattern* dialog box, the *Full-Color Pattern* dialog box would display the new pattern.

See the **Fill Tool** section in Chapter 3 for more information on applying two-color patterns and full-color patterns to objects.

CREATE ARROW

Figure 6. You can choose the *Create Arrow* command only if you have selected an object. It opens the *Create Arrow* screen prompt, which asks you whether you want to create an arrowhead with the selected object.

Clicking on *OK* inserts the selected object in the *Arrows* field of the *Outline Pen* dialog box. The larger you make the selected object, the larger it will appear as an arrowhead option.

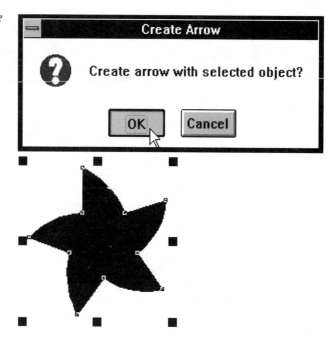

Figure 7. You can now use the arrowhead you created at the beginning or end of a line. See the **Outline Tool** section in Chapter 3 for more information on applying arrowheads to a line.

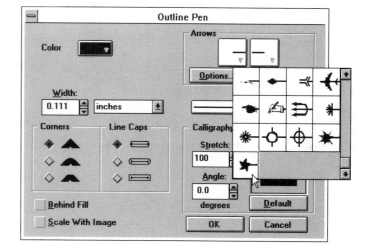

CREATE SYMBOL

You use the *Create Symbol* command to create symbols that will appear in the *Symbol* Roll-up. You can create a symbol from any closed object of any size.

Figure 8. With the Pick Tool, select the object you want to use as a symbol from, then choose *Create Symbol* from the **Special** menu. This opens the *Create Symbol* dialog box of the next figure.

In this example we combined the text with the object behind to make them all the one object.

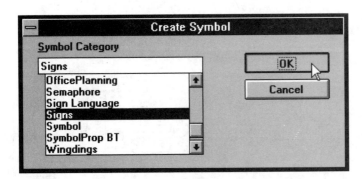

Figure 9. From the *Symbol Category* list in the *Create Symbol* dialog box, choose the library you want the new symbol to appear in and click on *OK*.

Figure 10. This object will now appear in the *Symbols* Roll-up in the category you choose in the *Create Symbol* dialog box. You can place it on the page and edit it as you can with any symbol in Corel-DRAW.

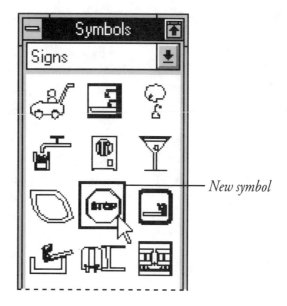

— *New symbol*

EXTRACT

You use the *Extract* command from the **Special** menu to save text created in CorelDRAW in an ASCII format for editing in a word processor. You must save the file before using the *Extract* command.

Figure 11. Select the appropriate text and choose *Extract* to open the *Extract* dialog box. Like the *Open Drawing, Save Drawing,* and *Export* dialog boxes, you must choose the destination of the file and give it a name. Click on the *OK* button once you have done this.

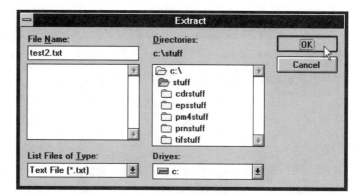

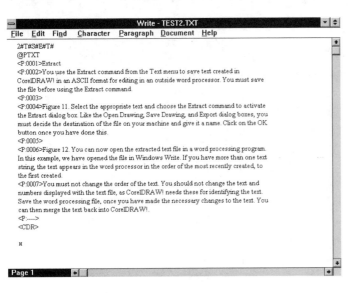

Figure 12. You can now open the extracted text file in a word processing program. In this example, we have opened the file in Windows Write. If you have more than one text string, the text appears in the word processor in the order of the most recently created, to the first created.

You must not change the order of the text. You should not change the text and numbers displayed within the less-than and greater-than symbols, because Corel-DRAW needs these to identify the text. Save the word processing file, once you have made the necessary changes to the text. You can then merge the text back into Corel-DRAW.

MERGE BACK

Use the *Merge Back* command to put extracted text back into the file from where you extracted it.

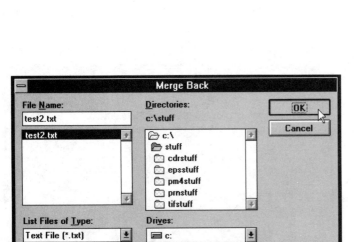

Figure 13. After opening the file that you originally extracted the text from, select *Merge Back* to open the *Merge Back* dialog box. Find the text file using the *Drives* and *Directories* lists and click on the *OK* button. This inserts the edited text file back into the Corel-DRAW file.

You merge the text back into the CorelDRAW document in the same format you extracted it, except for text that you blended, extruded, fitted to a path, or altered in the *Character Attributes* dialog box. The text returns to exactly the same position you extracted it from. If you added a lot more text in the word processor, it may overlap other text, but this is corrected by CorelDRAW itself.

If you made any changes to the text in the CorelDRAW file that you extracted the text from, the *Merge Back* procedure overwrites these changes.

PREFERENCES

Figure 14. Selecting the *Preferences* command from the **Special** menu opens the *Preferences* dialog box.

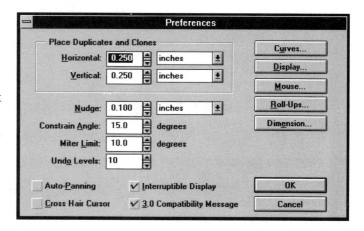

The *Place Duplicates and Clones* option in the *Preferences* dialog box sets the offset from the original of a duplicated or cloned object when you choose *Duplicate* or *Clone* from the **Edit** menu. Using a positive value for both the *Horizontal* and *Vertical* options puts the duplicate or clone up and to the right. A value of zero, for both *Horizontal* and *Vertical,* places the duplicate or clone directly behind the original object.

The *Nudge* option lets you set the amount of space you can move a selected object using the arrow keys on your keyboard.

The *Constrain Angle* sets the angular constraint when you use certain functions in conjunction with the Ctrl key. These include: rotating, skewing, drawing straight lines (*Freehand* mode), and manipulating control points when drawing curves in *Bezier* mode.

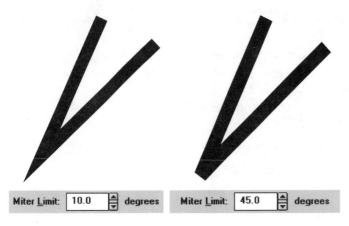

Figure 15. The *Miter Limit* sets the sharpness of a corner, or how far the vertex extends beyond the actual corner. The higher the value (between 5 and 45), the more beveled the corner. Compare the two corners in this example. Corel-DRAW bevels the joint below the specified angle.

The *Undo Levels* option lets you choose how many times you can undo commands. The more *Undo Levels* you have, the more memory it takes to run CorelDRAW.

Checking the *Auto-Panning* option in the *Preferences* dialog box scrolls the page when you resize, move, or drag an object past the edge of the screen.

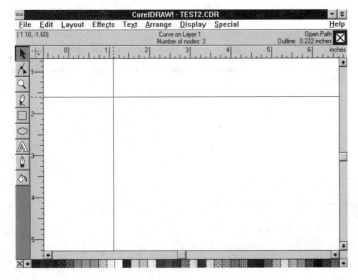

Figure 16. If you select *Cross Hair Cursor* in the *Preferences* dialog box, your mouse pointer turns into a cross-hair that covers the whole screen.

With the *Interruptible Display* option checked, you can interrupt redrawing on the screen if you click the mouse, press a key, or select a menu command or tool. This is useful for complex drawings, when you do not want to wait for CorelDRAW to redraw the entire graphic.

Figure 17. With the *3.0 Compatibility Message* option checked, Corel-DRAW displays a message when you open or import a version 3 CorelDRAW file.

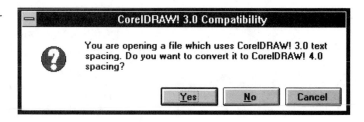

This message asks whether you want to convert the version 3 text spacing to version 4 text spacing. This occurs because CorelDRAW versions 3 and 4 calculate text spacing differently. If you decide to convert the text spacing, the difference will most likely be undetectable.

If you deselect the *3.0 Compatibility Message*, the spacing is automatically converted without displaying the message.

CURVES

Figure 18. The *Curves* button at the top right of the *Preferences* dialog box opens the *Preferences - Curves* dialog box. All the option settings in this dialog box range from 1 to 10, with 5 the default setting. You will find the default settings generally sufficient, but you may change them here if you wish.

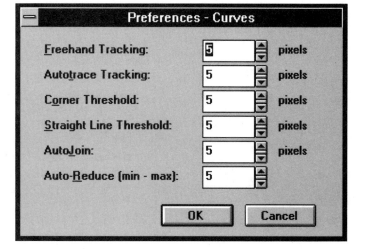

The lower the number you insert for *Freehand Tracking*, the closer the bezier curves follow the line you are drawing. This usually means more nodes and a rougher looking line. Inserting a higher number results in fewer nodes and smoother curves.

The *Autotrace Tracking* option works the same way as the *Freehand Tracking* option, but applies to the tracing of a bit-map. The lower the number, the closer the line will follow the outline of a bitmap when autotracing with the Pencil Tool. The curves appear smoother with a higher number, but they won't follow the outline of the bitmap as closely. See the *Autotrace* section in Chapter 2 for more information on autotracing.

Corner Threshold applies to both freehand drawing and auto-tracing; it determines the sharpness and smoothness of corners. If you set a low number, the corners are more likely to be cusps, and changes of direction are more acute. Setting a high number ensures that the corners are smoother, but the line might not necessarily follow the true outline of the bitmap.

The *Straight Line Threshold* option also applies to both free-hand drawing and autotracing. If you set a low number for this option, CorelDRAW is more likely to create curves when draw-ing or autotracing—except for definite straight lines. A higher number creates straighter lines, except for definite curved line sections.

The *AutoJoin* option determines how closely you must put an end node of a drawing to the beginning node before Corel-DRAW automatically joins them. The lower the number, the closer you have to put the cursor when ending a drawing. The higher the number, the less precise you need to be.

The higher the *Auto-Reduce (min - max)* value, the more nodes CorelDRAW removes when you *Auto Reduce* an object from the *Node Edit* Roll-up.

DISPLAY

Figure 19. The *Display* button at the top right of the *Preferences* dialog box opens the *Preferences - Display* dialog box. The first option is the *Preview Fountain Steps* option.

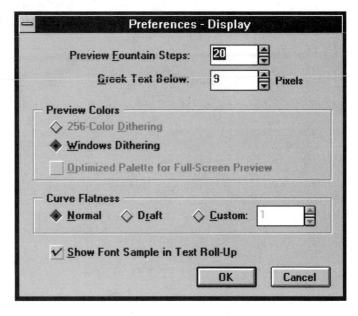

Figure 20. The *Preview Fountain Steps* option lets you set how many sections make up a fountain-filled object on the screen. The lower the number, the faster it is to re-draw, but you may not see a very smooth transition between the two colors.

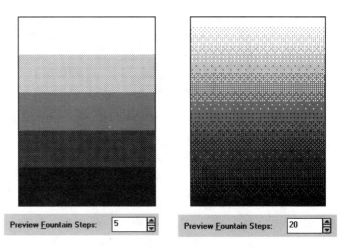

The *Greek Text Below* option in the *Preferences - Display* dialog box determines at what size CorelDRAW displays gray lines instead of paragraph text on the screen (greeked text). Greeked text for small point sizes speeds up redrawing time.

The *Preview Colors* section of the *Preferences - Display* dialog box determines how CorelDRAW displays colors on your screen. It automatically selects the *256-Color Dithering* option if your screen supports this. It selects the *Windows Dithering* option if your screen can't display 256 colors. The *Optimized Palette for Full-Screen Preview* option optimizes the colors on full-screen preview so that it uses up to 256 colors with no dithering. You can access this option only if your screen driver supports it.

The *Curve Flatness* option in the *Preferences - Display* dialog box sets the number of line segments in your drawing or text, on the screen, and on non-PostScript printers.

Increasing this figure can speed up redrawing and printing time. *Normal* is the lowest (on 1), and the highest setting is 10. *Custom* lets you choose any setting in between.

Deselecting the *Show Font Sample in Text Roll-Up* option in the *Preferences - Display* dialog box lets you disable the font sample window that appears when you choose a font in the *Text* Roll-up.

MOUSE

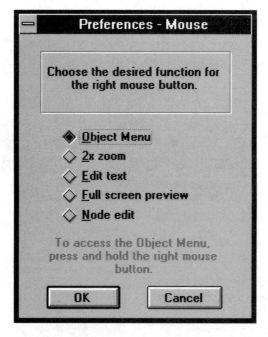

Figure 21. Clicking on the *Mouse* button at the top right of the *Preferences* dialog box opens the *Preferences - Mouse* dialog box. Here you can choose what the right mouse button does when you click it.

Figure 22. If you choose the *Object Menu* option from the *Preferences - Mouse* dialog box, you can click the right mouse button on an object to activate the **Object** menu. For more information on this menu see Chapter 12.

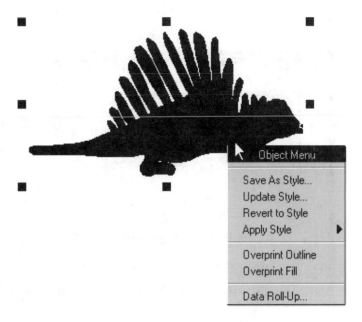

If you choose an option other than *Object Menu* from the *Preferences - Mouse* dialog box, you have to click and hold the right mouse button on an object to pop-up the **Object** menu.

If you choose the *2x zoom* option, you can click the right mouse button to magnify the area you click on by two.

Checking the *Edit Text* option lets you click the right mouse button to open either the *Artistic Text* or *Paragraph Text* dialog box. You must have some text selected with the Pick Tool before this will work.

If you want to click the right mouse button to see a preview of your drawing with nothing else on the screen, check the *Full screen preview* option. Click the right mouse button again to bring back the drawing.

Checking the *Node edit* option lets you select the Shape Tool (⚲) by clicking on the right mouse button.

ROLL-UPS

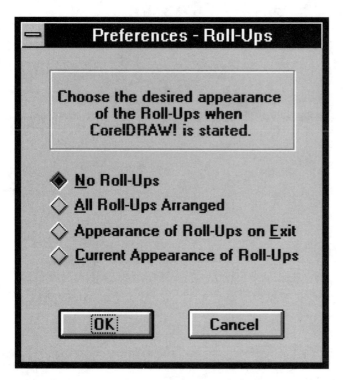

Figure 23. Clicking on the *Roll-Ups* button in the *Preferences* dialog box opens the *Preferences - Roll-Ups* dialog box. The options here set how the Roll-ups appear next time you open CorelDRAW

By default, the *No Roll-Ups* option is selected. This ensures none of the Roll-ups will be active.

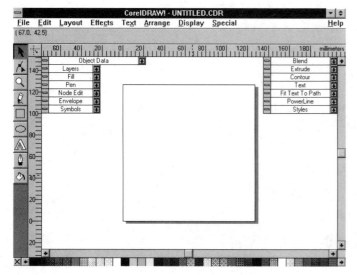

Figure 24. Checking *All Roll-Ups Arranged* will arrange all the Roll-ups at the top right and left of the screen.

Choosing *Appearance of Roll-Ups on Exit* opens the Roll-ups that are active when you exit next time you open CorelDRAW.

The *Current Appearance of Roll-Ups* option will open only the Roll-ups you have open when you choose this option.

DIMENSION

Figure 25. The *Dimension* button in the *Preferences* dialog box opens the *Preferences - Dimension* dialog box. The options in this dialog box set how the dimension text (labels) appear when you draw dimension lines with the Pencil Tool.

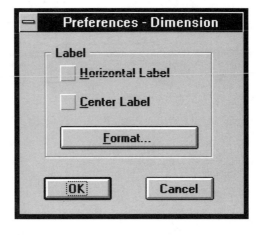

If you choose the *Horizontal Label* option, the label always appears in the horizontal position.

The *Center Label* option ensures that the label appears midway along the line. However this will only occur if you finish drawing the line by clicking inside the extension lines.

Figure 26. Click on the *Format* button in the *Preferences - Dimensions* dialog box opens the *Format Definition* dialog box. The options here let you further customize how the labels appear on dimension lines.

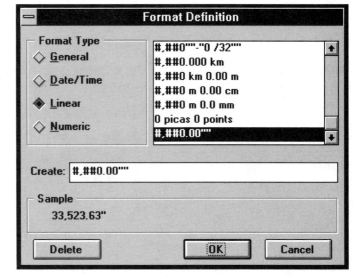

THE OBJECT MENU

THE OBJECT MENU COMMANDS

The **Object** menu commands cover a range of options. You can use this menu to save, update, revert to and apply styles, as well as assign overprint to an object's fill or outline, open the *Object Data* Roll-up, and change clone objects.

Figure 1. This figure displays the **Object** menu and its associated commands. Not all options in the **Object** menu are always available.

Figure 2. The way you bring up the **Object** menu differs slightly depending on what option you have selected in the *Preferences - Mouse* dialog box.

To open this dialog box, choose the *Preferences* command from the **Special** menu and, in the *Preferences* dialog box that appears, click on the *Mouse* button.

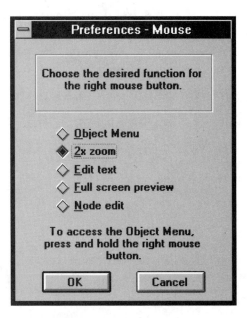

If you have the *Object Menu* option checked in this dialog box, you can click the right mouse button on an object to get the **Object** menu. If you have checked another option, you must hold the right mouse button down on the object to get this menu.

SAVE AS STYLE

The first command in the **Object** menu is the *Save As Style* command. This command lets you save and name the attributes applied to an object as a style. You can then quickly and easily apply these attributes to another object by assigning it that style.

Styles attributes can be saved and applied to graphics, Artistic Text, and Paragraph Text. When you are saving styles, CorelDRAW recognizes whether you are working with graphics, Artistic Text, or Paragraph Text.

Saving a Style in CorelDRAW!

Figure 3. Once you have applied all the necessary attributes to an object (in this case Artistic Text), you click (or hold) the right mouse button down on the text and choose *Save As Style* from the **Object** menu.

Figure 4. The *Save Style As* dialog box then appears. At the top of this dialog box you type in a name for the style. This name can be up to 15 characters long.

Then, in the *Include* section, check the attributes you want to include in the style and click on the *OK* button.

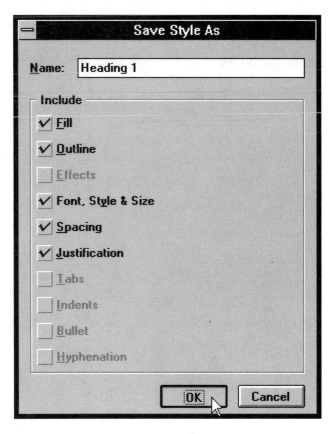

Figure 5. The style you create now appears in the *Styles* Roll-up. You can apply this style to other objects, which saves you from applying the attributes one by one to any new objects you want to format in the same way.

When you save styles, they are added to the current template.

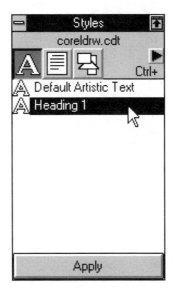

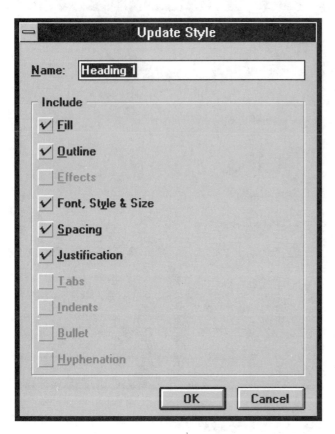

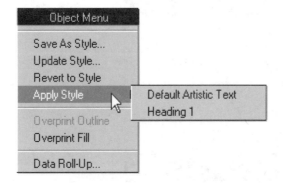

UPDATE STYLE

Figure 6. When you choose the *Update Style* command, this opens the *Update Style* dialog box. Use the *Update Style* command on an object if you have made changes to it since applying a style to it. In the *Include* section of the dialog box, choose the attributes you want to update and click on *OK* to add the new changes to the style.

CorelDRAW then updates all objects in the drawing that you have assigned this style. You can also change the name of the style in this dialog box.

REVERT TO STYLE

You use the *Revert to Style* command if you have made changes to an object since applying a style to it. CorelDRAW then changes the object's attributes to how they were before you applied the style to it.

APPLY STYLE

Figure 7. The *Apply Style* command pops-up a submenu of styles. The styles that appear here depend on what styles (if any) you have created, what template you have loaded, and what object you have activated the **Object** menu for. These are the same styles that appear in the *Styles* Roll-up.

If you are applying styles to Paragraph Text, you can apply a different style to each paragraph. To apply styles to just one paragraph, insert the Paragraph Text cursor in the paragraph you want to affect. To apply styles to all the Paragraph Text, select the text block with the Pick Tool.

For more information on *Styles*, see Chapter 6.

OVERPRINT OUTLINE AND OVERPRINT FILL

These two commands let you apply the *Overprint* feature to an object's outline and fill. When you create color separations from CorelDRAW, colors are "knocked out" where they overlap. This ensures a third color is not created where this overlap occurs. If, for some reason, you want the colors to overlap, you can apply the *Overprint* feature to the objects concerned and there is no knock out.

For more information on overprinting, see the *Print* command in Chapter 4.

DATA ROLL-UP

Figure 8. The *Data Roll-up* command from the **Object** menu opens the *Object Data* Roll-up. Use the options in this Roll-up primarily for creating a database of information about your drawing.

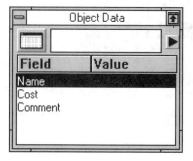

A database is a tool for organizing, managing, and retrieving information. This information is stored in columns of information. This feature is useful but not necessary for the day-to-day use of CorelDRAW.

Once you have set up the database and opened the *Object Data* Roll-up, you can click on an object in your drawing to find out the relevant information in the *Object Data* Roll-up.

Remember, to open the *Object Data* Roll-up, click or hold the right mouse button on an object to first bring up the **Object** menu; then select the *Data Roll-up* command. Once you have displayed this Roll-up, you can move it around the screen, roll it up, or remove it as you can any other Roll-up. You can also change the size of this Roll-up by holding the mouse down on any edge of the Roll-up and dragging it in or out.

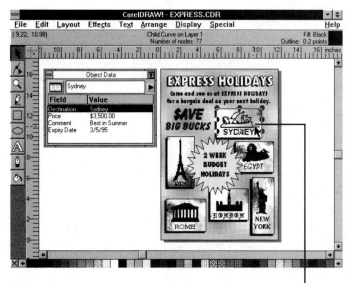

Selected object

Figure 9. In this travel flyer example you could include information in the database regarding the destination, price, general comment, and the expiration date of the offer. Here we have selected one of the destinations, and all the relevant information appears in the *Object Data* Roll-up. An employee can follow this procedure to find out this information for a customer.

Notice that the object selected in this example (Sydney Opera House) is a child object. This means it is part of a group of objects and we had to hold the Ctrl key down to select it by itself. You can include information on groups of objects as well as child objects.

See the following sections on how to create such a database.

CREATING FIELDS

Figure 10. The first step in creating the database is to establish and create the fields. Choose *Field Editor* from the *Object Data* Roll-up to open the *Object Data Field Editor* dialog box.

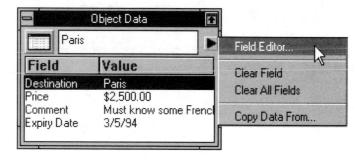

Figure 11. You create new fields in this dialog box by clicking on the *Create New Field* button at the top of the dialog box. This adds the *Field0* label to the text box and the list of fields below the button (a). You can type the name of your field directly over the top of the *Field0* text and click on the Enter key to add the field (b).

Follow the same procedure to add all the fields you want. If any fields already exist that you do not want, you can simply select them from the list of fields and click on the *Delete Field(s)* button, or type a new field name directly over them.

(a)

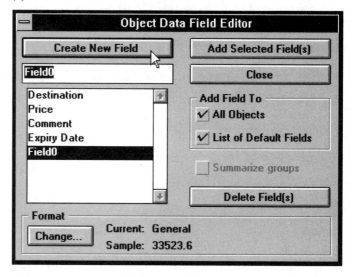

(b)

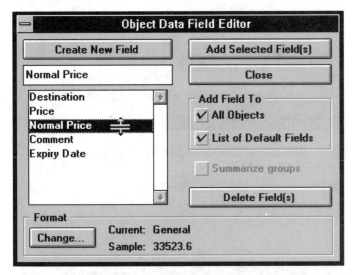

Figure 12. The order the fields appear in this dialog box is the order they will appear in the database and the *Object Data* Roll-up. If you want to change the order of the fields, hold the mouse button down when the cursor is on the field label you want to move, drag it to a new position in the list, and release the mouse button.

In this example we have moved the *Normal Price* field up underneath the *Price* field.

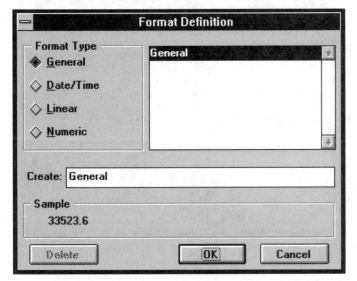

Figure 13. Once you have added all the fields and put them in the right order, you can format a field by clicking on the *Change* button at the bottom of the *Object Data Field Editor* dialog box. This opens the *Format Definition* dialog box. You have four format options.

When you choose one of the options other than *General*, you then have further formatting choices. CorelDRAW lists these options in the preview list to the right of the format choices.

Apply the *General* format option to fields that include general text.

Use the *Date/Time* format for fields that are going to contain the date. In the example of our travel brochure, we formatted the *Expiry Date* field with the *Date/Time* option.

Use the *Linear* format option for fields that are going to contain measurements, and the *Numeric* option for fields that will include currency or percentage information. We applied the *Numeric* option to the *Price* field in our travel brochure.

When you choose a new format option, the *Sample* section of the dialog box displays an example of how it will look. You can also customize your own format by typing it into the *Create* edit box in the *Format Definition* dialog box.

Choose a format separately for each field in your database.

Once back in the *Object Data Field Editor* dialog box, you must click on the *Add Selected Field(s)* button to close this dialog box and return to the *Object Data* Roll-up.

Figure 14. The field names you created appear under the *Field* heading in the *Object Data* Roll-up. You can now enter the information into the *Object Data* Roll-up for a selected object. You then select another object to add the information for that object, and so on. Here you can see that the list of fields contains the field names already there, plus the new one we added: *Normal Price*.

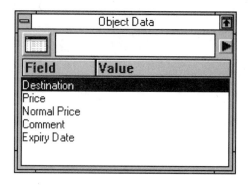

ADDING FIELD INFORMATION

Figure 15. With the Pick Tool, select the object that you want to insert the information in. If the object is part of a group, you must hold the Ctrl key down to select the object separately. Then, in the *Object Data* Roll-up, click on the field that you want to put the information in. In this example we selected the *Egypt* graphic.

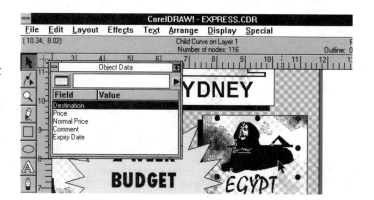

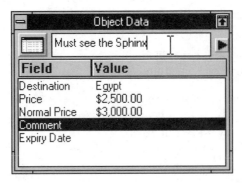

Figure 16. Next, insert the cursor in the text box at the top of the Roll-up and type in the information for the selected field. Press the Enter key (or the down arrow on your keyboard) to add the information to the *Value* list in the Roll-up.

You can then select the fields one by one and add the information in the same way as just described. In this example, we have added the *Destination, Price,* and *Normal Price* information and are about to enter the *Comment Value.*

You can edit the field information once you have entered it. To do this, select the field you want to edit from the *Object Data* Roll-up, and change the text that appears in the text box of the Roll-up.

THE OBJECT DATA MANAGER

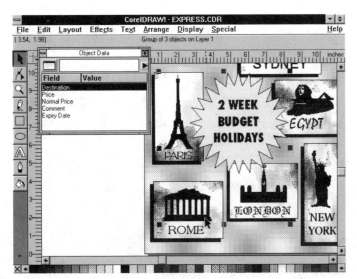

Figure 17. If you want to add information to the database—say for a group of objects, you can open the *Object Data Manager.* You do this by first selecting the relevant object or group of objects, and clicking on the ⬚ button from the *Object Data* Roll-up. In this example, we selected a group of objects that included the *Rome, Paris,* and *London* graphics.

The status line tells us we have a group of three objects selected.

Figure 18. When the *Object Data Manager* appears, you can type in the different field information for each object in the group. If you had already typed in this data, it would be displayed in the *Object Data Manager*.

	Destination	Price	Normal Price	Comment	Expiry Date
1					
2	London	$2,750.00	$3,500.00	Visit Buckingham Palace	9/6/94
3	Rome	$2,250.00	$3,000.00	When in Rome...	4/5/94
4	Paris	$2,500.00	$3,250.00	Must know some French	3/5/94
TOTAL					

Figure 19. Here we have added a main heading in each field for the three grouped items. You can also type this directly into the database.

To enter text directly into the database, click the mouse in the cell you want, and type in the relevant text. Use the arrow keys on the keyboard to move from cell to cell. Once you have entered text into the database, you can edit it directly to update any necessary changes.

	Destination	Price	Normal Price	Comment	Expiry Date
1	Europe	$5,000.00	$7,500.00	Three for the price of tw	9/12/93
2	London	$2,750.00	$3,500.00	Visit Buckingham Palace	9/6/94
3	Rome	$2,250.00	$3,000.00	When in Rome...	4/5/94
4	Paris	$2,500.00	$3,250.00	Must know some French	3/5/94
TOTAL					

Figure 20. You can change the size of columns in the database by holding the mouse button down when the cursor is on the bar between the columns, and dragging the column edge to a new position and releasing the mouse.

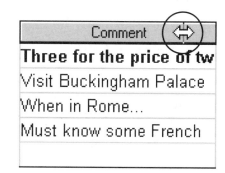

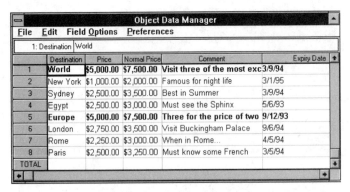

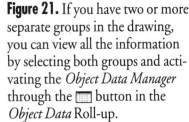

Figure 21. If you have two or more separate groups in the drawing, you can view all the information by selecting both groups and activating the *Object Data Manager* through the 🔲 button in the *Object Data* Roll-up.

In this example, the first group (*World*) contains the *Sydney*, *Egypt*, and *New York* graphics. The second group (*Europe*) contains the *Paris, Rome,* and *London* graphics. In this fashion, you can view the entire database of information.

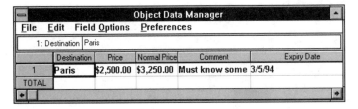

Figure 22. If we want to view any of these graphics individually, we first have to select them with the Ctrl key held down. The information in the *Object Data* Roll-up and, subsequently the *Object Data Manager,* applies to the selected object only.

OBJECT DATA ROLL-UP SUBMENU

FIELD EDITOR

Figure 23. The ▶ icon in the *Object Data* Roll-up pops-up this submenu.

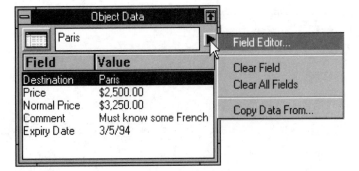

Figure 24. The *Field Editor* command in the *Object Data* Roll-up submenu opens the *Object Data Field Editor* dialog box. You use this dialog box to create and format new fields. For information on creating and formatting fields see **Creating New Fields** earlier in this chapter.

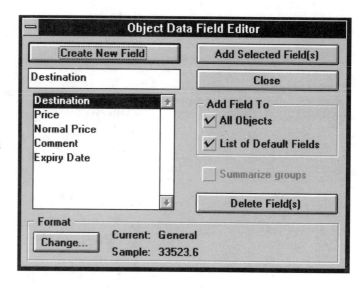

The *Add Field To* options in this dialog box let you apply the fields to all objects. Additionally, if you check the *List of Defaults Fields* option, you can add the fields in this dialog box to a list of default fields for all new CorelDRAW documents.

If you change the default list with the *List of Defaults* option active (by adding or deleting fields) in one document, it will affect all the documents that contain the same fields.

To select multiple fields in this dialog box, hold the Ctrl key down and click on the fields you want to select from the list.

Check the *Summarize groups* option to summarize the totals of a group of fields. The subtotals for each selected group then appear when you open the *Object Data Manager*.

Click on the *Delete Field(s)* button in the *Object Data Field Editor* to remove the selected fields. When you do this you are prompted to confirm your decision.

The *Change* button in the *Object Data Field Editor* opens the *Format Definition* dialog box. Here you can choose or customize a format type for each of the fields in the database.

CLEAR FIELD

The *Clear Field* command in the *Object Data* Roll-up submenu removes all the information from the selected field.

CLEAR ALL FIELDS

The *Clear All Fields* command deletes all the database information from the fields in the *Object Data* Roll-up.

COPY DATA FROM

The *Copy Data From* command lets you copy all the information associated with one object to another object, saving you from retyping it. This command works in the same way as the *Copy Attributes* command from the **Edit** menu in Corel-DRAW.

OBJECT DATA MANAGER MENU COMMANDS

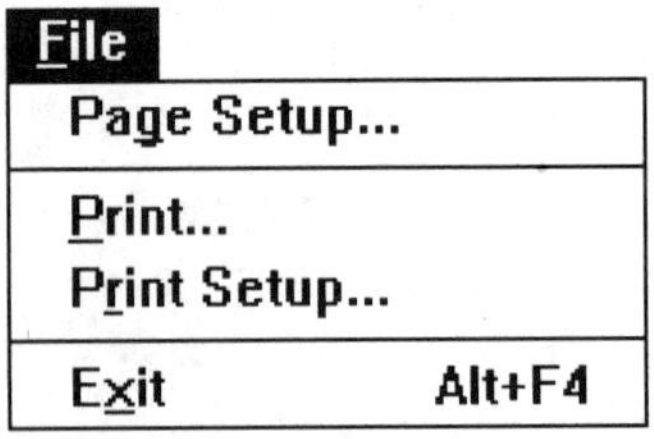

```
┌─────────────────────────────┐
│ File                        │
├─────────────────────────────┤
│ Page Setup...               │
├─────────────────────────────┤
│ Print...                    │
│ Print Setup...              │
├─────────────────────────────┤
│ Exit             Alt+F4     │
└─────────────────────────────┘
```

Figure 25. The first menu in the *Object Data Manager* is the **File** menu.

The *Page Setup* command lets you set up the database for printing.

The *Print* command lets you print the database.

The *Print Setup* command is to set up the printer before you print the database.

The *Exit* command closes the *Object Data Manager* and returns you to the *Object Data* Roll-up and your drawing.

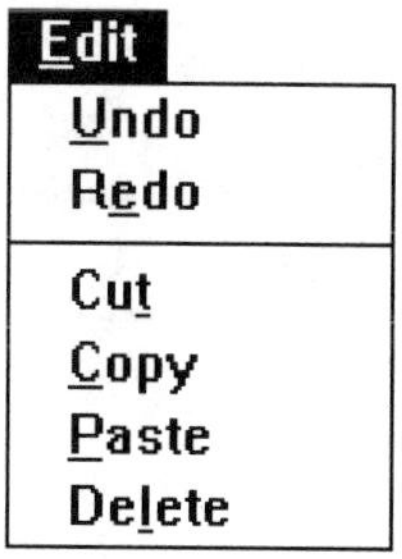

Figure 26. The **Edit** menu in the *Object Data Manager* contains these commands.

```
Edit
 Undo
 Redo

 Cut
 Copy
 Paste
 Delete
```

The *Undo* command reverses previous actions. For more information, see the *Undo* command in CorelDRAW

The *Redo* command reverses the action of the *Undo* command.

The *Cut* command removes information from selected cells and places it in the Windows Clipboard.

The *Copy* command makes a copy of the information in the selected cells and places it in the Windows Clipboard.

The *Paste* command pastes the contents of the Windows Clipboard into selected cells of the database.

The *Delete* command removes the contents of selected cells.

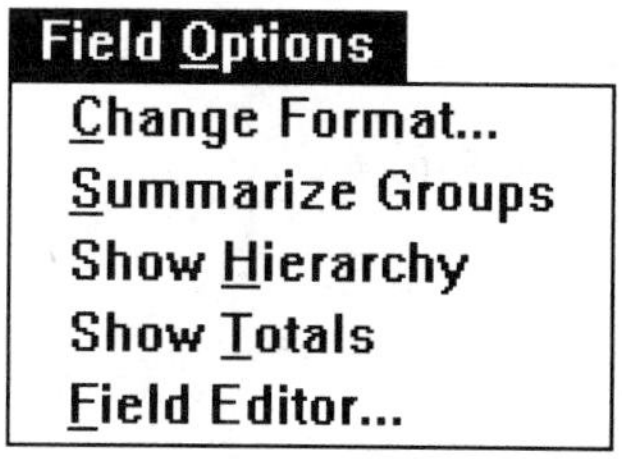

Figure 27. The **Field Options** menu in the *Object Data Manager* contains these commands.

```
Field Options
 Change Format...
 Summarize Groups
 Show Hierarchy
 Show Totals
 Field Editor...
```

The *Change Format* command opens the *Format Definition* dialog box (discussed earlier).

The *Summarize Groups* command displays the subtotals of individual groups when a field shares a multiple group.

The *Show Hierarchy* command indents objects within each group.

The *Show Totals* command adds the totals of a selected field.

The *Field Editor* command opens the *Object Data Field Editor* dialog box.

Preferences

Show Group Details ▶
√ Highlight Top-level Objects
√ Italicize Read-only Cells

Figure 28. The **Preferences** menu in the *Object Data Manager* contains these commands.

The *Show Group Details* command expands the datasheet to include all objects in a group of selected objects.

The *Highlight Top-level Objects* command emboldens the first level of a group.

The *Italicize Read-only Cells* italicizes cells you cannot edit directly, e.g. the *TOTAL* cell.

SELECT CLONES

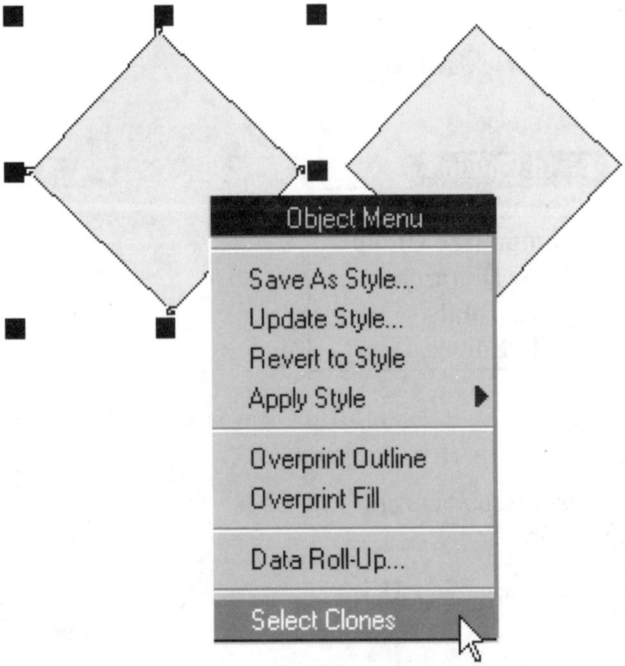

Figure 29. You can access the *Select Clones* command in the **Object** menu only when you have used the *Clone* command from the **Edit** menu. If you use the **Object** menu on a master object (the object a clone derives from), choosing the *Select Clones* command selects the cloned objects.

For more information on clones, see the section on the *Clone* command in Chapter 5.

Object Menu

Save As Style...
Update Style...
Revert to Style
Apply Style ▶

Overprint Outline
Overprint Fill

Data Roll-Up...

Select Clones

SELECT MASTER

Figure 30. You can access the *Select Master* command only when you use the **Object** menu on a cloned object. Choosing this command selects the master object that the clone was derived from.

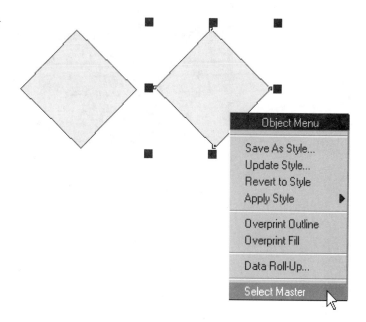

REVERT TO MASTER

Figure 31. You can access the *Revert To Master* command in the **Object** menu only when you have changed the cloned object independently of the master object.

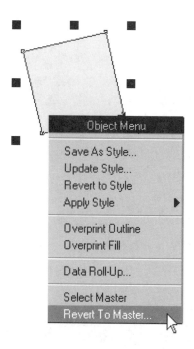

Figure 32. The *Revert To Master* command opens the *Revert To Master* dialog box. Here you select the option you have changed in the cloned object and click on *OK.* The cloned object then reverts to match the master object.

CorelTRACE 13

USING CorelTRACE

CorelTRACE is a tracing utility that comes with Corel-DRAW. It traces black and white, grayscale, and color bitmaps, and converts them into vector-based images. Vector images are superior to bitmaps because they take up less space and print faster, you can scale and rotate them without distortion, and they will always print at the highest resolution your output device allows.

You can then use and edit these traced images in Corel-DRAW, or place them directly into a page layout or word processing program. CorelTRACE is also capable of optical character recognition (OCR), which lets you trace scanned text and then edit it as text (rather than an image).

Figure 1. Open CorelTRACE by double-clicking on the Corel–TRACE icon in Windows.

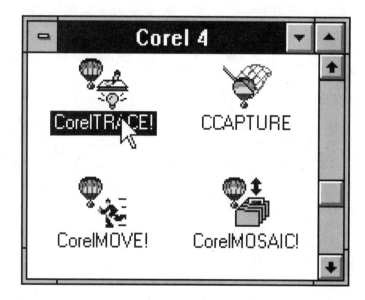

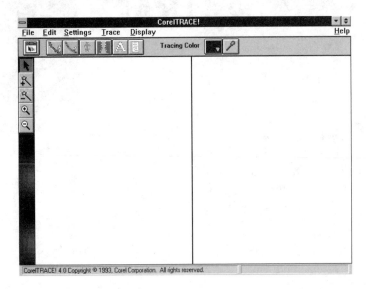

Figure 2. CorelTRACE is now running.

OPENING FILES TO TRACE

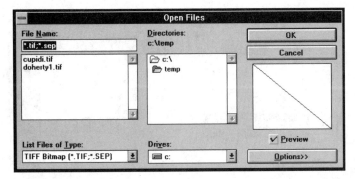

Figure 3. Choose *Open* from the File menu to bring up a dialog box to search for files to trace.

The *Open Files* dialog box works similarly to the *Open Drawing* dialog box in CorelDRAW. The *List Files of Type* drop-down list shows all the file types you can use for tracing.

You find your files in the normal way using the *Directories* and *Drives* lists.

Figure 4. Click on the *Options* button if you want information about any file you have selected in this dialog box. An image of the file appears in the *Preview* window when you select it from the list of files.

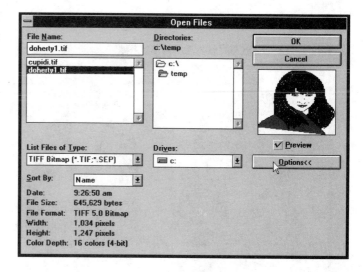

Figure 5. After you click on *OK* in the *Open Files* dialog box, the file you selected appears in the preview window of the dialog box.

TRACING FILES

Figure 6. To trace this file in the simplest way, click on the *Outline* trace button (circled). After a while (depending on the complexity of the image) the traced imaged appears in the right preview window.

You can, however, customize the way in which CorelTRACE traces your images.

THE TOOLS

PICK TOOL

Figure 7. Use the Pick Tool to marquee select the area of the image you want traced. With this option, you trace only the area that falls within the marquee selection.

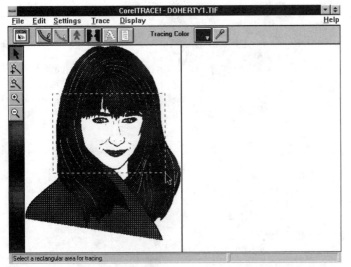

MAGIC WAND TOOLS

Figure 8. The first Magic Wand Tool (✳) selects an area that is similar in color. This lets you trace just certain colored areas of the image, or to build up the trace color by color.

After choosing the first Magic Wand Tool, click the mouse on the color you want, which then highlights all the connecting area with this color ready for tracing. In this example we clicked on the face, which selected all the face area because it is the same color.

The second Magic Wand Tool (✳) deselects areas of similar color.

ZOOM TOOLS

You use the Zoom In Tool (⊕) to magnify an area of the image you are going to trace.

The Zoom Out Tool (⊖) returns the view of the image back to normal.

Figure 9. The six buttons across the top of the left preview window are the tracing method buttons.

The first tracing method is the *Outline* method (shown earlier). This method traces the outline of the image and fills the traced object in relation to the original object. If the image you are tracing has a solid colored fill, this option traces the fill as well.

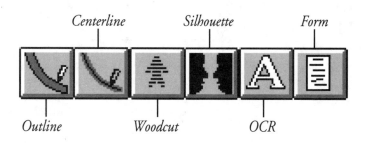

Centerline *Silhouette* *Form*

Outline *Woodcut* *OCR*

Figure 10. The *Centerline* method is the next method for tracing. This method traces thin bit-mapped images (black and white only) using varying outline widths and no fill.

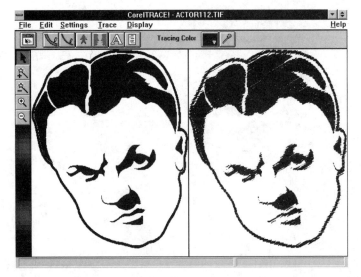

Figure 11. The *Woodcut* tracing method traces an image with a special woodcut effect.

Figure 12. The *Silhouette* method traces a selected area with a slab of the one color. In this example we selected a section of hair with the Magic Wand Tool and chose the *Silhouette* tracing method.

Figure 13. You determine the color for tracing with the *Silhouette* option by the color that appears in the *Tracing Color* quick-pick palette. You can choose a different color from the palette that appears when you click the mouse on the swatch.

Alternatively, click on the *More* button at the bottom of the quick-pick palette to activate the *Select Color* dialog box. This color dialog box works in the same way as the *Outline Color* dialog box works, described in Chapter 3.

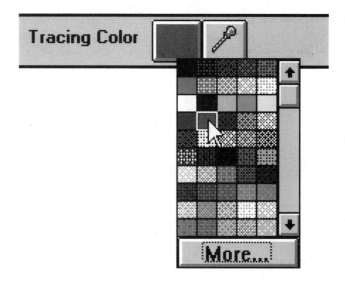

Figure 14. You can also use the Eye Dropper (🔑) to select the *Tracing Color*. Click on the Eye Dropper to select it, and then click on a color anywhere in your image to choose the *Tracing Color*. The color you click on with the Eye Dropper then appears in the *Tracing Color* swatch.

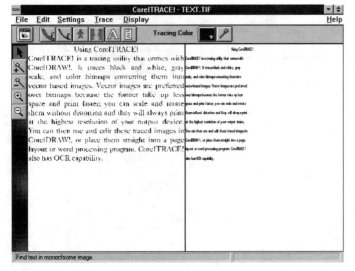

Figure 15. The next tracing method is the *OCR* option. With this option selected, you can trace text (black and white only) and in most cases you can then edit it as normal text when you import it into CorelDRAW.

You should set your scanner to scan the text at 300 dpi for the best results. The traced text will most likely not resemble the original text, as in this example.

Figure 16. You use the *Form* method to trace forms (black and white only) that include lines and text.

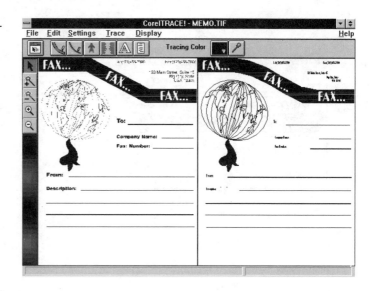

FILE MENU

Figure 17. The **File** menu and its associated commands.

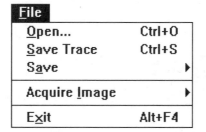

OPEN

The first command is *Open*. This brings up the *Open Files* dialog box (discussed earlier in Figure 3).

SAVE TRACE

You can choose the *Save Trace* command only when you have traced something. This command saves the traced file in the same directory as the file you are tracing.

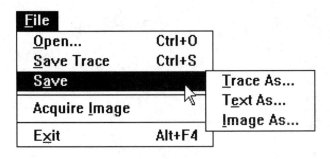

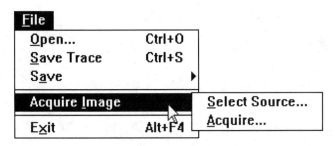

SAVE

Figure 18. The *Save* command pops-out this submenu. The *Trace As* option opens the *Save Trace As* dialog box which lets you specify the path and filename of the trace. This dialog box works in a similar way to the *Save Drawing* dialog box in CorelDRAW.

The *Text As* option in the *Save* submenu lets you save the traced image as text. The *Image As* option saves the image file. You may have to do this if you scanned the image directly into CorelTRACE.

Figure 19. The *Acquire Image* options let you scan an image directly into CorelTRACE. *Select Source* lets you choose your scanner, and *Acquire* starts scanning the image.

The *Exit* command in the **File** menu closes CorelTRACE. If you have made any changes since last saving the image or the traced file, CorelTRACE asks whether you want to save these changes.

EDIT MENU

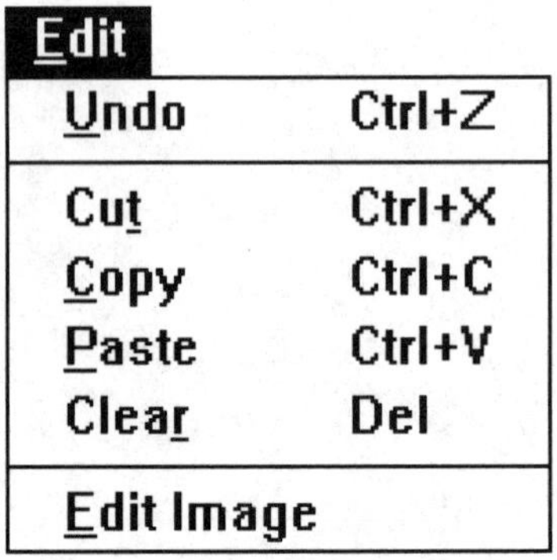

Figure 20. The **Edit** menu and its associated commands.

UNDO

The *Undo* command reverses the last action you did in Corel-TRACE.

CUT

You use the *Cut* command to cut the traced image and place it in the Windows Clipboard as a Windows Metafile (*.wmf*) file. You can then paste this into any program that accepts Windows Metafiles.

COPY

The *Copy* command makes a copy of the traced image and places it in the Windows Clipboard as a *.wmf* file.

PASTE

You use the *Paste* command to paste a *.dib* bitmap from the Windows Clipboard.

CLEAR

The *Clear* command deletes the traced image.

EDIT IMAGE

Selecting the *Edit Image* command opens CorelPHOTO-PAINT, letting you edit the image you are going to trace.

SETTINGS MENU

Figure 21. The *Settings* menu and its associated commands.

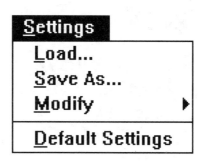

LOAD

The *Load* command opens a dialog box where you can load a custom trace settings file.

SAVE AS

The *Save As* command lets you save the current settings you have chosen as a file. You can save as many of these files as you like, and use the *Load* command to open each one.

MODIFY

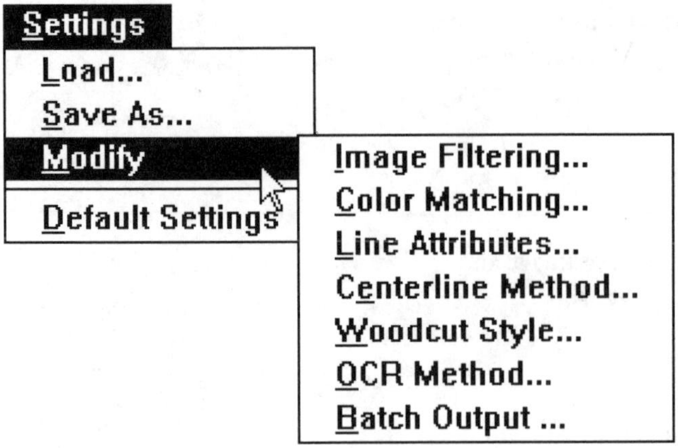

Figure 22. The *Modify* command pops-up this submenu. The options in this submenu let you set how you trace the image. Each option opens an associated dialog box where you can customize the way the image is traced. Once you have chosen your own settings, you can save these settings using the *Save As* command.

Settings
- Load...
- Save As...
- Modify
- Default Settings

Modify submenu
- Image Filtering...
- Color Matching...
- Line Attributes...
- Centerline Method...
- Woodcut Style...
- OCR Method...
- Batch Output ...

DEFAULT SETTINGS

The *Default Settings* command returns all the tracing settings back to their defaults. You use this command if you have adjusted any of the options in the *Modify* submenu and you want to return them to normal.

TRACE MENU

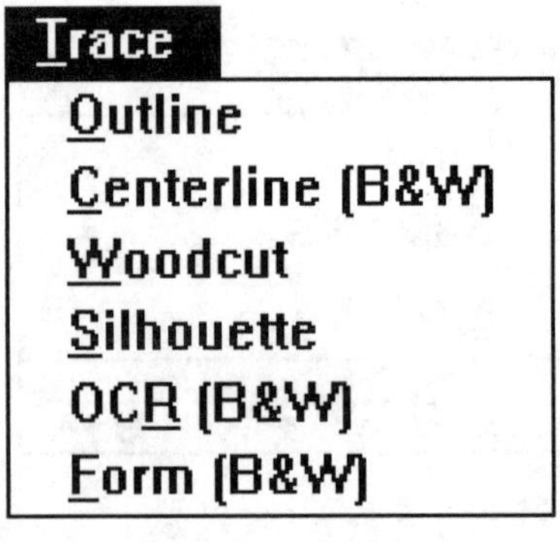

Figure 23. The options in the **Trace** menu are the different methods of tracing. You can also click on one of the six buttons below the menu bar. Selecting one of the options from the menu starts tracing.

Trace
- Outline
- Centerline (B&W)
- Woodcut
- Silhouette
- OCR (B&W)
- Form (B&W)

DISPLAY MENU

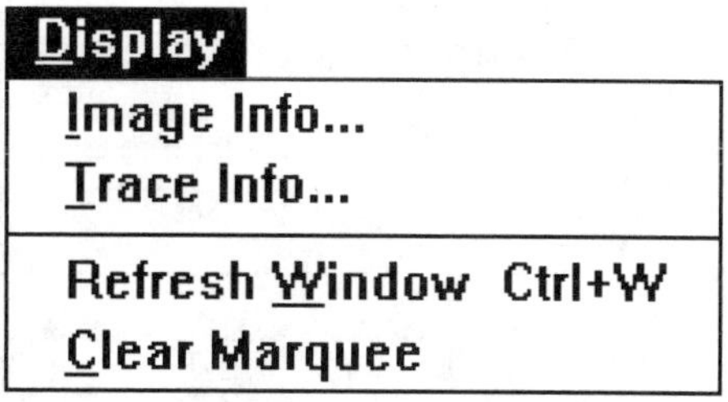

Figure 24. The **Display** menu and its associated commands.

IMAGE INFO

The *Image Info* command displays a dialog box that gives you current information about the image you are tracing.

TRACE INFO

The *Trace Info* command displays a dialog box that contains current information on the traced image.

REFRESH WINDOW

The *Refresh Window* command redraws both the window containing the image and the trace.

CLEAR MARQUEE

You use the *Clear Marquee* command to deselect any areas you have selected on the image you are about to trace.

TRACING MULTIPLE FILES

Figure 25. It is possible in the *Open Files* dialog box to select more than one file to trace. You do this by holding down the Ctrl key and clicking on all the files you want to trace before clicking on *OK* in the *Open Files* dialog box.

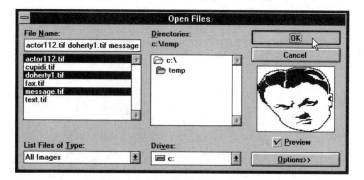

Figure 26. When you do choose more than one file to trace, Corel-TRACE automatically opens the *Batch Files* Roll-up. From this Roll-up you can choose to trace one file at a time, or all the files in the list. You can also choose the Tracing Method, among other things, from this Roll-up.

IMPORTING CorelTRACE IMAGES INTO CorelDRAW

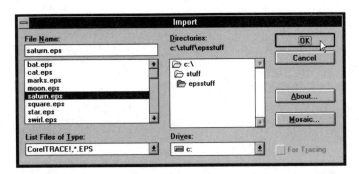

Figure 27. As an alternative to cutting and pasting a traced image from CorelTRACE into Corel-DRAW, you can use the *Import* command in CorelDRAW to insert a saved CorelTRACE image.

Choose the *CorelTRACE,*.EPS* option from the *List Files of Type* drop-down list in the Corel-DRAW *Import* dialog box and then use the *Drives* and *Directories* lists to find the file. Click on the *OK* button once you have selected the filename, and the traced image appears in CorelDRAW.

CorelMOSAIC  14

Using CorelMOSAIC

CorelMOSAIC is a file management utility that lets you view the contents of a directory. You can select more than one file at a time so that you can print and export multiple files. CorelMO-SAIC can also create libraries and catalogs of files. You can access CorelMOSAIC directly from Windows (*Standalone* mode) or through CorelDRAW (*Corel Application* mode). There are slight differences between these two modes.

Figure 1. To open CorelMOSAIC from Windows, double-click on the CorelMOSAIC icon in the Program Manager.

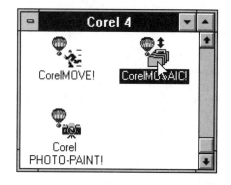

Figure 2. To open CorelMOSAIC from within CorelDRAW, click on the *Mosaic* button in the *Open Drawing* dialog box or the *Import* dialog box.

When you open CorelMOSAIC from within CorelDRAW, you cannot use all commands. However, the **Cancel** option in the menu bar is available only in *Corel Application* mode.

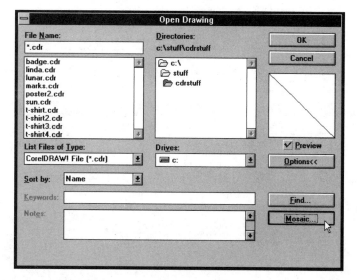

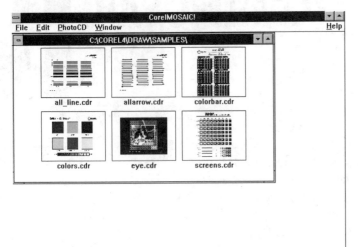

Figure 3. After starting Corel-MOSAIC, you will see a bitmap version of all graphic files, in the current directory, visible in the CorelMOSAIC display screen.

VIEWING DIRECTORIES

Figure 4. The first thing you do in CorelMOSAIC is select the directory that contains the files you want to work with. To do this, choose *View Directory* from the File menu.

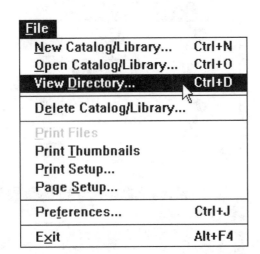

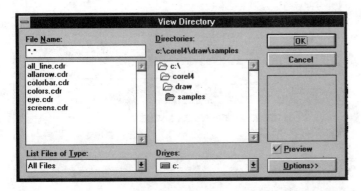

Figure 5. The *View Directory* command opens the *View Directory* dialog box. Using the *Directories* and *Drives* lists, you can choose the directory that contains the files you want to view.

The options in the *List Files of Type* drop-down list let you view all the files in the directory, all the image files, or just certain types of image files. Choose what you need and click on *OK.* Only the file-types you selected in the *List Files of Type* drop-down list appear.

Figure 6. Clicking on the *Options* button in the *View Directory* dialog box expands the dialog box to include further options.

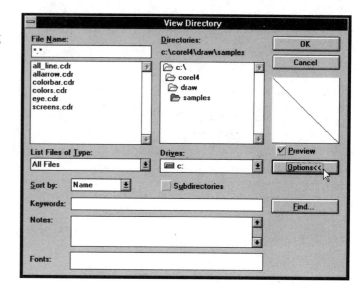

The *Sort by* option lets you determine in what order you display the files in the display screen, not in the *Open Directory* dialog box. Your choices here are by *Name, Date, Size,* and *Directory.*

If you have the *Subdirectories* option checked, CorelMOSAIC displays all files (in the file format selected in the *List Files of Type* list) in the current directory, and in any subdirectories below this one.

The *Preview* option lets you see a file you've selected from the *File Name* list.

The *Keywords* and *Notes* options work as they do in the *Open Drawing* dialog box in CorelDRAW. The *Find* button lets you search for files with certain keywords and display them in the CorelMOSAIC display screen.

The *Fonts* box lists the fonts you have used in the Corel-DRAW file you select from the list of files in this dialog box.

The other commands in the **File** menu are explained next.

THE FILE MENU

NEW CATALOG/LIBRARY

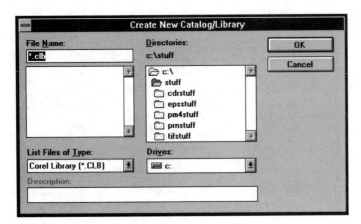

Figure 7. The first command from the **File** menu (Figure 4) opens the *Create New Catalog/Library* dialog box. From here you can use Corel-MOSAIC to create a library file or a catalog file.

Use a library file to store compressed versions of your graphics files. This can save you a lot of disk space because, after storing files in a library file, you can delete the original files.

A catalog file simply stores thumbnail images of files in the one catalog. The original files remain untouched in their respective directories.

You choose whether to create a *Corel Library* file or a *Corel Catalog* file from the *List Files of Type* drop-down list. If you choose to create a *Corel Catalog* file, you can enter some text in the *Description* edit frame about the catalog.

After deciding where to save the file and giving the file a name, click on the *OK* button. After doing this, an empty window appears in CorelMOSAIC with the name of the library or catalog in the title bar. You can now add files to your library or catalog file. For now we are going to discuss the remaining commands in the **File** menu.

OPEN CATALOG/LIBRARY

Figure 8. The *Open Catalog/Library* command brings up the *Open Catalog/Library* dialog box. Here you can open an existing catalog or library file. This dialog box works in the same way as other open dialog boxes in CorelDRAW. You search for the file, select it from the list of files, and click on the *OK* button. The library or catalog file then opens in CorelMOSAIC.

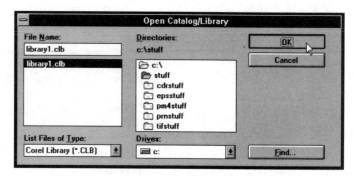

When you are searching for library or catalog files, remember that library files have an extension of *clb* and catalog files have an extension of *clc*. Make sure you choose the right option from the *List Files of Type* dialog box.

VIEW DIRECTORY

The *View Directory* command is discussed earlier in this chapter under **Viewing Directories**.

DELETE CATALOG/ LIBRARY

Figure 9. The *Delete Catalog/Library* command opens a dialog box where you can search for, select, and delete library and catalog files.

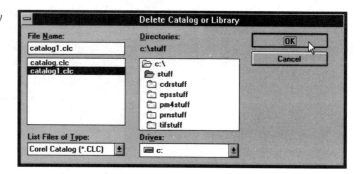

PRINT FILES

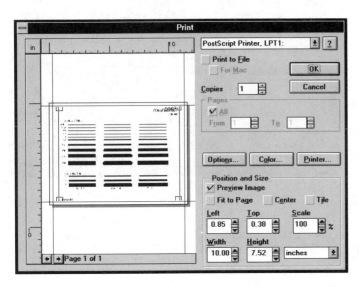

Figure 10. You can access the *Print Files* command only if you have one or more thumbnail images selected in CorelMOSAIC. To select a thumbnail image in Corel-MOSAIC, simply click on it with the mouse.

To select more than one file, hold the Shift key down and click on all the files you want selected. Use the scroll bar to the right of the thumbnail window to access thumbnails not currently in view. (See the **Edit** menu for other ways to select files.)

The *Print Files* command from the **File** menu opens Corel-DRAW and prints any files you have selected in the display screen. If any of the files you have selected are not in native CorelDRAW format, CorelDRAW imports and then prints them. All the images will be printed with the settings you choose in the *Print* dialog box after you open CorelDRAW.

PRINT THUMBNAILS

The *Print Thumbnails* command from the **File** menu prints the images within the display screen. CorelMOSAIC labels these bitmapped images in the display screen as thumbnails. The number of files in the directory determines the number of pages printed. Choose the thumbnails you want to print before selecting this command.

PRINT SETUP

Figure 11. The *Print Setup* command from the **File** menu opens the *Print Setup* dialog box, which is the standard Windows *Print Setup* box. From here you select the printer, page size, and paper orientation for printing your drawing.

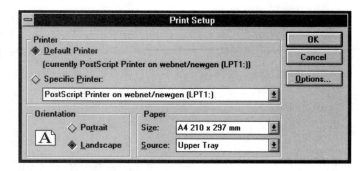

PAGE SETUP

Figure 12. The *Page Setup* command from the **File** menu opens the *Page Setup* dialog box. The options determine how you print the thumbnails.

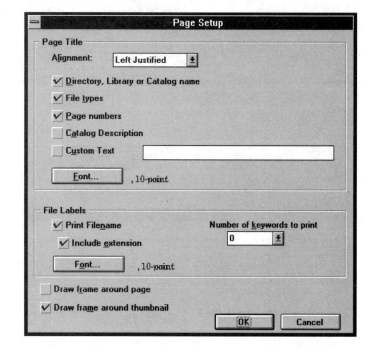

PREFERENCES

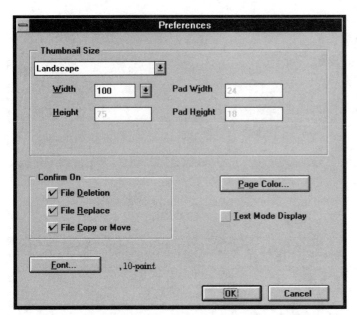

Figure 13. The *Preferences* command from the **File** menu brings up the *Preferences* dialog box. The options in this dialog box determine how CorelMOSAIC displays the thumbnails in the display screen.

The *Exit* command from the **File** menu closes CorelMOSAIC.

THE EDIT MENU

SELECT BY KEYWORD

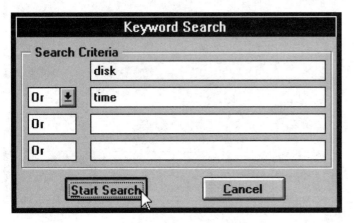

Figure 14. The *Select by Keyword* command lets you select all files with certain keywords. You can enter specific keywords that relate to a graphic CorelDRAW file. Insert the keyword into the *Search Criteria* frame at the top of the dialog box. If you have more than one keyword, you can add extra words in the frames below.

If you have the *And* option active in the drop-down lists to the left of the text frames, you will select all files with all keywords from this dialog box. The *Or* option selects files with any of the keywords you insert. In the display screen, Corel-MOSAIC highlights the files with your chosen keywords after you click on the *Start Search* button.

SELECT ALL

The *Select All* command from the **Edit** menu (available in both *Standalone* and *CorelDRAW* modes) highlights all files in the currently active directory.

CLEAR ALL

The *Clear All* command from the **Edit** menu (available in both *Standalone* and *CorelDRAW* modes) deselects all files selected in the display screen.

INSERT FILES

Figure 15. You can use *Insert Files* only when you have one or more thumbnail images selected in CorelMOSAIC. It then opens the *Open Catalog/Library* dialog box. Here you choose the library or catalog file you want to add the selected files to.

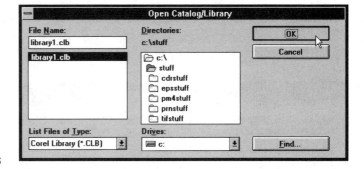

As an alternative to inserting files through this dialog box, you can also drag thumbnail images into a library or catalog window.

Figure 16. Hold the mouse button down with the cursor on the thumbnail image you want to copy into the library or catalog, then drag it across to the library or catalog window.

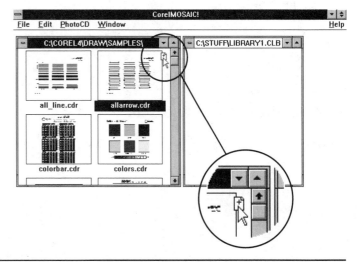

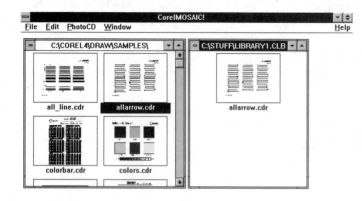

Figure 17. Release the mouse button in the library or catalog window. If you move the image into a library window, it's compressed into the Corel Library file. If it is a catalog window, only the thumbnail image is copied. If you hold the Shift key down, you can move the file into a library file. You cannot move a file into a catalog file.

Note: After you create a library and you intend to delete the original files to conserve disk space, you should first check that you can expand each compressed file.

EXPAND FILES

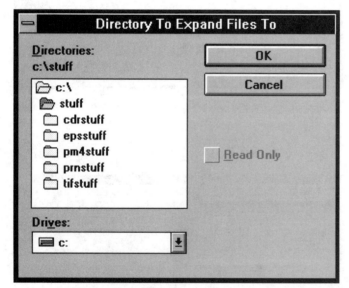

Figure 18. Use the *Expand Files* command to expand library files; before choosing this command, select the thumbnail images from the display window in CorelMO-SAIC. In the *Directory To Expand Files To* dialog box, choose which directory you want the Corel Library files to expand into.

UPDATE CATALOG

Use the *Update Catalog* command to update any changes you have made to a catalog file.

EDIT

The *Edit* command opens the selected file in the application it was created in, or the Corel application it can be edited in.

CONVERT FROM CORELDRAW

Figure 19. The *Convert from Corel-DRAW* command opens Corel-DRAW with the *Export* dialog box active, which lets you save the file you selected in CorelMOSAIC in a different file format. If the file you select in CorelMOSAIC is not a CorelDRAW file, it is imported into CorelDRAW first.

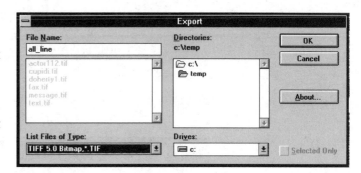

IMPORT INTO CORELDRAW

The *Import into CorelDRAW* command opens CorelDRAW and imports the selected image into this program. This command works on CorelDRAW files or graphic files that you can import into CorelDRAW.

DELETE

Figure 20. The *Delete* command from the **Edit** menu deletes any files you have selected. If you still have the *Confirm On/File Deletion* option checked in the *Preferences* dialog box (Figure 13), CorelMO-SAIC asks you to confirm you want to delete the files.

EXTRACT TEXT AND MERGE-BACK TEXT

The *Extract Text* and *Merge-Back Text* commands from the **Edit** menu are the same as the *Extract* and *Merge-Back* commands in CorelDRAW. Having these commands in CorelMOSAIC lets you extract and merge text on multiple CorelDRAW files.

KEYWORDS

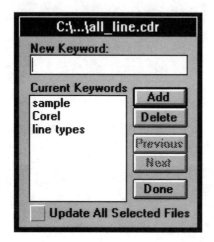

Figure 21. The *Keywords* command from the **Edit** menu opens this dialog box. The *Current Keywords* list displays any keywords for the selected file. To add any keywords to the selected file, key them into the *New Keyword* text frame at the top of the dialog box.

If you have more than one thumbnail selected when you chose the *Keywords* command, the *Next* and *Previous* buttons move you back and forth between all selected files.

After typing the word in the *New Keyword* text frame, click on the *Add* button to add this word to the *Current Keywords* list. You can use the *Delete* button to remove any keywords from the *Current Keywords* list.

If you check the *Update All Selected Files* option, Corel-MOSAIC updates all the keywords of the files selected in the display screen, according to the changes you make in this dialog box.

EDIT DESCRIPTION

You can use the *Edit Description* command only when you have a catalog file open. It lets you edit the description you have given to a *Corel Catalog* file.

GET INFO

Figure 22. The *Get Info* command from the **Edit** menu opens the *File Information* dialog box. This box reveals current information about, as well as displaying a large image of, the file.

Double-clicking on a thumbnail in the display screen with the right mouse button will also let you open this dialog box.

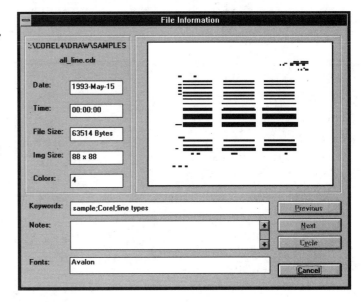

PHOTOCD

Figure 23. The commands in the PhotoCD menu let you view images from a Kodak Photo CD and to convert these images to other formats.

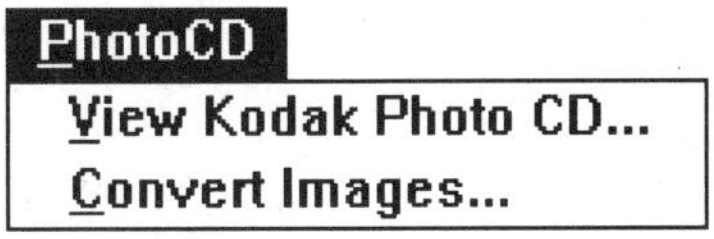

CANCEL

Figure 24. You can access the *Cancel* menu item only in *Corel Application* mode. Selecting this option returns you to CorelDRAW.

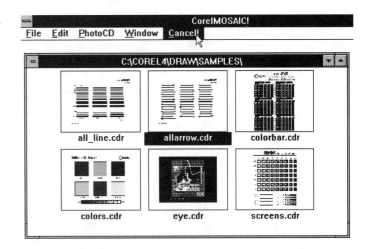

Index